Dynamic
Learning

by

Robert B. Dilts

and

Todd A. Epstein

Meta Publications
P.O. Box 1910
Capitola, California 95010
(408) 464 - 0254
FAX (408) 464 - 0517

Library of Congress Card Number 95-078653
I.S.B.N. 0-916990-37-X

Contents

Dedication

This book is dedicated with deepest love and respect to

Todd Epstein

the embodiment of *Dynamic Learning*.

Acknowledgments

We would like to acknowledge:

Teresa Epstein, Todd's wife and our colleague in the development and evolution of the Dynamic Learning Center. She has been and continues to be an invaluable part of carrying out the mission of Dynamic Learning.

Christine Amato, who has shared our vision and mission in the area of education and learning, and who opened the doors for Dynamic Learning in the school system.

The Pajaro Valley School District, for sponsoring the Dynamic Assessment project. And Richard Figuroa the State of California, for providing the impetus and the backing for the project.

Jeannie Higano, who sponsored the first Dynamic Learning seminar and coined the term.

John Grinder and Richard Bandler, who founded the technology upon which Dynamic Learning is based and taught us the true meaning of 'dynamic learning'.

Ami Sattinger, for her help with the editing and proof reading of the manuscripts for this book and for her enthusiasm and support for this project.

The students and teachers who participated in our Dynamic Learning seminars and the Dynamic Assessment project.

And many thanks to the exceptional individuals who served as the models for the learning strategies presented in this book.

Preface

In June of 1982 I conducted the first *Dynamic Learning* seminar in Vancouver, British Columbia. It was a five-day program made up of learning strategies that I had modeled from my studies of people who had demonstrated academic excellence in subjects such as memory, spelling, math, reading, language learning and creative writing. Over half of the participants of the seminar were school aged children. I had put together the program because I had received so many requests to work with people of various ages in that area who were having learning problems. The seminar also included the use of interactive computer programs that I had designed to teach spelling, math, typing, composition, and the development of certain perceptual skills.

The purpose of the Dynamic Learning seminar was to provide a set of basic learning skills in an experiential, interactive environment that would help people improve in all areas of academic performance. In other words, it was a seminar about 'learning to learn'. The mornings were for explanations and demonstrations of the various learning strategies and exercises. In the afternoons, the participants practiced these activities while I worked one-on-one with students who were having specific learning problems. The program was quite successful and seemed to me to be an innovative form of teaching and learning. I repeated the program several more times in British Columbia, tightening up the strategies and the structure.

In October of 1982, I co-presented a Dynamic Learning seminar in Palo Alto, California with Todd Epstein—it was the beginning of a partnership that was to last for the next thirteen years. Todd had been a colleague of mine for several years prior to this and we had conducted a number of NLP trainings together. Todd had been a professional guitar player, composer and band leader before getting involved in the field of NLP, so he had a natural zeal for creativity and performance; but he also had an intense passion for learning. When I had explained to him what I was doing in Vancouver, he had become very excited about the Dynamic Learning concept. It appealed to his innate curiosity, love for experiential learning and his strong sense of mission with respect to children and education.

We adapted the initial Dynamic Learning seminar structure to a somewhat more traditional workshop format but maintained the emphasis on experiential, interactive exercises and 'learning to learn strategies'. Our commitment to pursuing this path was so strong that we established *The Dynamic Learning Center* together to promote more of this form of teaching and learning. As it turns out, the Dynamic Learning seminar was only one of the many programs we would conduct together over the years. We also put together programs on creativity (the basis for our book *Tools for Dreamers*), leadership, presentation and training skills, dealing with addictions, and many other programs. This evolution culminated in the establishment of *NLP University*; an organization providing training for a full range of applications of NLP including health, business and organization, creativity and learning.

Another key development in the evolution of Dynamic Learning was the *Dynamic Assessment* project conducted for the Pajaro Valley School District. Christine Amato, a special education teacher who had attended the first Dynamic Learning seminar that Todd and I had done together, had become head of the special resources department of her district by the late 1980's. She brought us in to create a program for students with learning difficulties based on Dynamic Learning principles (described in Chapter 10 of this book). The success of this project was one of our most gratifying experiences together.

In 1992 Todd and I began work on the *Dynamic Learning* book, which was to be based upon transcripts from both our very first and most recent Dynamic Learning seminars. Work was slow because of the many other projects we had going on, both individually and together. Unfortunately, Todd died unexpectedly before the book was finished. But I know that he would be pleased and proud of it. I have tried to preserve, in the form of these transcripts, his curiosity, humor and sense of fascination with people and the learning process.

I hope that you enjoy reading this book as much as we enjoyed doing these seminars.

Robert B. Dilts
Santa Cruz, California
June, 1995

Introduction

Contrary to what many people might believe, much of our most fundamental learning does not take place through study and effort. Rather, it is a result of learning naturally through experience. For instance, how many of you readers learned to walk, speak your native tongue or ride a bicycle by laboriously studying them in a book? Probably none of you. Instead, in order to learn to ride a bicycle, you most likely got on your bike and tried to go somewhere. After falling down a few times you began to steadily improve until you had mastered the basic skills necessary to stay upright, move forward and stop. Your natural learning ability was engaged through the process of experience and feedback. You developed an 'unconscious competence' without ever consciously knowing exactly how your nervous system figured it out.

For most of us, our experience of learning how to ride a bicycle was different from our experience of learning how to spell, read or solve mathematical problems. Instead of learning in an interactive environment, with our parents, family or friends coaching and encouraging us, we did it sitting in a classroom looking at a book or a blackboard. Interacting with or encouraging our friends was looked upon as disruptive or even 'cheating'. One question we wish to pose with this book on Dynamic Learning is, "Is learning something like spelling or reading really so different from learning to ride a bicycle that they require such diverse methods of learning?"

Dynamic Learning is about the process of learning through experience. The techniques and exercises of Dynamic Learning involve learning by doing and by exploring different methods of thinking. In essence, Dynamic learning emphasizes the **how** of learning as opposed to the content or the 'what' of learning. Dynamic Learning also acknowledges that the relationships between people are a key factor in learning. It emphasizes skills of cooperative learning, co-coaching and mentoring. Thus, Dynamic Learning methods are very different from sitting at your desk, quietly keeping your hands folded and looking at a chalk board.

Dynamic Learning uses the modeling principles and tools of Neuro-Linguistic Programming (NLP) to release natural learning capabilities through awareness, exploration and discovery. A core presupposition in NLP is that when you are 'learning' you are using your brain and the other parts of your nervous system - which is in some ways more difficult than it sounds.

In fact, some people have so much trouble using their own nervous system that they begin to wonder if it really belongs to them. You might well ask, "If my brain was really mine why would it show me pictures of desserts when I'm trying to diet?" or "Why would it keep telling me that I'm going to mess up when I'm trying to do something that requires concentration?" Why would your own brain make you feel anxious about taking a test? Is it unhappy being in there and wants to get out? Or maybe it's that you have somebody else's brain. Richard Bandler, one of the co-founders of NLP, humorously proposes the explanation that, because the Earth is tilted a little on its axis, you actually have the brain of the person next to you. It's unhappy being in the wrong person, and that's why it's always picking on you. How else can you explain how you can be so competent doing one thing and then you turn around and do something else and suddenly feel so incompetent and stupid? How is it that you can be doing really well at one thing and doing really poorly at something else, all at the same time? Is it actually possible to learn to use your own brain in the way you want to at the times you want to? These are some of the questions that Dynamic Learning attempts to address.

For instance, what exactly is the difference between learning to spell and learning to ride a bicycle? Most people would say that the difference is that one process is essentially 'physical' while the other is 'mental'. But saying or writing a word is something that is as 'physical' as pushing the peddles of a bicycle. And the mental activity required to steer and balance a bicycle is at least as complex as that required to remember the spelling of a word. Certainly, both cases involve coordinating the activity of our nervous system in order to accomplish a goal.

So, just what activity **are** you engaging in when you are spelling? Somebody tells you to spell a word. The word comes into your ears as a sound. Your brain does something with it and you eventually say some letters outloud or write them down as a response. Somewhere between the time that somebody asks you to spell and you respond back, your nervous system has done something to that set of sounds. It is what happens in between the time that sounds go in and the letters come out that is the domain of Dynamic Learning.

According to NLP, when people think, learn and spell, etc., they do so by activating some combination of their sensory representational systems—that is, they are seeing, hearing, feeling, smelling or tasting to some degree. Our nervous systems are wired to naturally input, process and store the images, feelings, sounds, smells and tastes that we are exposed to during our daily activities. We can also imagine things. For instance, you could imagine what it would look like if you were floating above yourself, looking down on yourself as you are reading this book. In addition to storing various sensory representations, your nervous system can make up images, sounds and feelings. One of the most basic principles of NLP and Dynamic Learning is that when people are learning or thinking, they are putting together components of those sights, sounds, feelings, smells or tastes. The habitual structure through which a person sequences and combines his or her sensory experience is known as a 'strategy' in NLP.

In this book we are going to be exploring some fundamental strategies for learning. That is, we are going to be exploring the processes by which people 'learn how to learn'. Our approach is going to be somewhat different from what you would normally expect when you read a text book or go to a class. Normally when you go to a class or read a book, the material that you are supposed to learn is simply presented to you and, to a large degree, you have to figure out *how* to learn it yourself. In other words, you are exposed to the information or the material to study; but you are not necessarily told 'how specifically' to learn it. What this book is about is "how people learn."

We will be applying these 'learning to learn' strategies to some content areas like memory, spelling, reading, learning languages, composition and so forth. Yet, even though those might be the temporary focus of our exploration, the essence of this book is the process underlying *how people learn.*

To us, all learning shares the same kinds of structure and principles. The question is whether or not the particular strategy someone is using to apply those structures and principles is appropriate to complete the task in which he or she is engaged. A child who can learn to avoid handing his or her homework in every day has learned to do something. It does require a strategy. People tend to think of the mental processes that produce results that we don't like to see in children as not being related to good learning. But that is not true, because even if you are not able to do something well—you have to learn *how* to NOT do it. Especially when it involves something repetitive like many of the tasks required of children at school. For example, try to spell a word wrong the same way every time you spell that word. Some people actually spell a word the same incorrect way every time—they correctly remember the wrong spelling.

Certainly, somebody who has learned how to get to eighth grade or even high school without being able to spell, write, and read has also learned something. It may not be that they learned how to spell, write, or read, but they've learned something. Somebody who can't read a book, but can fix an automobile engine faster than you can stand on your head, has learned something. And for us, the process of learning is what 'education' is really all about. Once you've recognized that someone can learn and in what way, then you can begin to enrich and direct that process beyond its current manifestation.

So even though we will be focusing on some specific content areas, and you'll be learning some strategies which we think are effective strategies for those content areas, our ultimate goal is to offer you tools to learn how to learn anything more effectively, and to facilitate others to learn how to learn more effectively.

We think that developing your own learning skills and helping others to develop their learning skills go hand in hand with each other. We encourage you to first apply what you learn from this book to your own learning process, and then share it with other people. This approach is not necessarily unique, but it is unique in many ways when it comes to education. For instance, many teachers are not really taught how to do what is actually expected of the children that they are teaching. For example, how many grammar school teachers are required to show a competency in learning or acquiring a particular math skill? If a teacher is good at biology, is he or she ever taught how to teach kids in class 'how to' be good at biology as well? Typically a teacher teaches what they have to teach in class so the students will know the required amount of biology in order to pass on to the next grade.

In other words they emphasize the *what* to learn instead of *how*, specifically, to learn it most easily and effectively.

As you read this book, you'll be engaging in the activity of learning; you'll be learning to learn yourself. We believe that the learning strategies that help *you* to learn better will be the ones that you will be the most congruent about sharing with others. As you will see, most of the exercises are intended to be done with others in a 'cooperative learning' setting; but versions of them can also be done on your own. In most cases we have provided descriptions of the techniques and exercises that you can do on your own. We have also provided examples of the group exercises in the form of transcripts of demonstrations that can provide you with a sense of how the processes work in a group.

Dynamic Learning exercises and methods were designed to be done by people of all ages. Many of our Dynamic Learning seminars included as many children and young people as adults.

The reason that we call this 'Dynamic Learning', is because we are going to ask you to engage in activities that activate your neurology - that bring it alive. Some of those activities might seem to have nothing to do with traditional academic topics. One of the things that is most important about NLP is its emphasis on the fact that people learn through the activation of neurological processes. And the more you can use your neurology, the more you are going to be able to learn and the better you are going to be able to learn. Some of the exercises in this book may be considered a kind of mental calisthenics—calisthenics for the brain.

In a lot of ways the brain is like a muscle. When you first use a muscle that hasn't been exercised very much it might get sore for awhile. But if you keep doing your isometrics, you get used to it. Then you find that your abilities in areas that you are not even practicing begin to improve. Mental calisthenics can produce the same kinds of results. If you develop your mental capabilities you start to find that even without studying, you tend to learn new things more effectively. If you prepare the soil before you plant the seeds, the roots grow much more deeply and solidly.

Dynamic Learning involves engaging in activities and exercises that will be dealing with the multiple levels and dimensions of learning. Dynamic learning techniques address WHY issues of learning as well as HOW TO and WHAT TO and WHERE TO issues. Dynamic Learning strategies also address the function of *relationship* in the learning process. Within this framework, the emphasis of Dynamic Learning is on the HOW TO level. NLP is probably the one psychological model that has really built an actual technology around the HOW TO process: HOW TO communicate, establish and develop rapport and deal with other peoples' beliefs and values, HOW TO motivate people, HOW TO learn and perform effectively, and so on.

We believe interaction is an integral aspect of learning. In our Dynamic Learning Seminars we make sure people know it is OK to raise their hands and ask questions. As a matter of fact, we encourage it. It gives us more of a sense of who they are and how they are thinking. Seminar participants are also allowed to get up and move around, especially if they are one of those people that can't sit in his or her seat all the time. As far as we're concerned people can lie on the floor or stand on their heads if they want to. As long as they don't interfere with the experience of the persons sitting near them.

To preserve the experiential and interactive quality of Dynamic Learning, a major portion of this book will be drawn from transcripts of our Dynamic Learning Seminar. (We have indicated the names of the individual authors in relationship to their personal contributions in order to maintain the sense of diversity and dynamic interaction.) We have chosen to maintain the flavor of the seminar language at the risk of sacrificing literary fluency. But we feel that it is appropriate for a book on Dynamic Learning to preserve the spontaneity, humor and feel of a live seminar. We have also provided summaries of the basic Dynamic Learning principles, exercises and strategies in the appendices of this book as a reference, in case you want to skip over the explanations and examples and go directly to the strategies themselves.

Chapter 1

Fundamentals of Dynamic Learning

Overview of Chapter 1

- Levels of Learning
- The Influence of Relationships on Learning
- Cooperative Learning
- Neuro-Linguistic Programming
- Balancing Task and Relationship
- The R.O.L.E. Model
- The B.A.G.E.L. Model
- Identifying an Effective Learning State

Fundamentals of Dynamic Learning

RD: In this chapter we'd like to provide an overview of some of the fundamental principles, models and distinctions behind our Dynamic Learning exercises and strategies.

For instance, what makes an effective learning strategy? It is conventional wisdom that having a strategy is better than having no strategy at all. That is, that doing some kind of a systematic process to remember names, for example, is better than doing nothing or doing something unsystematically. However, systematic thinking is a 'double edge sword'. Ineffective learning methods may lead you to perform worse than having no method all. The danger of learning to think systematically is that the system that you use may be just as detrimental to some kinds of processes as it is advantageous to others.

TE: It's a lot like scotch tape—it's really great because it sticks to everything; and it's really lousy because it sticks to everything.

RD: For example, a process that allows you to spell well — to be very consistent and reproduce something you have seen exactly as you have seen it — might not be that great for creative writing. You might either be very repetitive or get in trouble for plagiarism.

I remember I used to get excellent grades in creative writing, but my creative spelling was never quite good enough. I didn't understand it because I was writing and spelling on the same paper. There were two distinct levels of processes going on there that I didn't initially know how to come to terms with. When I was writing, I was supposed to be creative, but not in the spelling aspect of the composition. If I applied the same values and strategies to both parts I got into trouble. I know a lot of people who have problems writing when they start correcting the spelling and grammar at the time that they're writing and then lose their whole creative train of thought.

TE: Their 'train of thought' jumps a track.

RD: The point is that writing, like many other learning tasks, is a multi-level process that requires several types of strategies in order to be effective. The values and strategies that you use for generating the content of a writing project are different from the values and strategies that you employ for checking the spelling or the grammar. The question we seek to explore through our work with strategies in the Dynamic Learning process is, what are the kinds of models, principles and ways of thinking that would tend to support certain kinds of learning and certain kinds of performance in the most effective manner?

Levels of Learning

RD: One very important presupposition of Dynamic Learning is that learning is a multi-level process. That is, learning doesn't just take place on one level. Learning takes place on many levels simultaneously. Beliefs and values are as important a part of learning as cognitive processes and behaviors. A person's sense of identity and self esteem are as much of an influence as environmental stimuli. All of these levels are important to consider whether you are teaching or learning.

People like Pavlov and Skinner, studied learning from the point of view of the relationship between environment and behavior. To them the cognitive capability level was just a black box. Other psychologies have focused up at the higher levels, studying self-esteem and motivation. People like Sigmund Freud, for instance, developed very brilliant and interesting models; but Freud's models didn't really give much insight into how to teach somebody to spell. Cognitive psychology, on the other hand, tends to isolate the capability level from behaviors and values. As a result, it hasn't really produced much of what you could call a "technology".

The goal of Dynamic Learning has been to follow an integrated multi-level approach that deals with the dynamic interplay between all of the different levels of the nervous system.

In the terms of my 'Neuro-Logical Levels' model, our capabilities connect our beliefs and values to our behaviors. Having beliefs and values without the capabilities to translate them into behavior makes them simply platitudes. Having behaviors without the capabilities to connect them to beliefs and values makes them simply reflexes. Dynamic Learning processes take all of these levels into account.

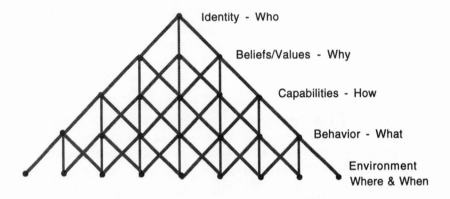

Levels of Influences on Learning

One of the most concrete influences on learning is the external environment. The environment that you are in will either be conducive and supportive or alternatively detrimental to learning. The 'dynamics' of the environment are a significant factor in the learning process. Sometimes you have to contend with environmental limitations—like distracting noises coming from another room.

TE: For instance, try to teach math in a Quonset hut on a hot day!

RD: The environment is going to be shaping the learning process. It may interfere with or may enhance learning. In our work with the Pajaro Valley school district in California we explored the creation of an environment that would be maximally conducive to learning. It was called the OLE classroom, the Optimal Learning Environment. The idea was to explore what kind of a setting would optimally support the process of leaning.

In addition to environment, learning requires behaviors and actions — not just the act of writing words and taking notes but through the act of doing something in relation to what you have learned. Of course, people tend to react to their environment, and reactions are a part of learning. But self motivated and directed actions tend to solidify learning more completely.

Self initiated behavior facilitates learning. Of course, part of the reason that you learn something is in order to do something with it that is relevant or important to you; in a particular environment, and at a particular place and time.

Environment relates to the **where** and **when** of learning and behavior relates to the **what** of learning. Beyond these, there is another important level of learning, the **how** of learning.

TE: It is at this level that we really start getting into the essence of Dynamic Learning. This level involves the development of internal capabilities and strategies. It is not about the content you're going to learn, but rather about the skills necessary to be able to learn - the capabilities and strategies that you need to learn new behaviors.

RD: According to NLP, people learn in proportion to how fully they use their senses. You learn through your senses—you learn by seeing things, you learn by hearing things, you learn by feeling things, you even learn by smelling and tasting; even though these last two senses are left out of traditional education most of the time. In fact, traditional education tends to emphasize primarily the visual and auditory parts of learning. But one of the things that we hope to demonstrate to you, through your own experience, is that the rest of your senses, especially you feelings and your body movements, are as important to learning as your eyes and ears. Even with what might be considered a very 'cerebral' skill—like math or spelling—your other senses are as important as what you see and hear or visualize.

TE: As any of you who work within the American school system know, there can be some formidable environmental limitations—that is, sometimes you have classrooms that are too small or too hot, or you have to make do with old books. There are a lot of limitations that can happen in the traditional educational environment. Some districts have the resources to get new books, while others do not. Equal opportunity in education is difficult to make happen on an environmental or even behavioral level. Equal opportunity in education only really begins to happen at the level of capability and strategy — at the level of neurology. That is, if everyone shares the same capabilities of how to learn something, then everybody starts out on the same foot; regardless of whether they are learning in a Quonset hut or whether they are learning in a brand new 20 million dollar school that has been built in a beautiful quiet location.

RD: Another level that is important to consider in the learning process is the level of beliefs and values. This level involves issues relating to *why* to learn. Why should somebody bother learning something? Values and beliefs have to do with the motivation to learn and the permission to learn.

Beliefs and values issues surface in many different places. They come up in relation to the student's own personal history, his or her peer group, the material to be learned, the teacher, and his or her cultural background. The influence of different cultural backgrounds and issues relating to students that come from multi-lingual and multi-cultural situations are becoming more and more prominent in our modern world.

For example, turning in homework is an action, and if a student doesn't carry out that action he is going to get a reaction from the teacher. The question is, if someone doesn't turn his homework in, is that because his didn't know how to do the homework or because he didn't want to do the homework?

TE: It may not be important in his culture to hand in homework.

RD: Perhaps he has some kind of a relationship problem with his teacher.

TE: Maybe his parents never handed their homework in and he thinks, "I want to be like them. That's what is important to me, not the homework."

RD: Or maybe his thinks, "If I turn my homework in, people are going to call me 'goody two-shoes', 'teacher's pet', or something like that."

These *why* issues are as important to learning as the *how to's* and the *what to*'s.

Beyond beliefs and values is the level of identity—*who* is learning, *who* is teaching. Who somebody perceives herself to be shapes and determines her beliefs, values and capabilities. Capabilities and values are often seen as direct expressions of identity.

An interesting learning process that is common in children is to take on the identity of something outside of themselves. When they are playing, they don't say "I'm going to learn how to act like a mommy." They say: "I'm going to *be* Mommy"; or, "I'm going to *be* a fireman"; or, "I'm going to *be* a puppy." Identifying with something is a very powerful learning process. Once you commit yourself to a particular identity the rest of the learning becomes a matter of adding in the details.

If you can't identify with what you are learning, it can be a real struggle. Let's take for example, learning a second language. I know people who have studied a particular language for years, and may have even lived in another country for years, and they still have problems with pronunciation They don't understand why they can't get rid of their accent. One of the things they don't realize is that the accent may be a way in which they keep and affirm their identity with respect to their native culture.

I once heard somebody say that if you want to learn a language, the best thing to do is to fall in love with someone that speaks that language. Why is that? Perhaps it is because you perceive something associated with someone you love as not being foreign to you but rather something that you have good feelings about— something you even begin to identify with.

Having a student identify with mathematics is really different than having them study it and try hard to learn it.

Sometimes, we'll work with somebody that has had a learning problem for a long time and discover other types of identity issues. For instance, I worked with a successful businessman who had been dyslexic for 30 years. He could do math perfectly, and he ran his business very well, but he could not spell. I was trying to teach him the NLP Spelling Strategy. But every time he started to spell a word, something got in the way and he became very anxious and upset. Finally I said "I notice that you keep getting this anxiety whenever you start spelling. I'm wondering what would happen if you were suddenly able to spell perfectly?" All of a sudden this guy blurted out in extreme anger, "Then I'd be finally giving in to that SOB after all these years!" It turns out that this person had an image of his third grade teacher etched in his mind. He could remember this teacher like it was yesterday. Apparently the teacher had been very abusive to this man and made his inability to spell such a personal issue that the man had polarized against the teacher and vowed he would never give in to him. It would have been a violation of his personal integrity to spell well. Of course, he hadn't had any conscious awareness of this vow. Once he became aware of it, he realized that spelling was simply a capability and that he was secure in his identity as an adult and could release himself from his vow. Needless to say, after this realization he was immediately able to spell words correctly, without having to learn a new strategy.

TE: The levels of belief and identity are good places to explore when other things don't work. If a child has a belief such as, "If I spell I am going to be just like the person who I don't want to be like", then you are not dealing with an inability to spell, you're dealing with a completely different issue. If you try to address it on the level that this kid isn't putting enough time in his spelling, then you are never going to get that child to learn to spell. In fact, you'll probably just end up frustrating him more.

RD: On the other side of the coin, sometimes things are perceived as identity or values issues that are not really at those levels. Sometimes a student who simply has an ineffective strategy for learning something is accused of having a poor attitude, being unmotivated or not trying hard enough. Having the "want to" without the "how to" is just as much of a problem as having the "how to" without the "want to".

I mentioned earlier that people tend to identify with what they can do and with what they can't do. You hear people say, "I'm a smoker" or "I'm a non-smoker." These are not statements about the behavior of smoking, they have to do with identity, which incorporates whole sets of values, abilities, behaviors, and environments. Similarly you will hear students say, "I'm a good speller," or "I'm a bad speller" instead of "I'm learning spelling." It is different to "be a mathematician" than to "know how to do math".

Calling yourself a mathematician or a writer or a good speller, becomes a statement about identity, not a statement about capability or behavior. To call somebody "a dyslexic" becomes an identity label more so than a description of that person's lack of capabilities.

TE: People do tend to identify with their symptoms. You can, in no time at all, convince young children and their parents that the child's identity is that they are learning disabled, or dyslexic or any number of other labels that you want to put on them. It is not so much the labeling process as it is the question of how the message is received. Is dyslexia the description of an ongoing process that can be influenced which has to do with the capability of spelling and reading, or is dyslexia the description of somebody's identity? As an identity statement it becomes a way to pigeonhole a student to keep them away from contaminating the rest of the class room. It is as if they had a bad identity virus that they have picked up somewhere along the way. You wouldn't want them to infect all the other kids in the class and then everybody would think that they were dyslexic. Who knows what you'd do after that.

RD: Invent a 'neural-antibiotic.'

The essential point of we are saying is that teaching and learning are multi-level processes. The lack of awareness of the influence of these different levels, or the confusion of one level with another can lead to problems. Sometimes it is important to address the *why* and *who* as well as *how to*. At other times it is important to keep issues of identity as far away from what you're learning or teaching as possible so that there isn't any confusion between capability and identity.

TE: Identity issues can apply not only to the student, but also to the perceived identity of the teacher. Not the teaching style, not the beliefs about learning, but the perception of the identity of the person who is standing up in front of the students teaching them.

The Influence of Relationships on Learning

RD: The teaching process minimally involves two dimensions: *task* and *relationship*. Learning often involves as much focus on the relationship as it does on the task. Ask a student that is really good at something, "What makes you good at that?" They rarely respond by describing the specific behaviors or mental capabilities that make them effective. Often the very first thing the student will say is, "I had a good teacher," or "I really liked the teacher." If you ask what makes someone a good teacher, you will get answers like, "She really supported me," or "He really believed in me," or "He really cared about me." These statements are focused more on identity and relationship than anything else. Another good example of this is that if you ask somebody who is a good athlete to think of their best performance, you get less response than if you ask them to think of their best coach. The recollection of an empowering coaching relationship activates a more complete and integrated set of neurology than the memory of a particular performance.

TE: On the down side, you can have a child who is doing extremely well in the fifth or sixth grade - an "A" student. But when the child goes to the following grade, suddenly he or she is getting C's and D's and maybe a few B's. The child studies just as much. He or she seems to be just as motivated about school. The counselors and parents can't quite figure out what's going on—until you go into the classroom and notice the interaction between the teacher and the child. The teacher may be totally mismatched with the child's learning style or perhaps so completely task oriented that the child feels no sense of connection to the subjects he or she is supposed to be learning.

RD: Disempowering or confusing relationships can have a negative influence on learning. I know a kid who was having all kinds of trouble learning math precisely because he hated his father and his father was good at math. The last thing he wanted to do was to be like his father in any way. It had nothing to do with the teacher or the classroom. He said: "If I learn math, then I'll be more like him. And I don't want to be like him."

I talked to a man recently who was teaching his son the NLP spelling strategy (which we will be going over later in this book). He was upset because the boy's mother, who was the one who helped him with his homework, was teaching the boy the standard phonetic methods of spelling. Now what's the kid supposed to do? He has to decide, "Am I going to align with Daddy or Mommy?" Spelling is no longer just a task, but becomes a decision on whether to do it "Daddy's way" or "Mommy's way." And, for a child, that can seem like a survival level issue.

TE: There was a kid we worked with whose father had taught him short cuts for doing algebra and geometry. When the child used his father's method in doing it, he succeeded in solving the problem. More importantly he understood the strategy for doing the problem. His conflict occurred when he got to school and discovered that is not how they taught it in school. He could do it the short way but they wanted him to do it the long way. The reason we ended up seeing this boy was because he was caught between doing it the way that was fun, easy and successful and doing it the way it was "supposed to" be done—and he was failing doing it that way. Children shouldn't be forced to make these kind of decisions in life—especially a child in the fifth grade.

RD: At least if they have to make that kind of decision, it should be clear that it is about cultural values and relationship, and not confuse it with learning.

Sometimes we find that task and relationship are confused in the educational process; at other times they are totally isolated from one another. For example, if a child does poorly on a learning task, like math or reading, you pull him out of school and make him get special attention to deal with his problem.

TE: You remove him from any possibility of maintaining relationships with the class he was in before.

RD: But also, if a student has no relationships at all at school — he is all alone in the schoolyard, he has no friends, he goes home lonely, and his best friend is the computer — nobody considers that that student might have a learning problem.

TE: Because he passes all of his classes. He does the tasks all right. Yet he has not learned how to establish or manage the kinds of relationships that are essential for education. In the educational system we don't tend to look at this factor.

RD: So, what we are saying is that learning intimately involves both dimensions. Because the two dimensions are not typically recognized and distinguished, they are often confused. On the other hand, they both need to be addressed for any kind of effective learning or any kind of effective teaching.

Dynamic Learning processes are based on the belief that both the task and relationship dimensions are equally important in learning. Even though the focus of many of our exercises will be on the development of learning strategies for specific tasks, the sense of identity and beliefs that go to support relationships as well as the capabilities, behavior and environment for the tasks will be equally as important. What we will be doing is studying principles that will cover the dynamics of all of these dimensions - levels of learning inside of the context of relationship as well as task.

When people get together in a context of learning, often the first thing they focus on is relationships. When people are uncertain about the task - when they don't know what they are supposed to do yet - they tend to place a stronger emphasis on relationship. Uncertainty in one area tends to put a need for stability in the other area. When people are uncertain about their relationships, they tend to focus on what they think they are supposed to be doing; they seek out some sort of task.

So, when a teacher is introducing new material or teaching a task that is either difficult, uncertain or new, then people's focus goes to the relationship. They are going to want to know why they should do it. They will want to know who else does it? For example, if the teacher is the only model a child has for why he would want to learn math, then the teacher is not just a carrier of information, he or she is a delegate or a role model of what it is like to be a mathematician or a speller, or a good reader, or an NLP trainer for that matter.

Cooperative Learning

RD: Another implication of this dual task and relationship aspect of learning is embodied in the process of cooperative learning. The process of cooperation has at least as much to do with relationship as it does with task—you don't cooperate except in terms of relationship.

TE: But it's obviously not the kind of relationship in which people are all just standing around hugging each other or sitting in a hot tub. There is a task to be accomplished. Cooperative learning is a description of utilizing both of these dimensions to their fullest.

RD: There are different levels of relationships as well. Some people are only in a relationship at an environmental level - for instance, they happen to meet each other in the break room.   Its a relationship in which they primarily react to each other because they happen to share the same space. However, when you have to coordinate your actions with somebody else, that is a more inti-mate relationship than the fact that you just happen to see them in the hall.   When they have to do something to coordinate their behavior with what you do, you've got a more involved relation-ship.   When you have to coordinate your thinking process with another person, an even more intimate relationship with that person starts to develop.   There is a tighter bond that begins to emerge when you are teaching and learning from each other on a capability level. A relationship built around shared values and motivations, or one in which the permission to do something becomes dependent on somebody else, involves a deeper level of interaction—which incidentally, is not only tighter but can lead to more potential friction. You can even have a relationship in which missions become intertwined. Your identity—the who you are—is coordinated with who somebody else is.

TE: That creates an interesting framework for accomplishment because it sets up a very deep basis for cooperation. Being on the same mission makes it easier to share the same beliefs and the same capabilities, the same behaviors and the same environment.

RD: We find that the more a teacher is able to fully be himself or herself while teaching, the easier it is to do everything. The more that what you're teaching relates to your mission, and embodies who you really are, the better teacher you are going to be.

A good example of this is portrayed in the movie "Stand and Deliver". It is about a man who chose to be a teacher in an inner city school in Los Angeles. He made it his mission to teach these kids algebra. He devoted 100% of himself to this one mission. Paradoxically, putting 100% of yourself into something often makes it seem like you are putting out less effort. Sometimes we find that just being yourself actually makes everything a lot easier. A lot of teachers might have the feeling, "I'm already tired at the end of a day, and you mean I'm supposed to put more of me into this—more of me into my teaching?" I think that when you do put yourself fully into what you are doing, it doesn't lead to exhaustion. In fact, it actually makes everything a lot easier. Because you're not in conflict—trying to be a different person than who you already are. You are totally congruent about what you are doing.

TE: If you have a strong mission, and a strong relationship it makes a seemingly impossible task possible. Then the total focus can shift to the *how,* the strategy for accomplishing the objective. In fact, a key element in the movie is that these students were accused of cheating because they all made the same mistakes on the test. He had so successfully taught them his own strategy for solving the algebra problems, that they all made the same mistakes. To me, that confirmed the importance of mission and relationship. It wasn't like all of a sudden these kids learned how to be smart and made up for all the years they had been going to school. It had to do with his relationship with them and his ability to transfer his sense of mission, that's what changed everything.

RD: You could call this a kind of a 'top down' strategy. Rather than beginning by saying, "This is what you are going to learn," you ask, "Who are you?" Then ask, "What is important to you?" Then you can ask, "What do you already know how to do?" After that you can begin to address the what, the content, of the learning task and connect it to their how, why and who.

The basic challenge in any teaching or training process is to get the learner to:

a) **want to** learn the target skills,

b) learn **how to** implement those skills and strategies in a pragmatic and effective manner, and

c) get a **chance to** practice them in appropriate increments and contexts that will actually make them a part of his or her behavior.

TE: A lot of problems happen when teachers or learners don't recognize the need for all three of these processes.

RD: For example, a teacher tells the class what to do and a student raises her hand and asks a question that boils down to something like "How?" or "Why?" The teacher either just re-explains what to do, or becomes indignant at the impertinence of the student.

In the Dynamic Learning process we believe an effective learning process is one that engages a person mentally, physically and emotionally and provides immediate feedback to the individual involved in the learning process. By interacting with the instructor, fellow learners, and the learning material within the teaching context, the learner comes away with some pragmatic skill that he or she is actually able to use in a real life context.

Neuro-Linguistic Programming

RD: Much of the Dynamic Learning process draws from the principles and technology of Neuro-Linguistic Programming. Neuro-Linguistic Programming (NLP) is about the dynamic interplay between the three essential processes through which we make up our models of the world. *Neuro* has to do with the nervous system. Not only the brain, the whole nervous system. People like Descartes tried to separate the mind from the body. Yet when you think about the mind as your nervous system, you realize that your nervous system extends down into your body. Moving your body engages your nervous system as much as sitting and thinking. Your heart and your stomach, for example, have their own internal neural wiring. The wiring of the stomach is in some ways as complex as certain brain structures. Its as if it is its own mini computer on line in your nervous system. We believe that your heart is as much a part of your whole nervous system as your brain is; not to mention your toes, your arms and your legs. Thus, learning takes place in the nervous system *as a whole*.

TE: If you don't believe that, take somebody that uses their hands a lot when they talk and tell them to sit on their hands and try to keep up the conversation. For some people, no words will come out of their mouths if they can't move their hands.

RD: The *linguistic* part of Neuro-Linguistic Programming has to do with the fact that as human beings we have evolved our communication systems, particularly in regards to language, to a very high degree. In the same way that the intricacy and sophistication of our language makes us so different from other animals, our ability to use language to a large degree reflects the ability of our nervous system. Of course, our language is influenced by our nervous system and, in the same way, our nervous system is shaped by our language. Language is one of the central tools and subjects in human learning and in all forms of education. Whether it's the language of mathematics, foreign language, spelling, grammar or creative writing, the bulk of what you do in school, revolves around the processes of language and linguistics. So,

Neuro-Linguistics is about the intimate interconnection between language and the nervous system.

The *programming* part of Neuro-Linguistic Programming has to do with how our neurological and language systems form structures which make up our models of the world. It is interesting that the field and technology of NLP emerged around the same time that the personal computer appeared. Certainly, one of the implications of Neuro-Linguistic programming is that the most important personal computer is the one between your two ears and behind your eyes. In the NLP view this is a personal computer that you can program and play with similarly to any other personal computer.

TE: The computer itself is designed to be user friendly but the programs are sometimes not so user friendly.

RD: It depends upon who programmed it. If you try to use other people's programs, they may not always be user friendly to you. But, in a way, this is what NLP is all about - how to get that computer up there to be more and more user friendly.

TE: Our belief is that the central processing unit of your body is extremely user friendly. As a matter of fact, it will go ahead and learn without you having to do anything at all - it is on your side. There's a difference, however, between the hardware, which in this case is what's biologically in there, and the software, which is how all this language and neurology is organized. People don't have bad brains. They may have programs that don't function well, but not broken brains.

RD: Now, not everybody's brain is exactly the same, just like not all personal computers are the same. IBM's are different from Macintoshes and so on and so forth. So, one goal of effective learning and teaching is to learn how to communicate with different kinds of 'computers'.

TE: Of course, people's brains work differently from computers in many significant ways. If computer programmers had their computers act like people's brains, it would freak them out. Your brain is always making new neurological connections. It would be like leaving your computer on over the weekend and returning on

Monday to find that it had soldered new connections within itself. It put new wires in by itself and soldered connections that you never put there. Computers don't work that way and that's the difference between the computer and a human brain. They're both programmable, but only humans can 'meta-program' or rewire their own computers. That's the difference—that's why you're not an automaton even though your brain has the ability to function in a strategic linear fashion. You can reprogram it, but the computer cannot reprogram itself. That's what makes you different from computers.

Balancing Task and Relationship

RD: We realize that a lot of people will think, "Oh, thinking of the brain as a computer is so mechanical and impersonal. I don't want to think of my child's brain as a computer or my students' brains as a computer." However, we've seen people do more inhumane things to children and students precisely because they *don't* conceive of their brain as being like a computer. A teacher will say, "That student is having a behavior problem and isn't learning. They must be resistant, or hyperactive, or not putting out enough effort." Yet maybe all that really needs to happen is for the teacher to talk to that student's brain in a language that it can understand. The paradox of this approach is that conceiving of the brain as a computer can make you a much more humane person, because you don't start thinking, "Ah, this stupid kid, they're resisting me, they're putting up a fight, or they're doing this on purpose." One of the things you'll realize, if you've ever tried to work with a computer, is that the computer does not have bad intentions. The computer is not resistant. The computer is not trying to do something just to get on your case or manipulate you. It can be useful to think about people being that way. It will sometimes help you to act more humanely because you don't project these kind of negative intentions. You realize that that person's brain is speaking in the only language that it knows.

TE: Once again, it's a balance of task and relationship. In terms of the task, you may want to think about the child's brain as being like a computer so that you can understand where the program is not functioning. This allows the relationship to be closer because you're not projecting problems with task into the relationship with the child.

RD: If you are able to be very skillful in relation to the task, then it frees you to really emphasize the human part of the relationship with a person. Having the choice to think about the brain as a computer actually gives you a lot more flexibility in figuring out how to deal with learning problems.

TE: Furthermore, if you have no technology with which to approach problems with the task, you end up doing some pretty inhumane things out of ignorance or because of the lack of other alternatives. For instance, periodically drugs like rytalin make a comeback in the school system. While I'm sure these drugs are championed by very well intentioned people, the message is that the brain is not even as sophisticated as a computer. Rather, the brain is like a motor and what it needs is heavier motor oil or something. "We'll just put in a higher octane gas and see if that changes the problem." Its the kind of thing that can make sense to someone who focuses on relationships but does not have an effective behavioral technology. It may seem like a cold, calculating, non-personal way of thinking about children to compare their brain to a computer. But you could perceive it as being just as non-personal, calculating or cold to force a child to take rytalin as opposed to finding out why his nervous system needs to be so excited and creative in class.

Man: I just want to make a comment regarding rytalin. I agree with you and I'd like to learn from these workshops how to deal differently with these kinds of behaviors, but I haven't had that much experience with them. Rytalin is another tool, if you don't have any other tool to work with that might be successful.

RD: That is our point, in a way. In the absence of other alternatives, drugs become a viable option. We are not saying it is not a viable tool if you have no other choices. All we're saying is that there may be other choices that are just as effective and perhaps may even be simpler and more ecological. We are not advocating using or not using rytalin, we are advocating the constant search for more options. NLP is about adding choices, not taking them away.

TE: I also see the periodic trend in the increased use of something like rytalin as a sign of an attitude shift. That is, rytalin doesn't deal with the issue of learning. It deals with the *behavior* of the child in the classroom. The question is, "What is your outcome?" Is it to facilitate learning and socialization or to simply stop problematic behavior? My concern is that the more interventions like rytalin become accepted, the more people use them. Not to aid in education and learning, but to control the classroom. It is more of a classroom management tool than it is a learning tool.

Woman: I read a scientific study not long ago that said rytalin did nothing at all to change the behavior that contributed to a child's learning process.

RD: Remember, in our multi-level approach to learning, behavioral and environmental influences have a place, but they are not the only factors that impact learning.

TE: Something like rytalin may be an effective tool for influencing behavior, but not necessarily for changing programming at the level of capabilities, beliefs, values or identity.

RD: Certainly, the mechanics of the computer is important. If the computer has all kinds of misconnections in it, the software will be misdirected, and you might need to go in there and deal with it mechanically. Through the technology of NLP we hope to add more choices for influencing those higher levels of programming. While you can certainly influence the functioning of a computer by oiling the parts or changing the power level it is receiving, these interventions will not correct bugs in the software.

Our primary point is that the more 'hi-tech' you get, the more 'hi-touch' you have to become. We really want to emphasize this balance. The more that we talk about thinking as programming, the more we'll also emphasize the relationship aspect as well. It is through broadening both of those dimensions, that you add more and more choices.

TE: Dynamic Learning isn't something that comes in a bottle or in a pill in which you have the same dosage everyday. If you 'administer' Dynamic Learning strategies as you would administer a drug, you are not really engaging in Dynamic Learning.

RD: When you forget about a child's identity, you forget about the child's motivation. Anytime that you take a 'cookie-cutter' type of approach, no matter what technology you're using, you begin to run that kind of risk of losing the important balance between task and relationship.

One of the basic principles of Dynamic Learning is that the more of your neurology you use to represent something, the more you will learn it. If you have to commit half of your neurology to fight against the teacher and the other half to focus on the task, you have less neurology available to commit to the learning task. If you commit half of your neurology to worry about what other people are thinking about you, and the other half to try to learn something, again, you're probably not going to be able to learn as well as if you are able to fully commit your neurology to learning.

TE: Commitment of neurology is not only affected by interpersonal issues. There are micro level influences as well. For example, some people involve a fair amount of their neurology fighting things like gravity. In other words, they even have a hard time holding themselves up, and being balanced because of their posture and other deep level habits. A lot of children have not had the experience of learning how to move their body effectively through the world. They use up half of their neurological capacity just to keep themselves from falling over or tripping over something, or to keep themselves awake and alert while sitting in this classroom. They're fighting gravity half of the time and half of the time they're trying to learn.

RD: Perhaps this how a drug like rytalin works. It reduces the amount of neurophysiological noise. I think that this is what readiness to learn is all about. Readiness to learn is a function of how much of my neurology is going to have to be used to manage the external situation - whether it be balancing myself, defending myself against other people's values or judgments, or trying to maintain a relationship - and how much of my neurology is actually committed to the learning process.

The R.O.L.E. Model

RD: It is within this framework that we would like to begin to look into the "Neuro-Linguistics" of learning. The basic model from which we operate, we call the R.O.L.E. Model. The R.O.L.E. Model has to do with how our senses and our sensory representational systems influence our abilities to be effective in the various tasks and relationships that make up our lives.

The goal of the R.O.L.E. modeling process is to identify the essential elements of thinking and behavior used to produce a particular response or outcome. This involves identifying the critical steps of the mental strategy and the role each step plays in the overall neurological "program." This role is determined by the following four factors which are indicated by the letters which make up name of the **R.O.L.E.** Model - *Representational systems; Orientation; Links; Effect.*

Representational Systems have to do with which of the five senses are most dominant for the particular mental step in the strategy: **Visual** (sight), **Auditory** (sound), **Kinesthetic** (feeling), **Olfactory** (smell), **Gustatory** (taste).

  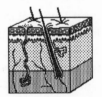

Our Primary Experience of the World is Through Our Senses of Sight, Sound and Touch.

Each representational system is designed to perceive certain basic qualities of the experiences it senses. These include characteristics such as *color, brightness, tone, loudness, temperature, pressure,* etc. These qualities are called "sub-modalities" in NLP since they are sub-components of each of the representational systems.

<u>Orientation</u> has to do with whether a particular sensory representation is focused (**e**)xternally toward the outside world or (**i**)nternally toward either (**r**)emembered or (**c**)onstructed experiences. For instance, when you are seeing something, is it in the outside world, in memory or in your imagination?

In the model of NLP, people will often have a preferred or most highly valued representational system and orientation for certain tasks and contexts. Differences in representational system preferences often account for differences in performance with respect to various learning activities. For instance, imagine the following interaction. A child who is having trouble with spelling is talking with his teacher:

Student: I just don't really *feel* excited about learning to spell.

Teacher: Well I think if we just take a closer *look* at your problem set you will *see* that its not so difficult to learn these words.

Student: It's not something that I can really get in *touch* with.

Teacher: You're not trying hard enough. Just *look* at them a little more carefully.

Student: I can't seem to get a *feel* for it.

Teacher: Pay attention to what I'm trying to *show* you. Just *focus* on your work. With a little effort it will *clear* up.

Student: Ah, well. I guess it *feels* like another boring day at school.

RD: Unfortunately, this exchange is typical of what frequently occurs in school between teachers and students. A well intentioned teacher and a student with a genuine desire to learn fail to connect around the process of learning. In the example above, the student was talking about the importance of *feelings* as a part of the learning process while the teacher was focussing on the *visual* aspects of the task. From the perspective of the R.O.L.E. Model, both student and teacher would benefit from widening their cognitive maps in different ways.

The student needs to learn how to expand his or her visual (and perhaps auditory) capabilities with respect to the task of spelling. The teacher needs to expand his or her ability to be aware of the language cues that the student is offering, and match the primary representational system of the student in order to establish a better relationship with him or her. For instance, the teacher could start by first acknowledging or 'pacing' the student's need for a different feeling about spelling and then 'leading' the student to develop a more visual strategy for learning spelling words.

The essential premise of the R.O.L.E. Model is that whether you are learning names, spelling, learning algebra, teaching a foreign language or interacting with other people, you do so by engaging your sensory representational systems—and by helping others to engage theirs. As you interact with the world around you, you see things, you hear them, you feel them, you smell them and you taste them. Then you make mental maps of these particular sensory inputs internally. You take in sensory input and store it and organize it by connecting it to other representations neurologically and linguistically - you connect it to other internal sights sounds, feelings, smells and tastes.

The "L" in the R.O.L.E. model stands for **Links**, which has to do with how a particular step or sensory representation is linked to the other representations. For example, is something seen in the external environment linked to internal feelings, remembered images, words? Is a particular feeling linked to constructed pictures, memories of sounds or other feelings?

There are two basic ways that representations can be linked together: sequentially and simultaneously. Sequential links act as *anchors* or triggers such that one representation follows another in a linear chain of events. Simultaneous links occur as what are called *synesthesias*. Synesthesia links have to do with the ongoing overlap between sensory representations. Certain qualities of feelings may be linked to certain qualities of imagery - for example, visualizing the shape of a sound or hearing a color. Certainly, both of these types of links are essential to thinking, learning, creativity and the general organization of our experiences.

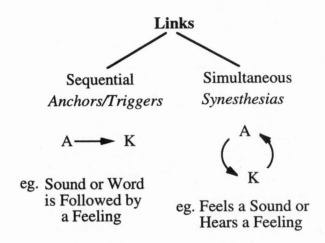

Types of Links Between Sensory Representations

Effect, the "E" in the R.O.L.E. model, has to do with the result, effect or purpose of each step in the thought process. For instance, the function of the step could be to generate or input a sensory representation, to test or evaluate a particular sensory representation or to operate to change some part of an experience or behavior in relationship to a sensory representation.

In our view, the thing that makes the difference between a 'good speller' and a 'poor speller' for example, is the way that they orient and link their various senses and sensory representations together. They have what you might call different 'recipes' for spelling.

TE: As an analogy, let's say there was a baking contest, and Tom, Julie and I each baked a chocolate cake for that contest. And let's say, as we were making our cakes, we all wrote down the amounts of the different ingredients that we used, the way in which we mixed them together, how long we baked the cakes, and at what temperature we baked them. Imagine that, when we were done, we all came out with different chocolate cakes. After the tasting contest, however, we all agreed that Tom had made the best one. If we wanted to know how Tom did it, so that we could make the same kind of cake ourselves, we'd have to go back over his recipe and find out how he put his cake together differently from what Julie did or I did.

RD: Similarly, we believe that the major difference between a 'good' speller and a 'poor' speller is in the mental 'recipe' they use to arrive at a particular spelling. As another analogy, having the right strategy for something is like dialing the right telephone number. If your house in on fire and you want help, you need to dial 911, or whatever your emergency code is. On the other hand, if you want to order a pizza, you will want to dial a different number.

TE: Or maybe call my uncle. He knows the number.

RD: One of the things that has been difficult in the educational field with respect to getting these mental 'telephone numbers' is that most people that excel in what they do have their telephone numbers unlisted. In other words, if you ask, "How do you do that?" They reply, "I don't know," or "Well, I just know it. I just think about it." Now that doesn't give you a heck of a lot of information to go from. They don't even give you the prefix.

So it is important to have some ways of getting that information from a person; because it's not that they're really trying to withhold it from you. I think that it's a result of a basic phenomenon of learning which is that 'the more that you learn something, the less you're aware of what you are doing'. For instance, when you are first learning to drive a car, you have to remind yourself to check the mirrors, release the parking break, look both ways, and so forth. Later on, these behaviors are so automatic that you do not need to be conscious of them at all. You can be consciously thinking of something else entirely and drive quite effectively and safely.

In other words, we know that we've learned something well when we can do it without paying attention to what we are doing anymore. When I was learning to play the guitar, I knew that I was beginning to really get the hang of it when I could talk to somebody else and still be playing, instead of needing to focus all of my attention on what the notes were. Now this is an advantage to the person that's learning because you don't have to waste your time thinking about what you're doing any more. But it is a problem for someone that's trying to figure out how you are doing what you do naturally. It can also be a problem if you're trying to modify what it is that you already do.

TE: Those of you who learned to drive a car with an automatic transmission first and then tried to learn to drive a car with a clutch can probably relate to what Robert is talking about.

RD: In order to adjust a strategy, it helps to know how you are already thinking about it. The ability to be aware of how you are thinking is called *'metacognition'*. One of the benefits of NLP is that it provides some tools for being able to 'read someone's mind', to a certain degree. There are certain kinds of verbal and non-verbal cues that people exhibit when they're dialing those internal telephone numbers that help you to know something about what's going on inside their minds.

The B.A.G.E.L. Model

RD: In our Dynamic Learning exercises we are going to be engaging in various learning tasks and noticing which parts of your neurology you're committing to which aspects of that task. In order to do that you will need some ways of identifying which senses or combinations of senses are being mobilized. NLP makes a number of different types of distinctions and strategies to help accomplish that. We have put these various cues together into what we call the B.A.G.E.L. model:

> **B**ody Posture.
> **A**ccessing cues
> **G**estures.
> **E**ye movements.
> **L**anguage Patterns.

Body Posture

People often assume systematic, habitual body postures when they are thinking or learning. These postures can indicate a great deal about the representational system the person is using. The following are some typical examples:

a. **Visual:** *Leaning back with head and shoulders up or rounded, shallow breathing*

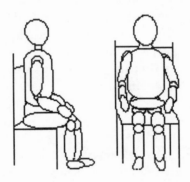

b. **Auditory:** *Body leaning forward, head cocked, shoulders back, arms folded.*

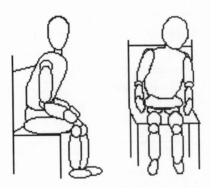

c. Kinesthetic: *Head and shoulders down, deep breathing.*

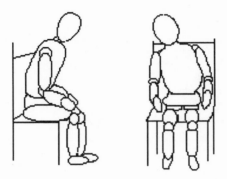

Accessing Cues

When people are thinking, they cue or trigger certain types of representations in a number of different ways including: breathing rate, non-verbal "grunts and groans", facial expressions, snapping their fingers, scratching their heads, and so on. Some of these are idiosyncratic to the individual and need to be 'calibrated' to that particular person. Many of these 'accessing cues', however, are associated with particular sensory processes:

a. Visual: High shallow breathing, squinting eyes, voice higher pitch and faster tempo.

b. Auditory: Diaphragmatic breathing, knitted brow, fluctuating voice tone and tempo.

c. Kinesthetic: Deep abdominal breathing, deep breathy voice in a slower tempo.

Gestures

People will also often touch, point to or use gestures indicating the sense organ they are using to think with. Some typical examples include:

a. **Visual:** *Touching or pointing to the eyes; gestures made above eye level.*

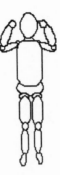

b. **Auditory:** *Pointing toward or gesturing near the ears; touching the mouth or jaw.*

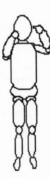

c. **Kinesthetic:** *Touching the chest and stomach area; gestures made below the neck.*

Eye Movements

Another kind of clue comes in the form of eye movements. In order to prepare the nervous system to sense or retrieve information, there are certain types of cues that place our neurology in a state of readiness. For instance, the position of the eyes plays a role in the neurophysiological organization that facilitates information representation or retrieval. If you want to help somebody become more ready to visualize something - to picture it in their mind's eye - you might have them move their head and eyes up. If you want to prepare somebody to feel something deeply, you might have them position their head and eyes down. In the model of NLP, the eyes are not only the 'windows into the soul', they are also windows into how somebody is thinking. They are also ways to help people get ready to use their neurology in order to learn. NLP has categorized these cues into the following pattern:

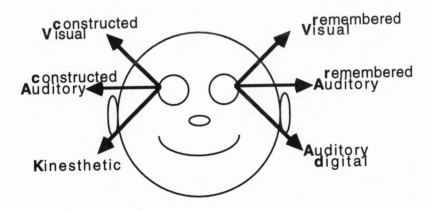

Eye Movements and Representational Systems

Language Patterns

A primary method of Neuro-Linguistic analysis is to search for particular linguistic patterns, such as 'predicates', which indicate a particular neurological representational system or sub-modality, and how that system or quality is being used in the overall program of thought. The NLP approach is to take what people say about their senses seriously. For example, if somebody says, "I get this *feeling* that something is going on." We believe that they are in fact having a feeling.

TE: If somebody says, "Oh, I *see* what you're *saying*." We infer that the person is actually making some kind of an image based upon the words. Likewise, if a student says, "I don't understand this. I don't see what you're saying," we would interpret the student to be saying, "I can't make a picture of your words; and until I can make a picture I won't understand."

RD: If a student says, "Something *tells* me that this is going to be difficult," we would believe that there probably is some program in there telling the student it is going to be difficult.

One of the interesting things about NLP is that you take people literally in a certain respect. Language is often a direct reflection or echo of the neurological process a person is using at a deeper level to form their language. Below is a list of the types of words that might be clues about visual, auditory, or kinesthetic (feelings and body sensations) processes. In addition to giving you clues about how people are thinking, these are also qualities of language that you can use in order to be more precise about either establishing rapport or giving instructions.

VISUAL	AUDITORY	KINESTHETIC
"see"	"hear"	"grasp"
"look"	"listen"	"touch"
"sight"	"sound"	"feeling"
"clear"	"resonant"	"solid"
"bright"	"loud"	"heavy"
"picture"	"word"	"handle"
"hazy"	'noisy"	"rough"
"brings to light"	"rings a bell"	"connects"
"show"	"tell"	"move"

Identifying an Effective Learning State

In Dynamic Learning, the state of a person's physiology is as important as the instructional material they are given. Your neurophysiological readiness is as important as the instructions you are receiving.

Reading a book without being in the state of readiness is not going to give you the full commitment of neurology required for full retention. As a teacher or author, you can offer great information to people, use all the right language, and all the right presentations and techniques, but the message that you're sending is only half of it. You have a 'receiver' on the other side who has to be ready to receive.

As a first Dynamic Learning activity, identify the cues that accompany your own effective learning states. Then, as you are reading this book, make sure that you are able to stay in that state as fully as you can.

Identifying the behavioral cues associated with a certain state is often most easily done through a process known as 'contrastive analysis' in NLP. Contrastive analysis involves comparing a particular process or experience with another experience that is quite different. This helps to bring the most significant differences into the foreground.

Body Posture and Learning

Remember a time in which you were able to learn easily and effectively. Put yourself fully into that experience and notice what happens to your physiology. Circle which of the pictures on the following page most clearly represents the posture you assume when you are in that effective learning state.

Remember a time in which you were trying to learn but became stuck or distracted. Put yourself back into that experience and notice what happens differently with your physiology. Put a square around the pictures that most represent your posture when you are stuck or distracted (choose both a front and a side view).

[Note: If you are a more auditory or kinesthetic learner, you may want to have a partner observe you, or look in a mirror when you are in the effective or distracted learning states.]

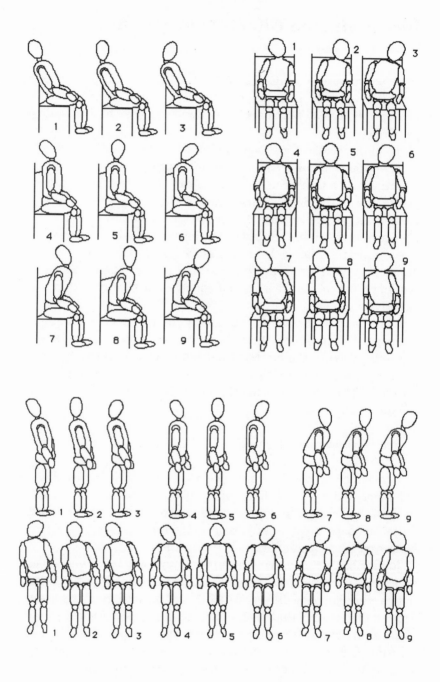

Gestures and Learning

Again, put yourself back into the experience in which you were able to learn easily and effectively and notice your physiology. Circle the picture among the following group that represents the gestures you most often use in an effective learning state, or draw the gestures on the picture provided on the right.

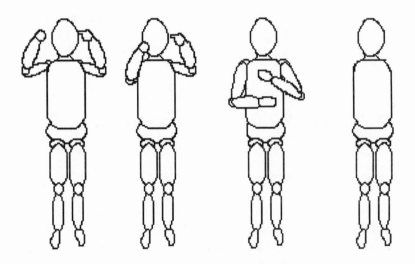

Gestures for Effective Learning State

Return to the experience in which you were stuck or distracted. Put a square around the picture among the following group that represents the gestures you most often use in a stuck or distracted state, or draw the gestures on the picture provided on the right.

[Again, if you are a more auditory or kinesthetic learner, you may want to have a partner observe you, or look in a mirror when you are in the effective or distracted learning states.]

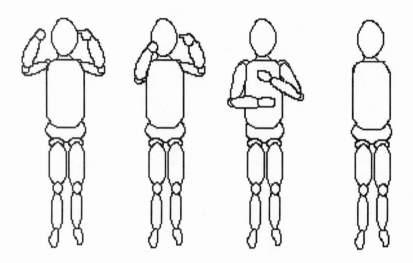

Gestures for Stuck or Distracted State

Eye Position and Learning

Once again, compare the experiences of the effective learning state with the stuck state. On the diagrams below indicate a) which eye position(s) are most associated with your effective learning state and b) which eye position(s) are most associated with a stuck or distracted state. If there is more than one, indicate the sequence or order the eye movements typically follow. You may use either numbers or arrows.

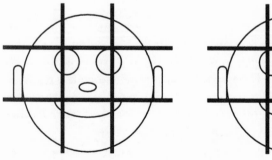
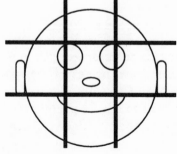

Effective Learning State   **Stuck or Distracted State**

Chapter 2

Remembering
Names

Overview of Chapter 2

- Name Tag Exercise
- Eliciting Strategies for Remembering Names
- Summary of Effective Name Remembering Strategies

Remembering Names

RD: To introduce people to how we use the fundamental Dynamic Learning principles and distinctions in our seminars we often begin by exploring some name remembering strategies. Remembering names is a good learning strategy to start with because it's a well defined learning task and has an obvious evidence for success. It's something that you can test out right away; a person will either remember someone else's name or they won't.

Name Tag Exercise

To expose people to one another's names, we begin our Dynamic Learning seminars by having people do a rapport building exercise in which people have a chance to meet each other. We ask them to turn their name tags over and write down on the back of the name tag "something that you can do well"—A capability. It could be anything from writing, to music, to creativity, to reading.

In an optimal learning environment each member could take advantage of what each of the other members had to offer in terms of their resources, skills and abilities.

So we ask people to write down a capability that they could share with other people and have that side showing instead of their name. They are then instructed to ask four questions:

1) *Who are you?* A name is only one answer to that; it's only a partial answer. What do you identify with yourself? What is something related to your personal or professional mission?

2) *Why are you here?* Why do you want to learn? Why are you involved in learning or teaching? Tell me something that's really important to you; what's a value to you about learning? Not at this particular seminar but about learning in general. You don't know that much about this seminar but you are here because learning is of value to you. It's something that's related to your mission because it has value, there's a motivation.

3) *What's some capability that you'd like to develop?* Not one that you already have that you've written on your name tag; rather, one that you'd like to develop more.

4) *What is a behavior you do well, but would like to learn more about how you do it?* Something that you do well, but you don't necessarily know how you do it so well. For example, someone may know how to ski but not know how to teach someone else how to ski. Someone might be able to communicate with certain students well, but doesn't know exactly how he or she does it. Someone might be creative in certain areas, but isn't entirely aware of how he does it. In essence, it is a behavior in which you know the what, but aren't conscious of the how.

After they ask these four questions—(1) who are you? (2) why are you here? why are you interested? (3) what is something that you'd like to learn how to do from being here? (4) what is a behavior that you have, but you don't know how you do it yet?— Then they can ask "What is your name?"

As the members of the course are meeting the other participants, they are able to notice capabilities that other members have to share or talk about. This creates a context in which both potentially shared relationships and tasks are discovered.

When they return from this exercise, we will ask if there is anybody who met a number of new people and can remember all the names of those people. We will also ask how many can't remember the names of the new people they have met. We will then begin to have them explore and compare their mental strategies for remembering names. The following is an example of how we go about 'eliciting' these strategies in a group.

Eliciting Name Remembering Strategies

RD: Linda, you were able to remember people's names well. How, specifically, do you go about learning someone's name?

Linda: I ask more than once.

RD: Do you just keep repeating, "What's your name?" "What's your name?" "What's your name?"

Linda: No, I talk a little bit, then I say, "What was your name again?" Then I really think and put it in there.

RD: How specifically do you do that?

Linda: I clean my window. Then I just do it. I put it in there.

RD: There is an interesting thing that I'm noticing when you talk about 'putting it in there'. Your eyes are moving up and to the left. In NLP, that tells us something important about what you are doing in your mind. Let's go through the sequence step-by-step. First of all, you say that you get ready for it, you 'clean your window'. When you ask for the name the second time, you are ready to "put it in there". That readiness is an important part of learning. Even the most simple tasks seem to involve the sequence characterized by: ready, aim, fire. Many people however, think learning is just fire, fire, fire! Ready or not.

Linda: I have to go back and get the person's name. I apologize and say, I'm sorry. What's your name again? And that's my anchor. Then I get it and I remember it.

RD: Of course, the most magical thing is what happens in between the time you "get it" and "remember it".

Linda: I worry about the fact that I don't remember what they told me the first time.

TE: That's your motivator to get them to tell you the second time?

Linda: Yeah. I don't remember their name and I'm talking to them about very personal things.

TE: So, you have the belief that it's important to remember someone's name if you are going to talk to them about something that's personal. And if you don't remember it the first time they say it, you can't go on with the conversation until you get it.

Linda: I can't support it any longer.

TE: What happens in the beginning when you first ask for the name. Is it kind of perfunctory?

Linda: I don't even hear it. Just courtesy stuff.

TE: It just goes right by. You're not even ready to know the name at that point.

Linda: I don't even remember hearing it.

RD: So that readiness prepares you to do whatever that magic is that happens in between the times you get the name and you remember it. When somebody tells you their name, what happens right after the time you get the name? Think of a particular person in this group whose name you learned. What did you do after you heard their name the second time?

Linda: I did it by association. Her name is Sue and I have a sister named Susan. I talked around the name a little bit. Then I asked her, "Do you like to be Susan or Sue?" She said "Sue". So, that's how I remembered it. I kind of loaded it a little bit.

RD: "Loaded it." Loaded it how?

Linda: I just made it important. I did a similar thing with Diane. I have a girlfriend named Diane, and Diane looks like her. Her name is Diana G. And so I thought of her.

RD: So what I am hearing is that you try to associate the name with other people who are important to you.

Linda: Always.

RD: (To group) This is a first approximation of the kind of thing we call a "strategy" in NLP. It's a sort of program: I take the person's name and try to associate it with other people whom I am already in a key relationship with. It is a program that attaches the name to something that is already important to me — things that belong to long term memory rather than short term memory. "Re-membering" something presupposes that it was already made a "member" at sometime already. In a sense, what Linda's saying is, "When I'm trying to remember a name, I want to bring more of a commitment of neurology into the process by connecting it to myself or things that are already important to me."

Linda: I make up names for people if I don't remember them or if they don't evoke something. I mean if Diane didn't look like Diana, or Sue didn't share the name of my sister and I couldn't relate to that; then I'll make up a name for them. I'll force them to let me use it. That could be like a nickname—it could even be 'Tiger', you know. I sound like a used car salesman, but I want to call them something other than a void. So, I'll use something. I'll say "Cookie," but whatever seems sweet, seems nice. I'm well brought up.

Lisa: Linda, you also add to the name. She calls me "Lisa-Bonita."

Linda: I change the value of the name so that I can remember it.

RD: (To Group) There are some things that we want you to be noticing that I'm going to call your attention to. Some of you initially may think that I'm dissecting Linda's experience and behavior, but it is not that at all. In fact, part of the reason I am going to bring your attention to these things, is because it's actually a way of getting to know somebody better. People have their own sign language while they talk. This sign language is often one that is shared by a lot of other people. But usually none of us pay much attention to it. For example, every time Linda said something like, "I make the name important to me." "I connect it to things." " I give it value." She made a gesture with her hands in which she touched her stomach with her hands.

TE: She moved them towards her. It is significant to us that her hands did not move out from her body. They came towards her body.

RD: Linda opened her hands away from her body when she said she wanted to call a person something other than, "a void". To us these are not just random movements. They begin to make a sign language that I might want to incorporate when I'm communicating with Linda, especially if it is something very important (gestures with hands toward his stomach — general amusement). In other words, these are gestures that I might want to begin to incorporate into our communication as messages and meta messages. I like to use them as a courtesy to show that I have really been paying attention to all the things that a person was doing while trying to communicate with me. Also, in NLP, these kind of gestures begin to indicate things to us about what kinds of senses somebody is using.

TE: Let's compare Linda's name remembering strategy with someone else's. What is your name?

Butch: Butch. Butch is a nickname.

TE: Linda didn't give you that nickname did she? (Laughter)

Butch: No.

TE: I just wanted to check how far she had spread this around. Butch did you meet someone new?

Butch: Yes.

TE: What was that person's name?

Butch: Patricia.

RD: How did you remember Patricia's name?

Butch: I made eye contact and tried to really hear the name.

RD: That's different from Linda's strategy.

Linda: Yeah. I don't hear it.

RD: Also, Butch makes eye contact. So, Butch, what does that do? When you really try to hear it, what does it mean for you to really hear the name?

Butch: Internalize it in some way. (Gestures toward his stomach.)

TE: (To Group) Did you just see some sign language here? He said he "internalizes it in some way," and gestured toward his stomach. There is probably some kind of feeling going inside of Butch when he is learning a name.

RD: I think it is important that he is not just hearing with his ears, but he's hearing with his body.

Butch: Also, I believe it is very important that I know their names. To know that they are someone I validate with a name. With my own students, I know all their names; in a classroom of 32 kids. I know everybody's name that first day, before they leave the classroom, I make it a point to do that.

RD: Butch says he "validates" someone with their name. It's as if names have to do with identity. Remembering names has to do with valuing a person. This may also have to do with which of our representational systems we value most highly. A lot of times, I think people don't remember names because they don't think they're important. They remember faces. Or they remember places, but not necessarily names. I think, for both Butch and Linda, it's very important that this auditory element—the name— is a sign of respect.

(To Butch) You say you make it a point to learn the names, do you go through processes similar to Linda? Do you try to associate the name with someone or something else that is important to you? Or do you have a different kind of strategy?

Butch: The faces. I definitely see the face—attach the face to the name.

RD: How specifically do you attach the face to the name?

TE: Like with the name of a child in your classroom, how do you hook the name to the face? How is that actually done? Are you aware of that at all?

Butch: There has to be something about the person—a character-istic of the person. Sometimes, I may find that the name fits perfectly with the person. So that helps me remember that person.

TE: Something about the way they look or the way they are?

Butch: The way they are. The style of dress, hair.

TE: Something that you can get the first day of class.

RD: Let's explore that a little bit. What kind of name would go with a particular style of dress?

TE: What do you do with George?

Butch: George has always had a particular appearance to me. For some reason, it fits that person, that make up of the person, not necessarily his dress—but his characteristics — the way he acts, walks, talks.

RD: (To Group) So, learning a name, for both Butch and Linda, is not a function of focusing on the sound or what the name is, but of focusing on the person. This focus seems really important. Linda says, "I don't even try to hear the name. I am trying to put my attention on the person." Both Butch and Linda feel that a person's name has something to do with the person. That name is not just a formality, but has something to do with a statement of relationship or quality of relationship.

TE: (To Butch) When the kids leave the class that first day, do you know that you know their names? When they're not there—they're gone. How do you know that, when they're gone, you know their names?

Butch: From having used their names throughout the day. Attaching the names to the face.

RD: "Attach". That word is interesting to me because in learning attaching one thing to another, of course, is very important. How, specifically, do you attach one to the other?

Butch: I see their face in my mind. I visualize.

RD: (To group) Notice how Butch's eyes move up when he talks about visualizing. (To Butch) Do you also create a picture of the name?

Butch: I believe I do. Yeah. Definitely the face is there.

TE: Do you imagine their name spelled there somewhere? Is it somehow represented?

Butch: It's a kind of a sight word.

RD: One common name-remembering strategy that we have come across in people who are able to recall names well is to make a picture of the face in their mind and then literally make a visual image of a name card and stick it on the forehead of the person. Some people imagine a little nameplate. You visualize the name going with the face. I think the glue that holds the name and the face together is not just that you've made a picture, the glue is that you've evoked that feeling of importance that Butch and Linda talked about, or that kind of association with something meaningful. Of course, you don't always get to see a person's name written down. But even if the name isn't written, do you make it a sight word up there Butch?

Butch: Yeah.

RD: Linda, when you remember people's names, do you have sight words for the name?

Linda: Not that I can recall. It's kind of hard to get in there and check it out...No. It's just evoked; not written down. It just comes up. It's recalled.

TE: (To group) Listen to one of the words she used there. She gestured with her hand toward her ear and she said it was "recalled".

RD: (To Linda) So you're "re-calling" it as opposed to "re-viewing" it.

TE: It's being resaid, recalled, somehow replayed, as opposed to being seen.

RD: On the other hand, I noticed that Linda's eyes are still moving up here, like Butch's eyes do when he's visualizing. And earlier Linda talked about "clearing her window" here. One of the things that has been said over the years, is that the eyes are like a window to the soul. In NLP, the eyes' placement will give you information about what kind of sensory process is going on inside of somebody's mind. Looking up is typically associated with visualizing.

Linda: It's funny, even though I know something about NLP and the eye movements, I couldn't help putting my eyes up there. I couldn't stop myself if I wanted to.

RD: You mean you're not doing it on purpose to make us look good — you're not a plant?

TE: A plant? (Laughter)

RD: I think I'd better branch on into something else before I get in trouble.

TE: Oh no you don't. Let's get to the root of things.

RD: I think you're barking up the wrong tree.

TE: I'm only trying to fertilize an idea here.

RD: Well I'm going to try to nip this in the bud.

TE: These people are having too much fun for such a serious subject as learning. If you're feeling good you must "leave".

RD: Look at what you've done Todd, now everyone else in the class is laughing. You've disrupted the class. You've put people in such a good state that they'll never forget this stuff now. Then they'll feel good every time they think about it. How can we allow this to happen? (To group) Quick, get out your books and start feeling bad. Think, "Effort, effort."

(To Linda) Now, back to more serious matters. If I was to say the name Sue, do you know who I'm talking about?

Linda: Sure.

RD: Do you have a picture of Sue at all?   Is there an image somewhere?

Linda: It's sort of a feeling. I know where she is. I'm kind of seeing her because I'm using her name all the time. But it's not really what she looks like.

RD: What is it then? Right there when you think about it, what is going on in your mind, or in your body?

Linda: It's kind of the experience of her. I'd really have to say that honestly. The time we spent chatting, I was feeling, "Now I'll probably see her face when I close my eyes tonight." It's mostly a feeling, but I probably could recall some of her features. But not her whole face.

RD: So you recall features. (To group) It is interesting to explore how you use and combine your senses while learning. Obviously, while talking with somebody, you engage all of your senses to a certain degree. Generally, there is not too much input with respect to taste and, hopefully, there isn't too much input in the area of smell (laughter); but you know, people wear perfumes or collognes. When you're trying to do something systematic, like systematically remember the names of 32 people in one day, you have to start coordinating your senses to make representations that are going to last or stay. What I am hearing Linda say is that she uses a name as a point of overlap for representations from her other senses that she associates with the person whose name it is. She uses vision as a lead-in system, to search for key features of the way a person looks. But the representational system that really brings it all together is her kinesthetic or feeling sense which unites all the other bits and pieces from her other senses.

Linda: For example, I remember if someone wears glasses.

RD: So some distinguishing feature like wearing glasses will come along with the feeling.

Linda: Yeah. I haven't looked at Diane. But I would see her hair. She has a cute little haircut. And her eyelashes.

RD: (To group) It is interesting to notice that when Linda's talking about Diane's hair and her eyelashes, Linda actually gestures toward herself. She does not point toward Diane, but rather toward her own hair and eyelashes. It is as if Linda has taken the other person in, and stood in their shoes for a second. (To Linda) So you've maybe tried some of their parts on you.

Linda: Yes, the things that I find attractive are the things that I take in.

TE: So, you have a tendency to find things attractive in the people whose names you want to remember?

Linda: No, it's because I want to remember everybody's name.

TE: Even if they're a jerk.

Linda: I'll find something.

RD: For example, what do you remember about Todd? (Laughter)

Linda: I remember his panning vision and his head going back and forth (moves her head from side to side).

TE: (To group) Did you see how she was imitating it? It is as if she has taken this behavior into herself.

RD: (To Butch) Butch, you said that you relate names to characteristics of a person as well. Do you do something similar to what Linda is describing?

Butch: Yeah. There is something that I take from the kid and put inside. Especially behaviors that are characteristic or different; "the bad kid," "the good type" or "the sad child". Definitely, it hits you.

TE: (To Group) Butch seems to chunk bigger than Linda. He finds larger categories of behaviors that go with the names. (To Butch and Linda) I have another very important question for both of you. Let me ask you first Butch. When you go through your name remembering strategy with all the children in your class, is it easy? Is it a laborious task in which you have to put out a lot of effort, or is it something that's easy to do?

Butch: No, it's easy for me to do.

TE: How about you Linda?

Linda: It's more than easy, it's fun. I take pleasure in it.

RD: This is another very important thing about every effective strategy that Todd and I have ever come across. They have both of those qualities—easy and fun. People who are good spellers don't feel that it's really hard every time they have to spell, or that they put a lot of effort into it. They say that it's easy and fun. One simple principle of the nervous system is that if something is pleasurable, the nervous system wants to do more of it. If something is not pleasurable, the nervous system doesn't want to do it anymore.

TE: At our first Dynamic Learning Seminar a boy was attending who told us, "I don't do my homework? Especially reading. It's too difficult and I don't put any time in it. I don't like it. It's too hard, I don't want to do it." We asked him to tell us about something that he liked to do. He said he liked Dungeons and Dragons. Now that is a very sophisticated game. In order to play you have to read a whole bunch of stuff. The amount of information and memory it requires has to be a lot more than you'd have to employ for most learning tasks at school. I asked how often he played this game. He said, "Whenever I get a chance." If it was up to him, he would do it 8, 9, 10 hours a day. I asked him, "How come you spend so much doing that? Isn't it hard to remember all that stuff?" He answered, "It's fun and it's easy, that's why I do it." The point is that if something is stimulating and enjoyable to you, it doesn't seem difficult, hard or effortful, even if it is a complex and sophisticated task.

The question in all of this becomes, "How do you make it fun?" How do you make remembering names interesting and fun? Those of you who have a hard time remembering names, is it fun and easy for you? Do you have to put a lot of effort into it?

Where do you start? The question is, where do you start from? When you are going to engage in the activity, do you start by thinking, "I'm not good at remembering names and therefore I'm not going to be able to do it. This has always been difficult. I've never been able to do it." Where do you start from?

Who else can remember names? John, how do you start?

John: I need to develop a rapport, and part of that mission is getting to know my students' identities. So it's important to me to know their names. In class we do this as a joke, that after thirty seconds I can rattle off 30 names. Then I tell them how I did it.

TE: How *do* you do it?

John: I make a picture of the student first and then I do the name.

RD: So, when the student is telling you the name you make a picture of that student in your mind?

John: Yes, I visualize their location and the environment. If I see them out of their seat, I'm in a little bit of trouble at first.

RD: So their spatial location is important at first. This could make this strategy a bit more difficult to use in social situations, because people move around.

John: Yeah, it's not so contained. But then I don't have the motivation to remember peoples' names in social situations either.

TE: John is a perfect example of somebody who has an excellent strategy for accomplishing something, yet only applies it in a certain context. I think it has less to do with the elegance or the effectiveness of the strategy. It has to do more likely with beliefs or identity issues.

John: In fact, when you asked, "Who remembers names well?" I didn't raise my hand. I remember names really well in the classroom. But I don't identify myself as that type of person.

RD: (To group) Did you hear how John was confusing the capability of remembering names with being a "type-of-person". This is a good illustration of how we limit ourselves from using or acknowledging capabilities that we have because we immediately mix them with identity.

TE: That is why I am so convinced that people are a hundred times smarter than they think they are.

RD: We'd like to give you all now the opportunity to discover how much smarter you are than you think you are by doing a cooperative learning exercise.

First, though, I'd like to thank our excellent models...er..Lisa?...ah...Bill?....and um... Jack? (Laughter, applause.)

Summary of Effective Name Remembering Strategies

We can summarize what we've learned about name remembering strategies by organizing the information into two parts: 1) the beliefs about remembering names and 2) cognitive steps that help to remember names.

The *beliefs* that seem the most relevant are:

A. A person's name has something to do with the person. A name is not just a formality, but has something to do with a statement of relationship or quality of relationship.

B. You "validate" someone through using their name. It's important to remember someone's name if you are going to talk to them about something personal.

C. Learning a name is not a function of focusing on the sound or what the name is, but of focusing on the person.

The *cognitive steps* involved in effective name remembering appear to be:

1. Start with the feeling that you want to get to know that person.

2. Make eye contact and try to really hear the name. Visualize the person's face, and attach the face to their name. For example, make a picture of the person's face in your mind, hear the person's name and then make a visual image of

the person's name on a name card and stick it on the forehead of the person.

3. Focus on a characteristic of the person. Find a feature that fits that person and the make up of that person; not necessarily his or her dress, but rather something that represents the way that person is — i.e., the style of dress or hair, or the way he or she acts, walks, talks, etc.

4. 'Try on' some of the characteristics of that person. Take in the ones that you find attractive.

5. Get a feeling for the person and use the name as a point of association for the distinguishing features related to that person.

Some other helpful strategies are:

a. Associate the person with other people who have a similar name and with whom you are already in a key relationship. This attaches the name to something that is already important to you — things that go into long term memory rather than short term memory.

b. Make up names for people if it is difficult to remember their actual name. If you can't get somebody's name, because it doesn't evoke something, then make up a name or nickname for them—such as 'Tiger', or 'Cookie'.

c. Add to the name; such as calling Lisa, "Lisa-Bonita."

Go try these strategies out. Find some people whose name you don't know yet. Ask them their names, then apply one of these strategies to remember it. If you want to, you can start from your own typical name remembering strategy and enhance it a little bit. Add some of the elements of the strategies we've touched on just now. Look the person in the eye, or relate their name to somebody else you already know. Perhaps you could try to rhyme the person's name with some feature that stands out to you about that person. Try starting from the feeling that you want to get to know that person and try to take something into you from that person.

TE: It was really evident in all three of our examples that the thing that was a key element was the desire to validate someone through using their name.

John: What do we get if we remember everyone's name? (Laughter)

RD: You get a really, really good feeling when you go home.

Actually, you won't need any external reward or reinforcement. Effective learning is self reinforcing.

TE: It pays to remember people's names, because you never can tell who you might meet. You never know who you might run into. My suggestion to you, John, would be: how would you get everybody to give you a little more money to remember them?

****

After the Exercise

RD: Did anyone learn anything that was interesting that you'd like to share with the rest of the group?

Linda: I discovered that I talk around names a lot. I'll say something like, "Your name is 'Irish', oh that goes well with your red hair."

RD: So you incorporate the name into the conversation.

Woman: I can't visualize a person as a snapshot, but I can remember someone in action. Like dropping a notebook. For me the movement holds more information about the person.

Woman: I find that if people say their name and then pull back, it is more difficult to remember their name. Its as if I keep going after their name, but they keep sucking it back in.

RD: There is a phenomenon that we call a 'meta message' - a message about a message. Most often meta messages are communicated by the non-verbal communication that accompanies verbal communication. So what you're pointing out is that if a person is giving their name and at the same time they are kind of pulling away, it's almost like another level of message that's saying, "Don't remember my name." Or "I'm not really revealing who I am."

Man: I was interested in developing the auditory aspect of the strategy, because if everyone in the whole world had a name tag, I'd be able to remember names very easily.

RD: You often learn as much about your own strategy when it gets interrupted as you do when it works perfectly. Truly effective learning strategies incorporate flexibility so that if you are blocked from using one particular approach you have two or three backups.

TE: Sometimes there are places where the auditory system is the only representational system you have access to. Certainly, if you do a lot of phone work, the only way you are going to get the name is by hearing it. Once you hear the name you can turn it into a mental image. But you don't start with the image.

RD: Another very important principle of learning is recess. Breaks from learning have been shown to be necessary to prevent fatigue, inhibition and habituation. Breaks allow your unconscious mind to think and mull over the information in a way that allows it to sink in. Many times the most important parts of learning don't take place while you're intensively focusing on it. But in those in between times where you're kind of letting it sit and integrate. Therefore, I recommend that...

TE: you

RD: take

TE: the

RD: opportunity

TE: to

RD: suggest

TE: to yourselves

RD: that you allow

TE: your unconscious mind

RD: to relax

TE: and to desperately try to not remember

RD: to remember all of the material

TE: that you've just learned

RD: in the most

TE: efficient

RD: appropriate

TE: and effective

RD: way possible.

Chapter 3

Memory Strategies

Overview of Chapter 3

- Memory Strategy Worksheet
- Memory Strategy Progress Report
- Visual Memory Exercise
- Auditory Memory Exercise
- Kinesthetic Memory Exercise
- Long Term and Short Term Memory Strategies

Memory Strategies

The purpose of the next Dynamic Learning exercises is to help you to determine which of your senses or combination of representational systems is most highly developed for memory. This will be done by leading you through the same learning task three times but limiting your input and output channel to a different representational system each time.

To prepare for this exercise refer to the following Memory Strategy Worksheet. At the top of the sheet are printed the digits from 0-9 and the letters from A-Z. Starting with the segment labeled "VISUAL," fill in the blank spaces provided under the heading "ORIGINAL SEQUENCE," with a series of randomly chosen letters and digits. You should end up with a total of ten random characters. Be sure to write legibly so someone else can read it.

Repeat this same process for the sections titled "AUDITORY" and "KINESTHETIC" choosing a *different* sequence of random characters for each "ORIGINAL SEQUENCE." Leave the spaces under the heading "GUESS" blank for now. (An example of a filled in worksheet has been provided for you.)

Divide the worksheet into four parts by tearing or cutting along the dotted lines in between each segment.

MEMORY STRATEGY WORKSHEET

0	1	2	3	4	5	6	7	8	9
A	B	C	D	E	F	G	H	I	J
K	L	M	N	O	P	Q	R	S	T
U	V	W	X	Y	Z	*	#	?	!

ORIGINAL SEQUENCE: **VISUAL**

— — — — — — — — — —

GUESS:

— — — — — — — — — —

ORIGINAL SEQUENCE: **AUDITORY**

— — — — — — — — — —

GUESS:

— — — — — — — — — —

ORIGINAL SEQUENCE: **KINESTHETIC**

— — — — — — — — — —

GUESS:

— — — — — — — — — —

MEMORY STRATEGY WORKSHEET - EXAMPLE

0	1	2	3	4	5	6	7	8	9
A	B	C	D	E	F	G	H	I	J
K	L	M	N	O	P	Q	R	S	T
U	V	W	X	Y	Z	*	#	?	!

ORIGINAL SEQUENCE: **VISUAL**

D L C 6 5 W 7 U 8 N

GUESS:

___ ___ ___ ___ ___ ___ ___ ___ ___ ___

ORIGINAL SEQUENCE: **AUDITORY**

E 2 8 C X K 9 T S J

GUESS:

___ ___ ___ ___ ___ ___ ___ ___ ___ ___

ORIGINAL SEQUENCE: **KINESTHETIC**

G Z Q I H 4 B 5 Y F

GUESS:

___ ___ ___ ___ ___ ___ ___ ___ ___ ___

MEMORY STRATEGY PROGRESS REPORT

Round 1

Rep. System Tested	No. of Characters	Time(s) Presented	Number Correct	Number Out of Order
Visual				
Auditory				
Kinesthetic				

Round 2

Rep. System Tested	No. of Characters	Time(s) Presented	Number Correct	Number Out of Order
Visual				
Auditory				
Kinesthetic				

Round 3

Rep. System Tested	No. of Characters	Time(s) Presented	Number Correct	Number Out of Order
Visual				
Auditory				
Kinesthetic				

Visual Memory Exercise

RD: Training all of your senses to input and receive information is important. One of the goals of this memory exercise is to have you explore what it is like to learn through different sensory modalities. We'd like to have you explore how well each one of your senses functions with respect to the same type of learning task. That is, if you tried to memorize something using just your eyes, or just your ears, or just your body, how well would you do? Some of you might be much more adept, for example, visually than kinesthetically; others may have a more highly developed auditory memory, and so on.

What we're going to have you do first is a *visual* memory task. It is best to do this in a group of three—a 'teacher' a 'learner' and an 'observer'. In order to demonstrate the process, I'm going to be in the role of the "teacher" or "operator", Todd will be the "learner/ student," Lisa will be the observer.

As the 'teacher' part of my job is to keep track of Todd's progress. If you refer to the *Memory Strategy Progress Report* on the previous page you will see that there are three 'scoring tables' set up to be used for three 'rounds' of practice. This is so you can expand the number of characters that you try to remember. This will give you a way to assess the development of your visual memory ability. I read an article on memory some time ago that stated that the world record for memorizing random characters is something like 80 characters in 3 minutes. As you develop the learning skills we will be presenting in this book, you might want to see how close you can come to this record—just for the fun of it.

Now, I've written down ten randomly chosen characters on the visual portion of the *Memory Strategy Worksheet*. So in the first box of the *Memory Strategy Progress Report* for Todd I am going to write in "10" under *Number of Characters*.

Rep. System Tested	No. of Characters	Time(s) Presented	Number Correct	Number Out of Order
Visual	10			
Auditory				
Kinesthetic				

In a moment, I'm going to hold up the group of 10 characters for Todd to look at, and he'll have up to 30 seconds to try to memorize them. If he does it in less time, that is fine. He's going to say, "I got it" when he believes he has committed it to memory. If 30 seconds runs out before he has said anything, then I will arbitrarily stop at that point. Thus, the longest time period for the task is 30 seconds. Lisa's job is to watch Todd carefully, as he is engaged in the process of memorizing the characters. She will try to notice any non-verbal cues that seem significant.

It is important that, during the time Todd is trying to memorize the characters, that we all remain silent. This task is to be done only through the eyes.

Question: Should you try any particular memory strategy at this point?

TE: It is not necessary, and in fact it is best to find out what you do naturally. You will have some kind of strategy that you engage; so you will want to discover what your existing strategy is.

RD: You will be getting the chance later on to try other strategies of course. But what we want you to do first is to find out what occurs to you naturally when presented with a visual memory task. (To Todd) "OK Todd, on your mark, get set, go." (Robert holds up paper for Todd to look at.) Lisa you watch him.

TE: (Looks at paper and moves eyes away briefly several times). I got it.

RD: OK, great. Now, Todd took about 21 seconds, so I would put "21 seconds" in that second box, under *Time(s) Presented*.

Now, I am going to ask Todd to silently point to the characters, at the top of the *Memory Strategy Worksheet*, in the sequence that he remembers them. So, rather than say anything to me, Todd will point to the particular characters that he recalls, in the order that he remembers them from the page I was holding up for him. Notice, we're doing this on purpose in order to see what happens if you have to do something completely visually. The purpose is to both input the characters visually and recall them visually. The 'learner' does not give the answer verbally nor does he or she write it since this would involve translating the information into other sensory modalities. Todd is going to merely point to the sequence of characters that he recalls. I, as the 'teacher', will write down what he points to on the line labeled *'Guess'* on the *Memory Strategy Worksheet*. Since this is a memory task, I want to be sure I keep the original sequence that I wrote down out of Todd's view while he is making his guess.

TE: So you want the sequence? (He begins pointing to various characters at the top of the Worksheet. Robert writes.) That's all I have.

RD: Alright. Todd pointed to a bunch of characters and I've written them down on the line labeled 'Guess'. As we compare Todd's guess to the original sequence, I see that they are generally the same but there are some differences.

ORIGINAL SEQUENCE: **VISUAL**

<u>D</u> <u>L</u> <u>C</u> <u>6</u> <u>5</u> <u>W</u> <u>7</u> <u>U</u> <u>8</u> <u>N</u>

GUESS:

<u>D</u> <u>L</u> <u>C</u> <u>6</u> <u>U</u> <u>7</u> <u>8</u> <u>N</u> __ __

For example, Todd pointed to the U in a different sequence than it had been originally. Obviously he remembered the character, even though he didn't necessarily remember exactly where it was placed in the sequence. This is why the Progress Report distinguishes between *Number Correct* and *Number Out of Order*.

TE: It is the difference between recalling characters and recalling the sequence. You can get all the characters correct and have them in the wrong sequence.

RD: So when it says Number Correct, what that means is how many did the 'learner' actually remember, even if he or she did not point to them in the same order that they were originally written. In Todd's case, I would write 8 under *Number Correct*. Then he pointed to 3 that were in a different order than in the original sequence. So I would write 3 under *Number Out of Order*.

Rep. System Tested	No. of Characters	Time(s) Presented	Number Correct	Number Out of Order
Visual	10	21 seconds	8	3
Auditory				
Kinesthetic				

It is important to keep in mind that there are different kinds of memory. For instance, there's sequential memory, which is memory related to order. On the other hand, there is what might be called 'gestalt' memory, which relates to how much of a whole I can remember—regardless of the sequence.

TE: You can either take all the information that's going to be presented to you as a whole, or you can take it as a sequence of information. The way you input what is presented to you is going to determine how you end up recalling it later on.

RD: So, Todd recalled some of the characters sequentially, and some in a more non-sequential way. What is most important, however, is not how many Todd remembered, but *how* he remembered them. That is, Todd used a particular strategy to perform this task. He got to look at the characters for 21 seconds. He said "OK, I think I have it." I then asked him to point to the characters in the order that he remembered them. There were 8 that he remembered out of the total 10—5 happened to be in the right order and the others were switched. It is the micro mental processes that Todd went through in those 21 seconds that is really the focus of the exercise. Because it is what happened inside Todd's nervous system in those few seconds that determined his eventual performance.

Actually, the test was a little more difficult for Todd than it would normally be because he had to wait and listen while I gave instructions.

TE: I was going to say I didn't know that this was going to be a long term memory strategy.

RD: And it is important to distinguish between short term and long term memory, because they are not necessarily the same thing. Had we asked Todd to make his recollection 30 seconds earlier, or hadn't gone through the same amount of explanation, his performance might have been different.

TE: I'd say, if you asked me to remember the characters later this afternoon, I'd probably get the same ones. They're in long term memory now.

RD: We will explore some of the differences between long term and short term memory a bit later. In fact, in either case, the focus of our attention is on the cognitive strategy employed by the 'learner' during the process of memorization. To do this we need the help of our 'observer'.

(To Lisa) Lisa what did you observe when Todd was learning this?

Lisa: When you said we're going to get started, his legs started to move a little bit. Getting ready, perhaps getting a little nervous. He then looked at the stimulus and then looked up and to the left four times. And when he said that he had it, he looked away.

TE: That was a very good observation that you made about movement—that I was moving my left leg first, when I started to move. However, I would caution you about interpreting what that movement means. Lisa said that I was "getting ready" and "perhaps getting a little nervous." She could have just as easily said I was "getting excited about it" or wanted to "show how well I could do." In other words, if you interpret a particular behavior right away you are in danger of projecting your own model of the world onto someone else. For instance, if you notice movement and you say something about "nervousness," it starts to connect that movement with nervousness. It's like you are giving the instruction that that is what this movement should mean. And even if it did not have anything to do with "nervousness" initially, the movement may begin to become associated with it (like a kind of hypnotic suggestion).

RD: Todd is making a very important point about the difference between observation and interpretation. As an example, there was an interesting study that was done with elderly people in nursing homes. The study related to a phenomenon called 'symptom labeling'. They noticed that elderly people tended to live a lot longer and be more in control of their lives, depending upon how they labeled their feelings. If somebody got up and they felt bad and started labeling the feelings as "illness", they would wind up feeling more depressed and helpless than people who just labeled it in terms of actual feelings rather than symptoms. For example, saying, "I have this queasy feeling in my stomach," is quite different than saying, "I feel like I have the flu;" even if both descriptions relate to the exact same sensations. The people who labeled their feelings as simply "feelings," tended to have a lot more control over their own experiences and to be a lot more independently than the people who were constantly and initially labeling them in terms of "illness."

The same point can be applied to learning processes. As soon as you say, for instance, that someone is acting like they are "dyslexic" or have an "attention deficit," you've begun to interpret rather than observe. So, when we describe behaviors in this exercise it is very important to separate your observations from your interpretations.

TE: At this stage, what we really want you to do, if you're the observer, is to be like a Martian. To be like 'Nerk-Nerk'. Nerk-Nerk is an imaginary character who doesn't know how to interpret things like we do. Nerk-Nerk sees what we see, hears what we hear, feels what we feel and can make all of the sensory distinctions that we make; but he doesn't know what they mean. For instance, Nerk-Nerk would not say, "You moved your legs— you were nervous." Instead Nerk-Nerk just says, "I noticed that you were moving your legs."

Once you notice such a movement, then you can ask, "What was going on inside of you when you were moving your legs?" If the 'learner' says, "I was feeling like I was on the spot," "I knew I had to perform," or "I was a little nervous," then, you can start to 'calibrate' the relationship between the behavior and the internal response. This type of 'calibration' relates to pattern recognition, as opposed to interpretation. Calibration involves building a model of the meaning of the behavior of an individual learner rather than making general judgments.

RD: This is a very important point. The observer watches and listens, tells her observations, then we ask the 'learner', "What was going on inside of you when you were doing that?" The reason you want to identify the behavioral cues is so you can find out, "what was happening inside your mind during that behavior?" So instead of just asking the question in general, we have something observable to anchor it to. This makes it much easier for the learner to give a specific and meaningful answer.

In Todd's case, Lisa noticed several significant things that he did. He was moving his legs, and he moved his eyes up and away four times. What we want to do now is ask Todd, "What were you doing at those times? Were you aware of looking away four times?"

TE: Yes, yes, yes.

RD: Were you trying to see the whole group of characters up there?

TE: I wasn't "trying" to see any of it. I just looked at it, looked away. I wasn't trying to engage any particular strategy at all. My natural propensity is to just look at something and look away. That's just what I did. I looked at the paper and then I looked up.

RD: Was there anything you're aware of that was going on in your mind at that time?

TE: Just quick flashes of what I'd just seen on the paper.

RD: Were they flashes of the whole thing, or was it in chunks?

TE: Chunks.

RD: OK, good. Now we are beginning to get something. (To audience) Initially, people are not necessarily going to be completely aware of all the little things that they are doing. So, Todd was first saying "I was just looking away, that's just how I do it." As we probed a little further, he said, "There were quick flashes of what I'd seen on the paper." But these weren't just random flashes. They were flashes of particular 'chunks' of the group of characters.
(To Todd) Was it the same chunks each time, or different ones?

TE: Different chunks.

RD: (To audience) So, even though Todd was not trying to do anything specific, he was spontaneously organizing the characters into chunks. Our next question to Todd would be, "Were those 'chunks' of three letters apiece? Were they in a specific order building up to the whole thing?"

TE: Well, actually, the size of the image was the first thing I tried to go for. I needed to see how much space I was going to have. In other words, as you're asking me now, I'm going back and looking at it and the first thing that I did. In fact, what I did was that I looked at the paper and then I thought, "How much space do I need to represent what's here? I need to have enough space to represent everything. So, how much room do I need on the screen?"

RD: So the first thing you did was to create the internal mental "space" you needed for what you were going to need to remember.

TE: I created the space for what I was going to remember, then chunked it.

RD: I think that creating this type of mental space is important with respect to memory. Sometimes we'll find that when a person is trying to remember 10 characters, they'll have this very large mental screen. By the time they are looking at the last characters they can no longer see the first characters any more because those characters are so far away mentally.

TE: Other times we'll find that when people have to remember 10 characters, their mental screen is so small that there's only enough room for three.

RD: Todd made the space yet had an easier time remembering the characters on either end of the sequence, and had more difficulty with the ones in the middle. This probably relates to how he was chunking it.

TE: It's interesting to me that now that you've started asking me about my strategy, all of a sudden, my brain finished what it didn't have time to do in the 21 seconds—which was not only to create the appropriate size of screen but also be clear about the chunk sizes within it. The chunk size that I had chosen in that short a time, didn't allow me to get all the pieces. They were randomly sized chunks. So the sizes that I chose to stick up there were not conducive to remembering all the characters. What I was trying to remember was a group of random characters, not a word where you'd sound it out by syllables. What I realized when it was over, was that had I expected the characters to naturally sort themselves into chunks like the syllables of a word. Now that I think about it, I would have had an easier time doing it if I had thought of the ten arbitrary digits of a telephone number and chunked it in groups of 3, 3 and 4—just like a telephone number. Then it would have been simple.

RD: What Todd is talking about now is one of the key points of doing this exercise. By developing a metacognition of his own natural process, Todd is able to spontaneously refine his own memory strategy. Todd and I have studied strategies for many years, and we're always learning something new from the same old tasks. By approaching the task spontaneously, Todd was able to learn something new and important about his own programming.

TE: If you only do what you're supposed to do, you never learn anything new.

RD: The goal is not to try to figure out the 'right' way to remember, but rather to develop the awareness or 'metacognition' of your own strategies so that you can constantly improve your own thinking process.

TE: The next time I do this I will do it better because now I can add more intelligence to my own natural process.

RD: Speaking of developing more awareness, there was something else I wanted to explore with you Todd. What about your internal state? Lisa did mention that she noticed movement in your legs. Was that connected to your internal state in some way?

TE: I was thinking, "OK, there's a task to be done now and I need to move out of this teacher state to get ready to take information in a different way." As a teacher I had been primarily outputting information. So I needed to shift my state to be more ready to input information.

RD: So that movement in your legs is about a change of state— getting ready to input information.

TE: Yes. Getting ready to change to do something else.

RD: Shifting your state from output mode to input mode.
Another thing I was curious about was whether you were aware of any of the other people in the room at the time. Because some people will say they were really aware of the environment or the time during a task like this.

TE: No, as a matter of fact, I was surprised that it had been 21 seconds. I had a total loss of time and the people out here just disappeared. They weren't part of the task. I was only aware of the relationship between the three of us.

RD: Some people will think, "I really hated the time constraint. It was really making me anxious." In fact, some people will actually commit more of their mental energy to thinking about all the issues surrounding what they are doing, more than to actually doing it.

TE: The most important thing that allowed it to happen, that just came to me, is that it didn't matter. That came right after I got kind of excited about doing it. I got excited and then thought to myself, "And it doesn't matter." Which let me get more excited about it. In other words, it doesn't matter if I get two or five or if I don't get any. None of my identity was tied up in remembering these characters at all.

RD: Some of you might find differences between your own experience and what Todd is talking about right now. You might find that you make it very important to yourself to remember these characters. In Todd's case, disconnecting the task from his sense of identity helped him to be more involved in the process of learning rather than concerning himself with the results of that process.

Todd, I'm also curious to ask, "How did you know when to stop?" Were you thinking at all about the time?

TE: Well, you see, time wasn't an issue. I thought it had been only about 10 seconds to be honest with you. I was surprised when you said 21 seconds. I had no idea how long it had been.

RD: This is another potential difference in learning strategies. Unlike Todd, some people will be aware of all 30 seconds. If someone really wants to insure that he or she gets a good 'score', that person might think, "I'll wait until they say my 30 seconds are up." Todd, on the other hand, went into a state in which his emphasis was more on the process than the result, and the time had no meaning in that state.

TE: If I had spent time thinking about the 30 seconds, I would have never gotten to the chunking, because I would have been trying to think of how much time I had already used while at looking at the words. Then my focus would have been on something else. Instead I thought, "All I'm going to do is this," and then I put my eyes up to the left to see what would happen, literally.

RD: I think a key point to this discussion relates to the question, "When you learn something, what state do you want to be in while learning it?" Todd decided, "Here's a state from which I want to learn and I want to make the strategy that I'm going to use to input information fit with this state. And I'm willing to allow myself to not need to be perfect at first. Because if this is the state that I want to be in when I'm learning, then I'll need to adjust my strategy to fit this state." This is a different approach then thinking, "If I really try hard I'll remember them all perfectly." Todd's strategy is what we would call a *'learning to learn'* strategy.

TE: That's right. I would not have made the realization about chunking the characters like a telephone number if I had been overly focused on the result. As Robert said, I wanted a certain state and I wanted to make sure that my strategy fit with that state. If I could not operate that strategy from the state that allows me to learn what I want to learn, then it says to me that I've got to change that strategy so that it fits. Because, otherwise, I'm going to spend half my neurological time, so to speak, fighting the difference between my state and my strategy and where they don't match; as opposed to concentrating on inputting the characters.

RD: From this perspective, Todd was showing you as much about learning how to learn, as he was about how to remember things.

TE: That's true. I really didn't care about the characters at all. What I became totally involved with was, "How is this going to happen? I'm going to let it happen and how's it going to happen when it happens?"

RD: But notice, if we had put pressure on Todd and said Todd, you have got to get all of the characters right. And Todd went Oh, I'm supposed to be demonstrating these things to these people, I'd better get them all right. See, where do you put the emphasis, on getting them right or on the state from which you want to develop the strategy. Because, I'll guarantee you, if you keep yourself in that state, your brain will get better and better at remembering those characters.

TE: Because it's having fun. It's not working hard.

RD: But if Todd had made it all important to get it all right, he might have gone into a different state.

TE: I just would have engaged the strategy that I know works all the time for remembering numbers, letters and characters. I would have consciously engaged the strategy as opposed to looking at the paper and just letting something happen. The interesting thing to me is that at the end I realized I already had a way of chunking that I've never used before to help me remember letters.

RD: So let's now review the steps. Get together with two other people (making a group of three) and test each other's memory strategies with the following procedure:

1. INPUTTING - Start with the section of paper marked "VISUAL." The 'teacher' will show the 'learner' a sequence of 10 characters for up to 30 seconds, no longer. During this time, the 'observer' is to carefully watch the learner for any significant patterns of micro-behavioral cues. If the 'learner' thinks that he or she has memorized the sequence in less time you may stop before 30 seconds. Record the time in the box marked "Time(s) Presented" on the MEMORY STRATEGY PROGRESS REPORT.

2. RETRIEVING - Have the 'learner' point (without speaking) to the sequence of characters in the order he or she remembers them on the segment of paper containing the list of all the numbers and letters. Write down the sequence in the spaces under the heading "GUESS" as the 'learner' points it out. Then compare it to the ORIGINAL SEQUENCE.

3. SCORING - Record the number of characters the 'learner' remembered correctly (regardless of whether or not they were in the right order) in the box marked "Number Correct" on your MEMORY STRATEGY PROGRESS REPORT. Then record the number of characters that were in the wrong sequence in the box marked "Number Out Of Order."

[NOTE: If the 'learner' has simply left out a character it does not mean that all of the ones following it are in the wrong sequence. So if your sequence is: DLC65W7U8N and the 'learner' forgets the "W" and points to DLC657U8N their score is 9 guessed correctly and 1 in the wrong place (the "7" is out of order). If the 'learner' points to a character that was not in the original sequence that is counted as a character that is "Out of Order."]

4. ELICITATION - Find out what kind of memory strategy the 'learner' used to try to remember the characters by discussing what he or she did mentally during the time you were showing the characters. The observer begins by recounting what he or she saw happening while the 'learner' was attempting to commit the characters to memory. It is important that the observer simply report what he or she has seen or heard, not attempt to interpret those observations. Then both the observer and the 'teacher' may start asking the 'learner' what was happening internally in relation to the observed behavioral cues. What was the 'leaner' aware of? Did the 'learner' attempt to make a picture of the characters in his or her mind's eye? Did s/he say them to his/herself? Observe the eye movements and other non-verbal behaviors that can help you tell which representational system(s) the 'learner' was using. Note how well this strategy worked by referring to the score. Discuss how the strategy could be refined or improved.

Then switch roles so that a different person is 'learner', 'teacher' and 'observer'. Repeat the process until all three members of the group have been in each role. (The process should take about ten minutes per person.)

RD: You might be surprised at how much occurs in this 30 second time period. You can learn a lot about yourself as well as about the memory process. Think of what happened in Todd's case. Look at how much came out of a total of 21 seconds. Dynamic learning is about how much can happen in a 21 second period of time, and how much that can tell you about what goes into the process of learning. When you imagine the hours that teachers spend with students, and realize how much learning can be packed into 21 seconds, perhaps you will develop a new respect for the capabilities of the brain and the possibilities that open up when you understand the micro structure of the learning process.

••••••

After the Exercise

TE: How many people were able to remember all ten out of ten? (Many hands are raised in the group) That's a lot.

RD: What did you do to remember them all?

Woman: Chunked them.

RD: Chunking is an important strategy for memory, and other kinds of learning as well, because it reduces the complexity of the task. In this last exercise, for instance, instead of having to remember ten things (i.e., the 10 characters), you only have to remember two or three things—the groups of characters.

TE: As an example, telephone numbers have seven to ten digits in them. If you remembered each digit as a separate piece of information— i.e., the 8 and then 0 and then the 0, as all separate units of information—then about all you could remember is seven numbers. If you take all of those numbers, as most people do, and collect them into two or three 'chunks' of information, it becomes a much smaller amount to remember. If you live in an area where everyone has the same area code or prefix, for instance, it is not necessary to remember those as separate pieces of information each time you learn a neighbor's telephone number. You are able to remember them as a single 'chunk'—such as "area code" or "local prefix."

RD: I used to have a phone number that had "1964" in it. Instead of having to remember 4 individual numbers, I just had to remember the year that the Beatles were on the Ed Sullivan Show. So I condensed four pieces of information into one.

This brings up the issue of the 'micro strategy' that you use to select the chunks you are going to work with. Remember in Todd's case, he was initially thinking that the chunks might be formed in terms of sound syllables —like a word. He realized afterwards that it would have been simpler to arrange them in arbitrary groups of three or four—like a telephone number.

One common micro strategy for chunking is related to what could be called the "rote" memorization approach. Some learners start with the first character and try to commit that one character to memory. When they are able to look away or close their eyes and still remember that one character, they will then try to commit the first *and* second characters together to memory. When they can remember those two, they expand to a combination of the first, second *and* third character, and so on. Each time they are repeating what they already know, and then preparing themselves to open up for the next one.

With random characters, chunks sometimes delineate themselves spontaneously because there is an odd character (like a "@" or a "&") positioned in between some others that naturally separates them. Another 'micro strategy' for chunking, however, would be like the one I described earlier for remembering my telephone number. In this case, the relationships between the characters form some larger meaning. So instead of arbitrarily taking groups of three or four characters, you chunk them according to relationships they might create. For instance, one group member remembered the characters "3D" as one chunk and "613AD" as another chunk. Even though the first is only two characters and the second was five characters, these were chunks that "went together" because they had meanings for her—she could relate "3D" to a type of visual imaging and "613AD" to an ancient date. This strategy involves finding patterns in seemingly patternless information; in addition to chunking. Patterning and chunking are not necessarily the same process. If I simply "chunk" a group of randomly selected characters, it is as if I have a set of boxes that I'm going to arbitrarily stick the information in. If I find patterns, I am creatively trying to find meanings in various combinations of characters.

Sometimes there is no obvious pattern or meaning in the group of characters you are attempting to remember, so you actually need to add something in order to create chunks that have meaning. For instance, you might find that the sound of the characters follows a certain rhythm, or that you can create a little melody that helps to remember them. I recall learning a little song about spelling "Mississippi" that simply put the letters into a particular melody and rhythm. This involves overlapping the visual image of the characters onto another representational system—namely auditory.

TE: Having a been a musician for 20-odd years, I really got confused when touch tone phones first came out; because I had my own melody for everybody's phone numbers. And the notes that I had in my mind for people's phone numbers did not match at all with those tones that they picked for the telephone machine. I'd start dialing and I'd notice the sounds and I'd forget the phone number, because it'd be the wrong notes for that person's phone number. I think you should be able to change or adjust the tones on those phones. The way they are now, you can't play music on them. I don't know who picked those notes. (laughter) They don't know anything about music. It was definitely a visual person who chose them.

RD: There is another strategy for creating patterns or meanings, that is more verbal and visual than it is tonal, that is typically known as "mnemonics." It involves adding words or images in order to produce a pattern or meaning on another level. For example, when I was in primary school, I was taught a mnemonic technique for spelling 'arithmetic' that involved a sentence made up of words starting with each letter in "arithmetic." It went something like, "A Red Indian Thought He Might Eat Turkey In Church." Again, the goal of mnemonics is to add something that helps to create order or meaning.

TE: It think it is important to keep in mind, however, that 'input', 'storage' and 'retrieval' are three distinct parts of memory. While "mnemonics" may be an effective method to facilitate the 'storage' of characters, it may not necessarily be the most efficient way to 'input' or 'retrieve' information in general. If you used it for everything you had to remember, it could become rather time consuming and inefficient. For example, the way I was taught "arithmetic" was, "A Rat In Tommy's House Might Eat Tommy's Ice Cream." That caught my attention when I was learning to spell, and made it a touch more amusing, but if I had to remember all those words every time I wanted to spell arithmetic, I'd be wasting a lot of time. Or, for instance, if I had a lot of numbers and letters I had to remember and I had to make a sentence and connect meanings to each one of those, it could become cumbersome. If you had 400 or 500 pieces of data to remember, you'd have an awful lot of sentences to make up and remember.

RD: Another important factor relating to the input, storage and retrieval of information relates to the 'state' that you are in while you are learning.

TE: Absolutely. Another strategy for memory is to start by selecting a particular state like I did, and let your brain do whatever it does. I actually made a conscious decision to turn off my internal voice. I gave the instruction to my brain to just see what would "stick." Some people will be able to have great success visually without verbally having to say the names of the characters in their minds. It is as if they can mentally drag the image of the character off the page and put it up onto a mental screen, just like you can do when you are editing a document on a Macintosh computer—they can mentally "cut and paste" characters into their memory. Of course, this type of strategy presupposes a strong ability to manipulate mental visual imagery.

But the other point is that the strategy you use also relates to your internal state. Often you will have several different types of memory strategies, but in order to get to them you have to go through the neurological "doorway" of your internal state. And sometimes you enter into a task through the "door" that is the state of nervousness, and you look around and the strategy that you want to use isn't there because it's not connected with that state. It's connected with some other state.

RD: For example, some people only have creativity behind the door marked "anxiety" or "pressure." I used to experience this when I was in school writing a term paper. I couldn't write until the last minute when the pressure got so great that the door would open up and 'zip', the words would suddenly come pouring out. But if I had plenty of time and went behind the door marked "relaxed," no strategy was there. It really became a bind because I didn't necessarily like the feeling of the pressure. But I think that's why some people become addicted to anxiety, or addicted to frustration because it's the only way that they can get to something they really need.

In fact, an important part of the dynamic learning process involves exploring how to put the appropriate choices behind the appropriate "doors". Because if you don't relate the strategies to the doorways, you end up just randomly trying all kinds of different things. And even though I believe that any strategy is probably going to be more effective than no strategy at all, trying a whole bunch of different methods at the same time is going to create difficulties of another kind.

TE: A point in all directions is the same as no point at all.

RD: Another important issue relating to this memory task involves beliefs and values. Some people end up spending 80% of their neurological time during this task questioning why they should remember this completely meaningless list of characters to begin with. In addition to your state and your sensory capabilities, your beliefs will determine a lot about how you approach this type of task, and how well you do at it. For example, if something doesn't have an obvious meaning, do you say "To heck with it," or do you say "It's up to me to give the meaning to it because the world won't change for me." In other words, do you put out the effort to give something meaning, or do you expect someone else to create the meaning for you?

Learning ability is not just a function of a person's cognitive capabilities, but also the beliefs that support or interfere with those capabilities. Todd gave the task meaning by deciding to learn something about his own learning process. In fact, one of the reasons that we use random characters in this exercise is so that you don't have to worry about whether or not the content is important. This gives you the freedom to focus on your own processes if you choose to.

Auditory Memory Exercise

RD: Let's move on to the 'auditory' version of this exercise. It is similar in many ways to the visual exercise, but there are some key differences. As in the visual memory task, you will work with groups of random characters (refer to the second part of the Memory Strategy Worksheet). You will continue in the same group of three people, maintaining the same set of roles— 'teacher', 'learner' and 'observer'. For our demonstration this time, I will be the 'learner', Todd will be the 'teacher' and Linda will again be the 'observer'. Instead of showing me the characters, however, Todd is going to read them to me. I don't get to see them.

TE: It's all auditory—auditory in, and auditory out.

RD: Todd is going to sit behind me and read aloud his sequence of 10 characters from the section of the Worksheet marked "AUDITORY." My task is to try to remember the characters that Todd has read out loud. If I can't remember all the characters after the first hearing, I can request to hear the sequence again; but I am limited to three repetitions, no more. If I can get it in one or two readings, that is fine; Todd would mark down a "1" or "2" on the Time(s) Presented portion of the Memory Strategy Progress Report. Otherwise, I must make my guess after the third presentation. So, in the same way that you had up to 30 seconds for the visual task, you get up to 3 repetitions for the auditory memory task.

While I am listening to Todd, I am going to keep my eyes open— even though I won't be looking at Todd or the characters—so that Lisa can observe my eye movements more easily. Some people will want to close their eyes during this task, which is OK if necessary. It is possible to see a person's eyes moving under their eyelids if you look closely enough.

One other thing that I would like to add is that the learner can have a certain degree of influence on how the 'teacher' reads the characters. For instance, after the 'teacher' reads the characters the first time, the 'learner' can ask the 'teacher' to say the characters a little faster or slower.

We are now going to demonstrate an example of the process. (Todd sits slightly behind Robert. Linda sits facing Robert.)

TE: Are you ready?

RD: Yes.

TE: 2-7-6-H-B-L-K-7-9-J.

RD: OK, I need it again. You can just read them at the same speed as last time. That was fine.

TE: OK, 2-7-6-H-B-L-K-7-9-J.

RD: OK, I've got it.

TE: You've got it? OK. Now since this is an auditory task, Robert will verbally repeat the characters he remembers, and I'll write down what he says in the spaces marked "Guess" on the Memory Strategy Worksheet. The 'scoring' is done the same as for the visual exercise. Go ahead Robert.

RD: 2-7-6...H-B-L-K. And then I think it's 7-9-J?

TE: Correct. You got all ten out of ten. Were you aware of what you were doing mentally?

RD: If you listened to the way I said the characters back, it was obvious that I was chunking them. I chunked the three numbers, then the four letters, and then there was the last bit there that I had to handle a bit differently.

TE: That's interesting because I put them down that way on purpose. They are random, but I put them down in groups of numbers and letters and then a mixture, in order to find out what would happen. 2-7-6 is all numbers, H-B-L-K is all letters, then I put 7-9-J so we could see what happened when you mix them together. Anyway, you got the whole sequence right.

RD: Lisa, what did you notice?

Lisa: When you started to answer, you sat up in readiness with your hands out in front of you. Throughout the task, your hands were moving rhythmically. And your eyes, to me, seemed focused slightly upwards. Then you sort of nodded your head as you received the different input. There was some mouth movement, but not a lot.

RD: I was aware of my eyes moving around to different places, although I wasn't trying to do anything with them specifically. Sometimes they felt like they were down and slightly to the left.

Lisa: I noticed that they were moving back and forth somewhat.

TE: (To Robert) Are you aware of what was going on when you were moving your hands as Lisa was describing?

RD: Well, it was related to a kind of feeling state.

TE: A feeling state as a 'starting state', or a feeling state in reaction to the characters or the task?

RD: It was a starting state.

TE: What was the starting state?

RD: It was just the state of 'readiness'. Just sort of anticipation. It served as a kind of fuel, to make things happen. I wanted to stick the characters in there, but I wasn't sure how I was going to do it.

TE: So you didn't make any conscious effort to try and organize the characters.

RD: Similar to you, I was waiting to discover what strategy I was going to use; and also what patterns might be in the characters. I found that, as I was taking the characters in, I was picturing them. Actually, at first I thought I might chunk the 2 and the 7 as an age—like 27— but as I was thinking about that Todd kept going and then I thought, "Whoa, he is getting ahead of me." So I had to stop trying to make a meaning and just let the sequence come out. Then I noticed the "H-B-L-K" which I thought would maybe make a word. But what was strange about it was that I never could make a word out of it; although I thought this should be a word—"H-B-L-K." In the end, the letters just happened to stick because of the feeling that "these letters should be a word."

TE: Did you repeat any of the letters to yourself as I said them to you?

RD: Yes, in a way. It was interesting that Lisa made the observation that I moved my mouth a little bit, but not very much. Half of what I was doing was replaying Todd's voice in my mind, but half hearing it in my own voice. It was part his voice and part my own voice. So, I wasn't really repeating the characters. I can do that now because I could read them off from my internal picture; but during the task it was like they were floating around waiting— and I didn't know if they were going to stick or go away. And that's part of what happened with the last group of characters. The first two groups I had more clearly, but the last bit I had to really just rely on my mind's ear to produce them. I thought that they were these numbers but I couldn't be sure. It was like the auditory and the visual weren't connected somehow.

TE: So, in summary, after trying one strategy with the first couple of letters, you said, "This is not going to work because I can't spend all my time on the '27'. Todd is not going to stop reading the letters while I'm doing that." And instead of thinking, "I should find another strategy," you decided, "I'll just let them go in and find out what happens."

RD: I have to say that a large part of it came down to trusting. Especially the last bit. It was like, "I just have to sit back and trust that it'll be there." Once I could trust myself, then the fact that you waited with the pen, gave the characters the opportunity to actually get clearer in my mind. It gave them time to stabilize. But since I didn't have a clear mental picture of the last group of mixed characters, I had to really just bring them up from sound memory only.

TE: When you say that you were bringing them back as sound, were you aware whether it was in my voice or your voice at that time?

RD: It wasn't like it really had a voice. It just came up.

TE: The reason I asked that is because I noticed that he put his eyes in one direction and his ears in the other direction. He shifted his head and ears to the left, but moved his eyes toward the right. In the model of NLP, a movement of the head and eyes to the left would accompany auditory memory (for a right handed person like Robert)—such as remembering my voice. A movement to the right would go along constructed or imagined sounds—such as Robert creating something in his own voice. In this case, Robert's eyes were over to the auditory construct location, but his head and ears were going in the direction of auditory memory. So, it is interesting that he said he wasn't hearing them in either of our voices.

RD: On the inside it felt like I was trying to open up both channels as much as possible. It would be like trying to tune a radio when the transmission is weak. You've got to tune it to just the right place. I was trying to get my mental 'radio' tuned since the signal associated with the last group of characters wasn't quite as strong as the others.

For instance, I think that if you had initially waited 5 or 10 minutes before asking me to guess the characters, I probably would have gotten the first two but I probably wouldn't have gotten the last ones at all. Now, I would get the last group because by saying them aloud I was getting the confirmation that those were the right characters, which made my internal representation stronger. The fact that I guessed and wasn't sure, then found I was right, increased the clarity of that last group and my confidence in my ability to remember them.

Initially, they were more or less out in front of me, almost like vague holographic images. I don't know if you've ever seen holograms, but they're not solid pictures like a photograph. It is more like they are floating out in space. The letters themselves are made out of light rather than being a concrete picture on a solid background. That's why I wasn't able to get all the characters so clearly. It wasn't like seeing them printed out. Now they have a more tangible quality as a mental image.

TE: In summary, Robert was essentially using a strategy that involved transforming something that was auditory into a visual image—in the same way that many of you may have found yourselves mentally verbalizing the visual characters in the last exercise. We think it will be interesting for you to notice if your performance stays the same with this exercise; since your strategy

will certainly have to be somewhat different because of the constraints of the exercise.

RD: To review:

The 'teacher' is to sit behind the 'learner' and the 'observer' will
sit facing the 'learner'. The 'teacher' is to read aloud the sequence
of characters on the section of paper marked "AUDITORY." The
'teacher' should read the characters at a consistent rhythm (without any attempt to chunk them for the 'learner'—so that the
'learner' may chunk them in his or her own way). The 'learner' may
request to hear the sequence again (either faster, slower or at the
same rate) but may hear it no more than three times. The 'teacher'
is to record how many times the 'learner' needed to hear the
sequence in the box marked "Time(s) Presented." Without looking
at the characters, the 'learner' will then verbally repeat the
sequence that was previously read aloud by the 'teacher'. The
'teacher' will write down the 'learner's' recollection in the spaces
beneath "GUESS" and score it as you did in the previous exercise.
Then the 'observer' will make his or her observations and the
group will explore the 'learners' mental strategy for memorizing
this sequence. For instance, you can ask, "Does it differ from the
strategy used for the visual task? How well did it work for this type
of memory?" Then rotate the roles until all three group members
have had a chance to try the auditory memory task.

•••••••

After the Exercise

RD: How did you do with this task? Was it the same or different
from the previous exercise?

Man: It was more difficult for me. I kept trying to form a picture of
the various characters, but they got jumbled up as my partner kept
saying more letters and numbers. I need to be able to write things
down in order to be clear. When I can't do that I get confused.

TE: Your strategy is similar to the structure of how music is
taught — and why kids can get confused about music. When

children are taught music, they are instructed to shift between something they see on a piece of sheet music to a particular behavioral operation or output—typically in the form of some kind of finger position on a musical instrument. Unfortunately, that's all the music eventually comes to mean to the child—that note means this movement, not this sound or this internal feeling. When composers create music, they don't start with the notes; they typically start with a feeling that they want to express. Then they turn that feeling into a sound and finally it becomes a picture, in the form of the notes on a page. Yet, people are taught how to play the music the opposite way. You don't get to start with the feeling that goes along with the music, and listen to what it sounds like when it's being played. You are typically first taught the visual-to-kinesthetic aspects of reading music and playing an instrument.

The Suzuki method is a refreshing alternative to the traditional approach. The method involves a group of people standing together, each with a musical instrument—such as a violin. They might have 400 kids in a room, and one instructor. They all play the same note, but they play the living life out of that note; until they all have internalized the form and the feel and the sound of that note. Their theory is that if you can play by ear, you can always learn the visual part of it—the notes—later on.

RD: Another alternative is the strategy we modeled from Michael Colgrass; who is a Pulitzer prize winning symphony composer (see *Tools for Dreamers* and *Strategies of Genius Volume I*). He teaches people music according to the same strategy that he uses to compose. He actually has them start with a feeling that they want to express and then make noises that fit with that feeling. Then he has the children draw their noises on a blackboard with different colors of chalk. What they draw are not notes, but rather abstract images of their noises—a kind of visual map of the sounds. They use these pictures to recall their sounds and conduct a group to perform their composition. They can even select the instruments that best represent their sounds.

After the students have successfully accomplished all these basic aspects of music—and had a lot of fun doing it—Michael shows them how their compositions can be translated into the traditional visual representations of notes and the fingerings of various instruments.

TE: I think that the typical way music is taught is a reflection of how the visual representational system has become the most highly valued sensory modality in education in Western culture. For music, however, that way of teaching brings with it some inherent problems. I was a musician for 20 years, and have friends who are still concert musicians that play in the symphony. They cannot do anything without a piece of paper. You ask them to play something, and they request the sheet music. You ask, "Can you jam? Can you make it up? Let's just play and make it up." They respond, "What do you mean make it up? "What's it made of? If you have it written out, I'll play my part if you have it." It is as if their creativity has been stifled because of their strategy. I think that is a reflection of the way that they were taught.

Kinesthetic Memory Exercise

TE: The last memory exercise is to be done through the kinesthetic channel. The 'learner' will input the characters totally by touch; no sound and no sight. The learner's output will also be completely kinesthetic.

RD: The structure of this exercise is similar to the auditory memory exercise, but there are some key differences. For this task, the 'teacher' is to instruct the 'learner' to close his or her eyes and is to guide the 'learner's' hand through the act of writing the sequence of characters. The characters to be used will be the set that you created for the section marked "KINESTHETIC" on the Memory Strategy Worksheet. The 'learner' may choose to use a pen or his or her index finger.

TE: The 'learner' could also choose to have the 'teacher' write out the sequence of characters on his or her back or the palm of the hand.

RD: As with the auditory test, up to three repetitions may be requested. Then, with eyes closed, the 'learner' is to write out the sequence of characters on a piece of paper. Scoring is done the same way as in the previous exercises.

When you are finished, the observer is to make comments on what he or she noticed about the 'learner's' physiology during the task. The 'observer' and the 'teacher' will then help to elicit the memory strategy that the 'learner' used for this task and compare the process and results to the previous exercises.

TE: Some of you who did well on the first two exercises might find this one a bit more challenging. We are much more used to recognizing characters visually and auditorily than kinesthetically.

RD: In fact, one issue that comes up with this exercise is whether or not you can remember something without knowing specifically 'what it is'.

TE: When you can see and hear the characters then you take for granted that you know 'what they are'; i.e., that "that shape is an 'A' and that is a '7'", etc. You can't always do that with kinesthetic input. For instance, Lisa close your eyes for a second. I'll be in the role of 'teacher' for a moment. (Todd traces a character on the palm of Lisa's hand.) Can you remember that shape?

Lisa: I think so.

TE: Take this pencil and draw it on this piece of paper without telling me what it is. (Lisa draws a character.) OK, did you have determine what character it was first?

Lisa: I don't know what it is, I can only say what it felt like.

TE: Good.

RD: You see, Lisa can remember the character as a kinesthetic pattern without having to know what it looks like or what 'name' to call it.

TE: It is a different experience to remember the characters as kinesthetic patterns than to try to figure out what they look or sound like. Because the task doesn't require Lisa to say if a character that she has felt is a particular letter or number. All she needs to do is to repeat the shape that she has felt. She doesn't have to know what it is.

RD: Many of you will probably try to visualize the characters that correspond to the pattern you are feeling. Others will say to yourself internally, "That's a 4...that's a Q...that's a 7". But it is also possible to do this completely kinesthetically. Go try it out.

• • • • • •

After the Exercise

TE: Any comments about this last exercise? Did any one find this task more difficult than the previous ones?

Mike: Yes.

TE: What was the part that made it difficult?

Mike: The characters were not recognizable.

TE: Did you try and figure out what the characters were, or did you just go with the kinesthetic memory of whatever the shape was?

Mike: I tried to figure out what the characters were.

TE: So you tried to figure out whether the pattern you were feeling was a 'D', or an 'A', or a 'star', or a number. I'm sure that many people did that. Just realize that was not a necessary part of the task. The task was just to reproduce whatever you were given as input. So the question is, do you just take the shapes in and give the shapes back, or do you try and figure what the shapes are by translating them into another representational system?

Beth: I did well with this exercise. The first thing I did was let my mind float free and feel where the letters were. If I identified a letter, that was fine; if I didn't, that was also fine. The second time, I tried to do what I did with the other letters—to try to make an association. When I was all done, I had eleven figures, because I had drawn a '4' as an 'L' and a '1'.

TE: Interesting. Who else did well?

Patrick: I did. I had my 'teacher' write the characters on my back and then I wrote them at the same time on my hand with my finger.

TE: That's interesting, because you were using two kinesthetic inputs. You've got the feeling of the character being drawn and you also have the motion—muscle motion. You learn a lot by moving your hand. You don't learn to write all in your head, you have to move your hand too.

RD: I know many high speed typists who do their initial 'proofing' through this kind of 'muscle memory'. They are typing along at 90 or 100 words per minute and suddenly 'feel' that there was a mistake. Because their hands know how it is supposed to feel to type a particular word, they are able to sense if it comes out differently while they are typing.

Ella: First I tried to make a picture of what I was feeling; but it wasn't strong enough for me to be sure I would remember — it didn't feel right. So I started writing on my leg and at the same time she was writing it, and then I talked to myself.

TE: So, you used all of the systems.

Ella: It wasn't something that I knew I was going to do. It developed while I was doing the task.

Long Term and Short Term Memory Strategies

RD: We often find that a person with a good short term memory for a particular set of characters will have an internal strategy that matches the representational system used to present the characters. For instance, a high scorer in the visual task will exhibit visual accessing cues and a completely visual strategy, while a poor visual performer will attempt auditory or kinesthetic accessing cues and strategies. An auditory high performer may show exclusively auditory accessing and representation while a poor performer will show a mix of other accessing cues and representational systems. Similarly, a kinesthetic high performer will go with the feeling of the kinesthetic pattern, while a poor kinesthetic scorer (who may be a high scorer for memory in a different representational system) may use an exclusively auditory or visual approach and become confused.

Longer term memory, on the other hand, is better facilitated by strategies that connect the information from one sense to other representational systems. For instance, some time has now past since we did the visual and auditory versions of this exercise. See if you can still remember any of those characters (even if you only got a few of them right).

[Some reactions from the group.]

RD: I noticed that many of you were moving your eyes to many different places. How many of you found that you had to use other representational systems to recall the characters this time?

Man: I remembered mine because of the discussion we had about them afterward.

Man: I got 10 out of 10 when I first did it, but can hardly remember any of them now.

Woman: I originally remembered mine initially through sound, but found myself trying to picture them in order to remember them now.

RD: In the model of NLP, the difference between long term and short term memory is a function of the strategy that you use to encode the information. Long term memory is a function of the process that you go through in relationship to the content you want to remember. One simple principle of long term memory is that 'the more of your neurology you mobilize to encode something, the easier it is going to be to remember it'. Long term memory is more a function of chunking and overlapping information to other senses than simply matching the representational system to the input channel. Mozart, for instance, had a phenomenal memory for music. He claimed that he could feel, see and even taste music (see *Strategies of Genius Volume I*). It seems obvious that it would be a little more difficult to forget something if you had it that fully represented.

For example, in one seminar, a woman was able to have perfect recall for the random sequence: 'A24705S58B'. She described her strategy for memorizing in the following way, *"I work in the food service business so I related the characters to my work. For instance, 'A' is for Apple and is at the beginning of the alphabet. '24' is how old I was when I changed jobs last. '705' means I'm 5 minutes late getting up. 'S' is for Salmon - and it kind of looks likes a fish swimming. '5' and '8' were difficult to find an easy meaning for so I just imagined that they were twice as big as all of the other characters and were bright red. 'B' is for Bacon and it follows A in the alphabet, so A and B kind of bracketed the whole group."*

Often, just by hearing this story, people will be able to remember these characters very easily, demonstrating that it is the strategy, not the degree of effort, that is responsible for effective learning.

TE: The type of long term memory strategy people habitually use can have a major impact on a number of aspects of their patterns of behavior and personality. For instance, these strategies are often reflected in the different degrees of memory loss people experience with certain illnesses that effect memory. (I worked with an Altzheimer patient just recently, who had trouble trying to remember all kinds of things). Not only do you habituate the strategy that you use for memory, but you habituate the entrance point (the input or 'lead in' system) that you use for the strategy. For example, you might habitually begin with an auditory input and then seek the pictures and the feelings that go with those sounds or words; or, you can start with feelings and then find the pictures and the sounds or vice versa. In other words, you can use any combination. But what happens is that you tend to habitually use a particular passageway for input or retrieval. If those are the particular nerve cells that become damaged through age or disease, the person will experience difficulties when trying to remember using that particular strategy or pathway to input or recall information. It is not so much that the individual cannot remember as it is that the way that the person is attempting to access his or her memory is not available.

The Altzheimer patient that I mentioned earlier, for instance, tended to rely on her visual representational system for memory. So, in order to help her, I took her in through the 'back door', so to speak. I taught her how to access memories through feelings and sounds. She began to remember things that she had not been able to recall previously. She was even able to get access to stored images.

RD: In summary, memory strategies involve several distinct aspects: (1) how you input the information, (2) how you store the information and (3) how you retrieve what has been stored. Another issue involves whether you intend to retain the information for a short period or need to remember it for the long term. Some things you may only need to know for a short period of time. Other information may need to be retained for a long period of time; and in many different contexts. The 'strategy' that you use will determine your success in these various aspects of memory and learning.

TE: We have already mentioned how learning and memory strategies may be dependent on certain internal 'states'. There is also the phenomenon of 'context dependent' learning. As an illustration, a classic study was done in which the researchers took a group of students that had been taught in a particular classroom and randomly divided them into two separate sub-groups. The two sub groups were given a test on some material that they had been taught in that classroom. One half of the group, however, was tested in a different room than the one they had been in when they learned the material. Then they switched the two groups—so that the one that had been initially tested in the classroom was moved to a different room and the other group returned to their initial classroom—and retested both groups. The results of the scores showed that whichever group was outside of the classroom in which they originally learned the material, dropped significantly— anywhere from 20% to 50%. In other words, many of the cues relating to the retrieval of the information was attached to that particular classroom environment. When they left the classroom, much of the information was suddenly not available to them.

For instance, let's say that there is a greenboard up in the front of the room that the teacher has been writing on during the whole time that you have been taking a particular class. Even though the information is no longer written on the board, that board has served as the primary context for the presentation of the information. That board can become a cue for your mind's eye when you are attempting to retrieve the information that was presented on that board. But if you go down to the auditorium or gymnasium to take the test, nothing is the same. There is no greenboard, there is nothing to provide the cues, except yourself.

This is a good example of where a strategy that is effective in one context is not effective in another context. There's something about the way in which the information was input and stored that influences how it needs to be retrieved.

Chapter 4

Strengthening The Senses

Overview of Chapter 4

- Developing Visual Skill
- Developing Auditory Skill
- Developing Kinesthetic Skill
- Summary: Strategies for Developing the Senses
- Exploring Perceptual Filters

Strengthening the Senses

RD: The next set of exercises involve developing the different sensory representational systems. These exercises will help you to develop richness and flexibility in using your senses so that you don't become trapped in only one sensory modality. In fact, I call these 'sensory calisthenics' because their purpose is to help you develop fundamental sensory strengths. It is the NLP view that these basic perceptual abilities are at the core of such things as our educational success and even our personalities. Developing these capabilities can make a fundamental impact on our lives.

TE: Often, people are locked into one type of learning strategy. For example, on one hand, you have the 'computer nerd' who goes through twelve years of school with no friends other than his computer; and maybe somebody that he shares software with. These people tend to be highly visual with a little bit of auditory ability dabbed in there; and very little kinesthetic development. On the other hand, you have the kid who sails through the air 14 feet, jumps 6 feet off the ground, and can dunk a basketball, and he's only 5'11"; yet he can't add two numbers together. This kid has really high 'kinesthetic IQ'. And, since you don't play basketball by yourself, this type of kid also develops many social skills. He can't pass a test in math to save his life, but he can do extremely complex things with his body and has developed many relational skills in order to play with a team. There's got to be a way to give the computer kids some of the physical and social skills and give the kinesthetic kids some of the computer skills.

The way to make that crossover is through representational system development. As I said before, I believe that this is where equal opportunity in education begins; at the level of capability. When a child first comes to school, his or her past personal history—including his or her parents, aunts, brother, uncles, sisters, where he or she fits into the family system— determines what strategies that child will use in order to learn. For instance, you may come to school with a well developed visual strategy, but I come with a kinesthetic strategy. By the time you get to school you can already recognize letters, words and numbers. When I get to school, I can kick the ball a mile and run like crazy. On the first day of school, the teacher says, "OK everybody, we're going to walk to class together." She says "We'll all be meeting in this classroom and it's room 4A." You're sitting back there and, because of your past personal history, your eyes naturally drift up and to the left, and you make this visual image of '4A'. While you are looking up and left, I am looking down at my shoelaces—even though we both entered through the same door, on the same day; both with the same preschool background.

On the second day of school, you're in the classroom on time, with your books, sitting in the right chair. I'm still out in the hallway trying to figure out where the heck I'm supposed to be—just walking around. A teacher sees me and asks, "Aren't you supposed to be in school now?" I say, "Yes, I am, but I don't know what classroom it is." He asks, "Who's your teacher?" "I don't remember." "Well, do you know anybody that was in your class with you?" I kind of remember one kid in class. So he takes me around, trying to find that kid. This literally happened to me when I started school. I'm the 'yo-yo' who couldn't find his way to class. Why? Because I walked in the door with a different strategy than you did. It doesn't make me worse, and doesn't make you better, or vice versa. But it is important to know that people start with different skills and strengths.

RD: It is also important to have some ways to help people recognize and develop these basic skills.

TE: The optimal NLP approach to education would be to take every child and first help them to develop all of the sensory representational systems. We'd develop their visual, auditory, kinesthetic, olfactory and gustatory representational systems. Then we'd teach them effective learning strategies. For the first six months of school we'd teach them to learn 'how to learn'. We'd first teach them how to use their brains.

RD: We had a person in one of our Dynamic Learning seminars who was forty years old and hadn't made it past the eighth grade. He was convinced that he was unable to learn; until we started doing the kinds of exercises that we did in the previous section and will be doing in this section of the book. By the third day, he was starting to read and spell words that he thought were impossible for him. He, like many people, had tremendous capacities for learning that he had never recognized or tapped into as being relevant for learning.

For instance, how many of you would like to have a photographic memory and think you don't have one; but, when you're trying to diet, you can remember the exact contents of your refrigerator?

TE: Or how many of you have gone home after seeing a movie, and remembered parts of the movie quite vividly?

RD: In other words, you laid down in bed and all of a sudden, you remembered some particular scene over and over again—whether you wanted to or not. For instance, how many of you can remember the scene in which Indiana Jones is falling down into that snake pit in *Raiders of the Lost Ark?* Now, anybody that can visualize that has the capability of having a photographic memory. You just need a way to harness that capability.

TE: It's like people who say that they can't carry a tune, and then find themselves unable to get the annoying music from the latest television commercial out of their heads—it just keeps playing over and over again.

RD: We believe that these experiences are a result of neurological processes that can be developed and harnessed. We've had people tell us, "I can't spell" or "I can't remember how to spell certain words," but they can remember something else that's just as complex. For instance, they can recognize their own bicycle or their car. That's just as sophisticated as recognizing the 'correct' spelling of a word.

TE: So is recognizing your own face in the mirror. (Of course, some days it's more difficult than others.)

RD: The purpose of these next exercises is to help you tap into and strengthen basic sensory skills. The first one involves developing visual acuity and recall. Before we begin the exercise I want to emphasize the distinction between a 'skill' or a 'process' and the 'content' to which that skill or process is applied. Visual acuity and recall are skills that can be applied to many different contents; such as faces, objects, movies, words, photographs, etc. When the skill is developed in one area it can be transferred to another. Skills are a 'deeper structure'; content relates to 'surface structures'.

As an example, we learn to write by holding a pen or pencil in our hand and moving our wrist and fingers. Yet, once we have mastered the skill of making letters, we can transfer that skill to other parts of the body without any practice. For instance, you can trace letters in the sand with your left foot. You can hold a pencil in your mouth and make readable letters. You can even trace reasonable facsimiles of letters with your knee or elbow—even though the types and combinations of muscles, bones and tendons are completely different from those in your wrist, hand and fingers. This type of phenomena contradicts the more mechanical view of learning proposed by people like Pavlov and Skinner. You cannot account for this kind of skill transfer through simple stimulus-response and reinforcement.

TE: Yeh. Who taught your elbow how to write? (Laughter)

RD: According to NLP, skill development occurs at a higher level of learning. It is a deep structure that can be transformed into multiple surface structures. So keep in mind that, even though the contents we will be using to develop sensory skills may not seem directly relevant to 'academic' topics, the skill to use your sensory representational systems is the foundation of all learning. The following is an overview of the basic steps of the exercise.

Developing Visual Skill

Get into pairs of two people (**A** & **B**):

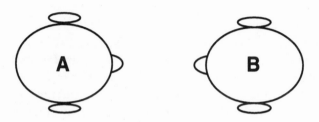

STEP 1. **A** and **B** stand facing one another. **A** gives instructions to **B** to visualize **A**'s body position and look up to the left (for right handers) or the right (for left handers) to remember it.

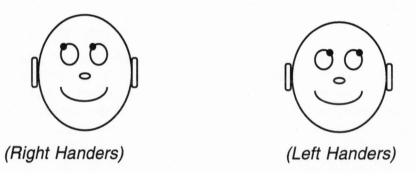

(Right Handers)   *(Left Handers)*

STEP 2. **B** closes his or her eyes. **A** moves some part of his or her body (i.e. hand, leg, finger, head tilt, etc.) while **B**'s eyes are closed.

STEP 3. **A** then tells **B** to open his or her eyes. **B** looks up to the left (or right) and compares what he or she sees to the remembered image and guesses which part of the body **A** moved.

STEP 4. If **B** misguesses then **A** instructs **B** to close his or her eyes again. **A** does not tell **B** what part was moved but goes back to the original body position and then instructs **B** to open his or her eyes once more and guess (go back to STEP 2).

TE: As an example, let's have Stephanie and Lisa come up and stand facing one another. Find a distance that is comfortable for you. Lisa, you look at Stephanie and then put your eyes up and left (since you are right-handed). As you do, make a mental 'snapshot' of Stephanie. If you want, you can look at her again, and double check your mental image. Now, close your eyes Lisa, and Stephanie you move something. (Stephanie moves her hand.) OK Lisa you can open your eyes. What changed?

Lisa: Her hand. (Cheers from audience.)

TE: Start by moving something fairly obvious such as an arm or a leg. This is not about tricking your partner; it's about allowing him or her to develop a visual skill. If Lisa had not been able to perceive the change, then we would have had her close her eyes again and instructed Stephanie to move back to the original position she had been in. Lisa would then be asked to open her eyes and look at Stephanie again and see if she could detect what has changed.

RD: Stephanie would keep going back and forth with that same movement until Lisa was able to perceive what was changing. Once Lisa was able to perceive the change, Stephanie and Lisa would repeat the cycle again with Stephanie making a more subtle movement.

TE: So, you start with macro level changes and continue to make them more and more subtle. You should be able to get to the point with this game where the observer is able to perceive a subtle curl in the fingers, a slight eye movement, a missing ear ring or any number of things changing. Thus, when the observer becomes good at picking up macro movements, you will want to begin to make smaller increments of change in order to find out how acute the person's perception can become.

RD: If the observer is able to master very subtle movements, you can make the exercise more challenging by moving more than one part of the body. In this case, the observer would have to detect more than one change.

TE: Another variation is to do the exercise in groups involving more than two people. To make the exercise more challenging you could have 4 or 5 people each moving something and one person observing. This will expand the number of 'chunks' of information that the observer is sorting for visually.

Also, keep in mind that the content we used for this exercise happens to be another person, but you can make many creative variations. For instance, a teacher could have all of her students look around the classroom and see who is there. The students would then be told to close their eyes. The teacher then sends one of the kids out of the classroom. The rest of the class is then told to open their eyes and guess who is missing. There are lots of creative ways that you could vary this process to help develop visual skill.

RD: For instance, let's say you wanted to adapt this exercise to a more 'academically' recognized content. We have developed a variation that can be used to help children learn to develop their visual acuity and recall to better recognize correct spellings. To make an analogy, words are made out of different variations of the same letters in the same way that different body attitudes are made out of variations of body parts. The skill required to remember different combinations of letters is really no different than remembering which parts of the body someone has moved. In Dynamic Learning we consider an academic task to be just another variation of the way we naturally use our nervous systems. In other words, we believe that if you can recognize your own coat and your own bicycle, or if you can recognize which part of someone's body has subtly moved, then you can recognize correct spellings.

To develop this kind of visual recognition skill we also organize people into pairs or groups. We give each group a few sets of flashcards. Each set of cards is made up of the same base word spelled in different ways—the standard or 'correct' version and a number of variations as in the following example:

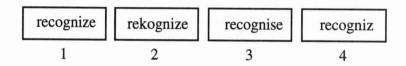

recognize	rekognize	recognise	recogniz
1	2	3	4

The 'observer' is shown the first card, which is always the standard or 'correct' spelling of the word. The observer is instructed to look at the card and then up and to the right or left (as in the exercise we have just described) and take a 'snapshot' of the card in his or her mind's eye. The observer is then asked to shut his or her eyes. At this point the observer's partner may either change cards or choose to stay with the first card. When the observer opens his or her eyes again, the task is simply to say whether the word showing on the card is the 'same' or 'different' from the original word.

TE: So all you do is take the very process that we described in this first visual development exercise and shift the content words. The task is to simply recognize variations from the starting state.

It boils down to whether or not you can recognize the set of letters that you started with.

RD: Once the observer is able to successfully recognize the set of letters, you can increase the challenge by asking which letters, specifically, have changed, if there is a difference. Another level of challenge would be to let a little time pass, and then see if the observer can recognize whether a particular card that is being shown is the original or 'correct' version without showing it to him or her first. That is you choose a card from one of the sets and without showing the observer the standard one that you started with, see if he or she can recognize whether or not it is the first word.

TE: If you do this variation of the exercise, however, it is important to keep in mind that it is a sensory development exercise, not a 'spelling' exercise. Spelling, Math, Science and Geography are subject areas. This exercise is about learning 'how to learn'—not learning a particular subject. It's a different way to approach learning.

RD: In other words, this variation of the visual development exercise is not about succeeding or failing at spelling. It is about how to develop the ability to recognize something visually. So if the observer is unable to recognize whether a word is the same or different, his or her partner needs to simply go back and forth between the first word and the variations in order to help the observer 're-calibrate'. The point we want to emphasize is that if you miss recognizing a variation, it doesn't mean that you did anything wrong; nor does it mean that you're 'slow' or 'stupid'. It simply means that your picture wasn't clear enough yet.

Developing Auditory Skill

RD: The Dynamic Learning exercise for developing auditory recognition and recall is similar in many respects to the visual development exercise but incorporates sound instead of sight. The basic steps of the exercise are summarized below.

Form a group of four people (**A,B,C** & **D**)

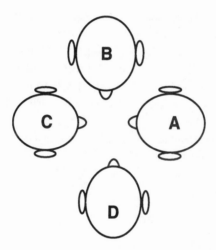

STEP 1. **A** sits or stands and **B,C** & **D** stand around **A** in a semi circle. **B, C** & **D** each in turn make a sound (i.e. snap fingers, tap chair with pencil, clap hands, as long as each person makes the same kind of sound) and as they do each repeats his or her name following their sound. **B, C** & **D** repeat the sound and the name until **A** indicates she can identify each person by their corresponding sound.

STEP 2. **A** closes his or her eyes and **B, C** or **D** makes the sound. **A** is to guess which of them has made the sound.

STEP 3. If **A** misguesses then **B, C & D** repeat the original sound and his or her name until **A** indicates he or she can identify the match between name and corresponding sound. The group then repeats STEP 2.

STEP   4. To add an interesting twist, persons **B, C & D** can attempt to imitate each others sounds and person **A** must guess who is imitating who. For example, **A** may guess "**B** is imitating **C**" or "**B** is imitating **D**."

RD: We'd like to demonstrate this next sensory 'calisthenic'; and get your ears doing some push ups and pulls ups. Eileen and Marsha would you come up and help us? Eileen sit here. You will be person **A**—the 'learner'. Todd, Marsha and I each are going to make the same kind of sound. Your task is to be able to distinguish which one of us is making the sound. First you will need to 'calibrate' our different ways of making the sounds. So begin by closing your eyes Eileen. We're going to snap our fingers, all in the same general area in front of you. As we do, we will say our names so that you can associate the sound with the name.
  [*Snap*]—Robert.

Marsha: [*Snap*]—Marsha.

TE: [*Snap*]—Todd.

RD: OK, do you need to hear it again? You can ask for another calibration.

Eileen: Yes. I'd like to hear them again.

RD: [*Snap*]—Robert.

Marsha: [*Snap*]—Marsha.

TE: [*Snap*]—Todd.

Eileen: OK. I think I can recognize the differences.

RD: Good. Now one of us will snap our fingers and Eileen you try to guess who it is.

Marsha: [*Snap*]

Eileen: Marsha.

TE: [*Snap*]

Eileen: Todd.

RD: [*Snap*]

Eileen: Robert.

RD: [*Snap*]

Eileen: Robert.

TE: [*Snap*]

Eileen: Robert. Ah, OK, now wait, that was Todd.

TE: Yes, that's good. I did that on purpose to increase the challenge. I moved my hand over to where Robert had been snapping his fingers.

RD: Eileen was beginning to calibrate on the basis of location; but, as it mentions in the exercise, once the person beings to guess you can make the task more challenging by trying to make your sounds more alike. Now if Eileen had not been able to distinguish between Todd and me, when Todd tried to make his sound more like mine, then we'd want her to re-calibrate between the two of us with her eyes closed. Todd and I would go back and forth snapping our fingers in that particular location until Eileen was able to tell the difference. And, for your information Eileen, you could even say something like "that's Robert trying to imitate Todd." Remember the purpose of this exercise is to refine your listening abilities. OK. Let's try it again.

Marsha: [*Snap*]

Eileen: It was Marsha.

TE: [*Snap*]

Eileen: Robert? No, it was Todd. But, it was Todd imitating Robert.

RD: That's correct.

TE: [*Snap*]

Eileen: Todd.

RD: [*Snap*]

Eileen: Robert.

Marsha: [*Snap*]

Eileen: Marsha.

RD: [*Snap*]

Eileen: Robert.

TE: [*Snap*]

Eileen: Todd?

RD: That's right. That was a Todd trying to sound like a Robert.

TE: In all fairness to the person who is in the position of doing the listening, you need to initially be as consistent in making your sound as you can, so that the person can calibrate and distinguish your sound from the others. If Eileen is trying to calibrate and distinguish between these different sounds, and they keep changing then that makes it harder for her to be successful. The object is to repeat the same sound in the beginning for the benefit of the person trying to do the calibration. It's not about fooling them— it's about giving them real sensory based evidence that they can use in their brain in order to sort out and determine which person is making which sound.

RD: By the way, there are many different kinds of sounds you can make—snapping your fingers, clapping your hands, clearing your throat, even tapping on some object.

TE: If you choose to tap on an object, all three sound makers will need to share the same object. If it was a spoon, for instance, we'd have to use the same spoon; or if we picked a pen, we'd all have to use the same pen and hit it on the same spot.

RD: That would be a very challenging task. What you would have to start listening for would be the unique signature of the way that person actually taps something. Things like clearing your throat are interesting because you have your own unique voice qualities. And it can be fun to try to imitate one another.

By the way, realize that this task is not simply about auditory input. Eileen had to hold three different sound templates in her mind in order to try to distinguish the current input and match it with one of these templates. So this task isn't just about hearing things. It is about internally representing information auditorily and then matching some ongoing input to one of the three internal templates in your mind. It's a fairly sophisticated skill—and a valuable one to build.

TE: Your degree of success with this exercise will tell you a lot about your unconscious 'micro strategies' for listening and hearing. For example — similar to the auditory memory exercise in the previous section—do you attempt to hear a particular person's sound and connect it to a visual image; such as a picture of the face of the person who is making the sound? That is, did Eileen sit there and form a mental a picture of Robert making his sound; or did she not have any picture at all? Perhaps she just took in sounds and mentally recorded both the sound of the noise and associated it with the sound of Robert's voice.

Since the purpose of this exercise is to develop your auditory system, it would be an interesting challenge to try to do it purely auditorily. In fact, before beginning the exercise you may want to review some of the basic qualities or 'submodalities' of the auditory representational system; such as volume, tone, pitch, tempo, distance, location and so forth. If you were to take the sounds that you hear and break them into their purely auditory components, not turning them into any other representational system, but just representing them as sounds—these submodalities would be some of the qualities that you would sort for. Is one person louder than the other? Does one person's sound last longer than the others? Is the pitch of a particular person's voice higher or lower than another's? If you want to try it as a purely auditory skill, that's the kind of sorting that you might want to use to distinguish the characteristics of the particular sounds associated with individual people.

RD: The type of fundamental micro strategies that Todd is talking about can have a tremendous influence on your ability to perform auditory tasks. For example, I have done some modeling contrasting 'non-musical' people with individuals who have so called "perfect pitch" and with those having "relative pitch." People who have 'relative pitch' are able to accurately distinguish musical notes relative to one another. That is, if you give them one note and tell them it's an "A," "B" or "C," then they can begin to accurately determine other notes that they hear relative to that one. However, it is necessary for them to first hear a baseline note. People who have 'perfect pitch' do not need any external reference. For instance, if I play any random note on the piano, the person can immediately they'll you, "That's a D-flat" or "That's an F." And they can tell you what octave the note is without any external reference at all.

In other words, their reference for sound is totally inside their own nervous system. Typically, what they will do is overlap the sound into the two major representational systems—sight and feeling in particular. The sound goes directly into a particular feeling, and that's how they know what the pitch is. One of the questions we were attempting to explore with the study was whether or not perfect pitch and or relative pitch could be taught or developed in people that were not born with it. The goal of this study was to model people who had perfect pitch and relative pitch, and then teach the strategy to other people to see if they could improve their ability to distinguish musical notes. As you can imagine, relative pitch was easier to teach than perfect pitch; but you'd be surprised at how fast people were able to identify notes on the piano once they had an effective strategy.

As Todd pointed out, you do have to initially connect the sound with the name, like 'D', 'F-minor', and so on. It is the same as connecting a particular sound with a person, as in this exercise. So, this seemingly simple little exercise or game is actually the same kind of process that would go into developing something like perfect pitch.

TE: Incidentally, people who have perfect pitch don't just have that ability only for sounds coming from musical instruments. They hear all sounds and know what notes they are. It's like they can't not know what note it is. In other words, you close the door, and they respond with, "B-flat." It's a part of how they relate to the world.

RD: It is a part of their identity and way of living. When they hear sounds, it's as if the tones resonate with other parts of their nervous system. That's a really powerful way of relating to sound. For instance, Mozart wrote that he felt, tasted and saw his music, as well as hearing it. Other composers, such as Beethoven, also described these kinds of 'synesthesias' (see *Strategies of Genius Volume I*).

TE: One of the strategies that I have used to teach music is to have students sing anything that they are playing. It doesn't matter what they were playing, what scales or what notes. They are supposed to sing what they play. This creates an internal reference for music. For instance, if somebody says to me, "Play 'do dah dee do dee dah'," I know where that is both on the instrument, on the scale, and inside my head. Let's say you're skipping down the street and a melody comes into your head. For a lot of people, if they don't run home and write it down, they forget it. For me, once I start singing it in my head, then the visual image of the guitar or the piano pops up in my mind's eye and it becomes like a movie. Then when I go home, I just play the movie back. These mental links allow me to make a direct correlation between the sound and what the hands are actually doing.

It gets bizarre sometimes. Weird things happen when I get about 14 instruments going at the same time. Where they are all playing, the whole orchestra plays at once in your head.

RD: Now you understand why he acts the way he does sometimes. (Laughter)

TE: How else would you write for fifteen people if you don't have fifteen instruments playing in your head at the same time? Otherwise you'd put the music together one chunk at a time; and if you do it that way, how do you know if all the pieces are going to fit?

RD: Learning, thinking and your ability to function in this world, come from being able to drink in that world through your senses. Imagine that you were thirsty in your auditory system and that sounds were something you could just drink into your ears. That's the kind of state that you'd be in during this exercise. Start with three sounds (then you can try to go up to 14 or 15, like Todd was talking about). It can be snaps, claps, whistles, clearing your throat, or all singing the same notes.

•••••••

After the Exercise

RD: Are there any reports, questions or comments generated by this last exercise?

Man: It was more difficult than the visual practice, because we weren't taught to really listen when we were little kids; unless, we were musicians.

TE: We're not taught to think in sound increments at all. Generally speaking, in Western culture, we describe things visually. Our language is full of references to visual submodalities; such as size, shape color, intensity, and so on. We're not really taught as children how to describe sound in the same degree of detail that we are taught to describe the visual world. Most children when asked what something sounds like, will make or imitate the sound. They don't say, "It was a high pitched frequency, about 2000 herz, and lasted for approximately 3.5 milliseconds." But, you do describe things visually almost that accurately. People say things like, "It was circular, about a foot and a half across..." You are not trained to think about the auditory system in that way.

RD: In fact, you're more likely to be taught to think about the details of your auditory experience in visual terms. When I was in the third grade, I had a teacher who loved music. I remember one time when she played a classical record during class and gave us crayons and asked us to draw the music. I went, "What?!" Music was more kinesthetic to me. I remember looking around and seeing the rest of the class drawing all kinds of pictures that they saw in the music; and I had no idea what she was talking about. I ended up doing a kind of kinesthetic strategy, where I just moved my hand up and down when the sound went up and down; and I made a terrible looking picture. I can still recall the disappointed look on her face when she saw my drawing. She said, "That's what that looks like to you?" Overlapping sounds onto imagery was a skill that I had to learn how to develop.

TE: I do think you can also train your ear to listen more closely. I do believe that. I hear light bulbs. I walk into the house, and I can tell you when a light bulb is about to go out. A week before it happens, I know it is about to go out. This ability probably relates to all the listening training that I have done throughout the twenty years of my music career.

As an example, I was involved in a research study once whose purpose was to develop auditory acuity. Now, in music, there is something called "timbre." Timbre is what makes the saxophone sound like a saxophone, as opposed to a flute. That is, there is a difference between the pure tone of the notes a, b, c, etc., and the sound of a saxophone or piano playing the notes a, b, c, etc. This difference has to do with the other frequencies that the instrument is adding to the pure note. If you heard a "pure note" generated on a sound machine, it wouldn't be all that pleasing to your ear. What makes the sound of instruments pleasing to your ear is that they have what are called "overtones."   Those overtones are what creates the sounds of the flute, versus the piano or the violin.

In this study, they recorded a saxophone playing the melody to the song, "Moon over Vermont" — just a single saxophone playing the song. They played this recording to people and asked, "How many instruments do you hear? How many melodies do you follow?" Initially people responded, "Just the saxophone, just one instrument is playing the one melody line."

Then, they electronically separated out the pure tone and the 'overtones'. You could both see and hear that there were other frequencies above and below the pure note being played, and that they had their own patterns. These are known as "harmonics." As the primary note moves, the harmonic line moves in relationship to it. This pattern of frequencies automatically happens; it's a function of the design of the instrument.

They had the people in the study listen to each of the separate harmonic lines over and over again for about two days at three hours a day. On the following day, they played the initial saxophone recording again and asked the people how many melodies they heard playing. The minimum they heard was five. In other words, they didn't hear the saxophone any longer as just a saxophone, they heard the pure note being played and they heard the movement of all the harmonics around it. Instead of just hearing the saxophone, now, they heard this rich piece of music with only one instrument playing. That goes to show you how much you can train people's ears to discern the difference between things—just by exposing them to it. Eventually the people were even able to tell you which one of the overtones it was. Naturally, these people said that their experience with music from that point on was completely different.

RD: It would be like listening to a barbershop quartet. You hear everybody singing together, then you just hear each one singing their own part.

TE: You learn what the individual parts sound like.

RD: Then when you hear it again, you're not just hearing this one mass of sound, you're hearing all the parts working and playing between each other.

TE: Most importantly, these people developed more choice about what they heard. I think choice is important for any skill. For instance, I can selectively not listen to light bulbs now and not hear them. I think that it is important to be able to hear if you want to, or decide that you don't need to listen.

RD: Again, part of what we are talking about is control over hearing as well as just heightened hearing. One thing that happens to people is that they become fearful that if they hear any more, then they will be overwhelmed. But the kind of thing that Todd was describing has to do with making choices.

TE: You organize things so that you are not overwhelmed. For example, I can create an internal sound in my ears where I cannot hear anything on the outside. I grew up in an apartment building right across the street from a railroad track. The trains ran from 5 AM in the morning until 2 AM the following morning. So, if you wanted any sleep you had to learn to make 'earlids'.

RD: By the way, you can also help people remove 'earlids' that are no longer necessary. I once worked with a lady who had a hearing problem in one of her ears. She had what they call physical and perceived deficit. She had an especially hard time hearing things in the range of the human voice. She supposedly had some kind of organic damage and had been through multiple operations. I found out that she'd had a difficult childhood, and that there were a number of reasons she didn't want to hear. I assisted her in changing some beliefs about hearing and when she went back and had her hearing retested, her deficit had all but disappeared; especially in the range of human voices. She was able to hear out of her previously damaged ear.

The work we did together essentially involved helping her to disconnect certain sounds from feelings. Speaking of feelings, the Dynamic Learning exercise for developing kinesthetic recognition and recall is very similar to the auditory development exercise. The basic steps of the exercise are summarized below.

Developing Kinesthetic Skill

Form a group of four people (**A,B,C & D**)

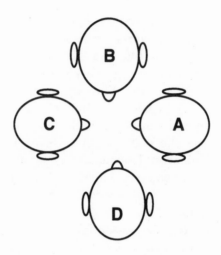

STEP 1. **A** sits or stands and persons **B, C & D** stand around in a semi-circle.

STEP 2. Person **A** is to orient his or her eyes down and to the right (or to the left if **A** is left handed) and take a deep breath in order to promote the maximum access to his or her feelings.

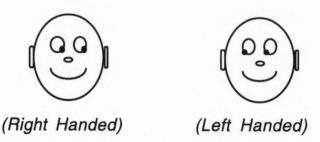

(Right Handed)   *(Left Handed)*

A is then instructed to close his or her eyes and **B, C & D** each take turns touching person **A**. They should each touch person **A** in the same place. Initially, **B, C & D** will each say his or her own name while touching person **A**. This is so that **A** can associate each person's touch with that person's name.

For example: **B, C & D** touch **A** on the back of the hand with their fingers or hands. **B, C & D** could also use an inanimate object such as a pencil or a piece of plastic. The important thing to remember is that each person use the same object and touch **A** on the same area (i.e. **B, C & D** could touch **A** on the right first knuckle with their index fingers as they say their name). This process is repeated until **A** indicates that he or she can identify the touch associated with the name.

STEP 3. While **A** keeps his or her eyes closed either **B, C** or **D** will touch **A** without saying his or her name. **A** must then guess the name of who just touched him or her. Specifically, **A** looks down and right (or left) and compares the feelings of the touch he or she just received with the memory of the three touches he or she experienced previously. **A** picks the one that matches most closely and says aloud the name he or she has associated with that touch.

STEP 4. If **A** is unsuccessful in correctly guessing who just touched him or her, **A** should "recalibrate" by repeating STEPS 2 and 3.

When **A** has guessed the correct person three times in a row proceed to the next section for the next level of the exercise.

STEP 5. **A** is again instructed to close his eyes and orient his eyes down and to the right or left. While **A** has his eyes shut

B, C & D each touch A, in sequence, without verbally identifying themselves. A then has to match the names with the touches and guess the appropriate sequence. The sequences should be random, for example, <B, D, C> or <C, D, B>, etc.

STEP 6. If A is unsuccessful in identifying the correct sequence he or she may call for a "recalibration" by repeating STEP 2 (associating touches with names).

When A has correctly identified three sequences in a row proceed to the next step.

STEP 7. In order to really stretch A's ability to use his sense of touch, B, C & D can try to imitate each other's touch. With his eyes closed, A should attempt to guess who is imitating who. For example, B tries to make his quality of touch match that of D and C attempts to touch like B.

This one can be a lot of fun.

RD: Jean and Mary Beth would you help us demonstrate this? Jean, you will close your eyes, and Todd and Mary Beth and I will touch you in the same place on your hand. We'll touch you in the same place, say our names, and then you try to distinguish us by the differences between our touches. OK, close your eyes.

TE: [*Touches Jean's hand*] Todd.

RD: [*Touches Jean's hand*] Robert.

Mary Beth: [*Touches Jean's hand*] Mary Beth.

RD: We'll do it one more time:

TE: [*Touches Jean's hand*] Todd.

RD: [*Touches Jean's hand*] Robert.

Mary Beth:: [*Touches Jean's hand*] Mary Beth.

RD: Now, you tell which one of us is touching your hand. We won't say our names this time.

TE: [*Touches Jean's hand*]

Jean: Todd.

Mary Beth: [*Touches Jean's hand*]

Jean: Robert?

RD: Actually, that was Mary Beth. So, we'll go back and forth between me and Mary Beth.

Mary Beth: [*Touches Jean's hand*] Mary Beth.

RD: [*Touches Jean's hand*] Robert.

Mary Beth: [*Touches Jean's hand*] Mary Beth.

RD: [*Touches Jean's hand*] Robert. Now you tell who this one is [*Touches Jean's hand*].

Jean: Robert.

RD: Right. Now we'll continue.

Mary Beth: [*Touches Jean's hand*]

Jean: Mary Beth.

RD: Right.

Mary Beth: [*Touches Jean's hand*]

Jean: Mary Beth.

RD: Right again.

TE: [*Touches Jean's hand*]

Jean: Todd.

Mary Beth: [*Touches Jean's hand*]

Jean: Robert.

RD: No, that was actually Mary Beth.

Jean: I should have known. Mary Beth's touch is harder. Todd, you're impossible not to catch. You're temperature is different.

TE: As you can see, Jean is beginning to make some pretty refined kinesthetic distinctions. One of the things that Jean said that made my touch easier to recognize is that the temperature was different. Before starting the exercise you may want to review some of the kinesthetic submodalities such as temperature, size, pressure, and, if there's movement, the speed of the movement. These will help you to sensitize yourself to some of the qualities that will help you to recognize differences between the touch of various people.

RD: There is also a second part to the kinesthetic development exercise, in which, similar to the auditory exercise, you try to imitate each other. This can be as interesting for the people doing the touching as the one getting touched. For instance, it may be fascinating to notice what changes for you internally when you imitate the touch of another person.

TE: In other words, if I'm going to imitate how Linda touches, do I have to change something in my feelings or shift my state?

RD: Imitating someone else is a form of 'modeling' them. You may pick up intuitions about other people just by touching somebody the way that they touch that person.

Since we've touched on that subject, I'm sure you'll all be tickled to go and do this exercise now. It is a good way to get in touch with each other.

TE: Go out and 'finger' out how to do it.

RD: I've got to 'hand' it to you Todd, you really seem to have grasped the Dynamic Learning process.

Summary:
Strategies for Developing the Senses

RD: It is our belief that everybody was born with the capacity to fully utilize all of their senses. Almost every child that we have met has had an exceptionally robust contact with their minds' eyes, ears and feelings. People often ask, "How do you use NLP with children who don't know anything about cognitive psychology and the senses?" Our response is that children are actually the real experts on it! They are usually much more in touch with their senses and their imaginations than adults. In fact one way to help adults reactivate some of these capabilities is to help them get back in touch with their childhoods.

NLP provides several methods· by which people can learn to develop and enhance their ability to more fully use any of their representational systems (see also *Strategies of Genius Volume III*). The following is a summary of some of the various ways to develop the senses that we have introduced in this book. These methods include the utilization of :

    Adjusting Physiology
    Pacing and Leading Reference Experiences
    Chunking
    Reducing Interferences from the Other Senses
    Encouraging Positive Overlap with Other Senses
    Clearing Personal History and Limiting Beliefs

Adjusting Physiology

Accessing cues are subtle behaviors that accompany the activation of a particular representational system. The B.A.G.E.L. model identifies a number of types of micro behavioral cues, involving one's eyes and other physical features, that are associated with cognitive processes - in particular, those involving the five senses.

Eye movement patterns, for example, are one of the most interesting of these "minimal reflexes" or micro behavioral cues; and the one most closely associated with NLP. The movement of the eyes up and to the left or right tends to accompany visualization. An upward eye movement to the left typically coincides with the recollection of visual memories, whereas a movement up and to the right would accompany the formation of constructed imagery or fantasy. Horizontal movement of the eyes tends to go along with listening. Eyes down accompany feeling. An eye position to the left hand side is often indicative of memory, while a movement to the right hand side indicates imagination.

Body posture is another important influence and reflection of a person's internal processes. For example, most people would probably find it very difficult to be creative with their head down and their shoulders hunched forward. If you put yourself into that physiology you will find it's going to be difficult to feel inspired. NLP has discovered that when people are visualizing they tend to be in a more erect posture. When people are listening, they tend to lean back a bit with their arms folded or head tilted. When people are having feelings, they tend to lean forward and breath more deeply.

People also often gesture to the sense organ that is most active for them in a moment. People will touch or point to their eyes when they are attempting to visualize something or when they get an insight. People gesture toward their ears when they are talking about something they heard or are trying to hear. Likewise people will touch their mouth when they are thinking verbally (like Rodin's The Thinker). When people touch their chest or stomach it generally indicates feeling.

Various constellations of these types of cues, then, can either support or inhibit the development and use of particular representational systems. It would not be surprising if a person who was sitting slumped forward, staring at the ground and stroking his or her chin would experience difficulties in visualizing. Effective visualizing, for instance, would involve a posture in which the head and eyes were lifted upward. For a right handed person, visual memory would be most facilitated by shifting the head and eyes to the left; visual imagination would be enhanced by positioning the head and eyes to the right.

Incidentally, trying out these cues is not going to automatically make one start seeing technicolor fantasies. Our nervous system is not a machine and accessing cues are not simple cause-effect triggers. Adjusting one's accessing cue can be likened to what you do when you are turning the dial on your television set. The picture on the screen does not actually come from inside your television set. The picture has been transmitted from somewhere else. The tuning of the television set allows you to pick up the images and sounds that are currently being broadcast. Accessing cues function in a similar fashion. They help a person to tune into whatever mental representations are active. Just as one would find with a television set, if the signal being broadcast is weak or distant, you may not pick it up clearly no matter how hard you try to adjust the knobs. If one lives near a transmission tower or has a satellite dish, however, the precision of the tuning is less essential.

The point is that if you want to develop the skill of visualizing, you should make sure that your 'equipment' is tuned properly. Many people, for instance, find it strenuous or uncomfortable to put their eyes in certain positions. By practicing and becoming aware of the body postures and cues that facilitate visualization, one can help to facilitate the natural development of that capacity. At the age of three, for example, my daughter already knew how to look up in order to visualize words. She is able to easily spell simple words both frontwards and backwards.

Pacing and Leading Reference Experiences

Once the 'circuitry' of your nervous system is 'tuned' appropriately, you can focus on the signal to be 'broadcast'. Even if someone is not a good visualizer, for instance, there will usually be some mental images that he or she is aware of—dreams, for instance.

By starting with one image, even one that is very simple, trivial or indistinct, one can eventually succeed in "fixing" it so that it does not "flit away." By returning to this basic reference image and incrementally adjusting it, it will eventually gain in "strength and distinctness." For example, close your eyes and see what images you can bring up naturally. Maybe it is easy to recall the faces of the people you love, a favorite movie character, an emotionally charged experience from your past, a special vacation spot, the sunset, your automobile or a simple household object. Once you have formed such a picture, even if it is at first very indistinct, keep coming back to it, and see if you can add more depth, detail or color.

Often, people have access to a great deal of sensory information, even if they are not immediately conscious of it. For instance, I have worked with many people who initially claim that they cannot visualize. One of the first questions I ask is, "If you could visualize, what would you see?" For instance, "If you could visualize a big balloon suspended in front of you, what would it look like, if you could see it?" Most people will begin to respond, "Well, it would be red and round, about this far away from me..." and so on. The point is that the information and details may be there, but just not as a conscious image or 'positive hallucination." From there it is a matter of pacing and leading the unconscious images into consciousness.

Chunking

'Chunking' is the process of either taking small pieces of information and assembling them into a larger whole, or of taking a complete object and breaking it into smaller elements. Some people are able to make a picture of small details but are unable to see the whole object. Other people can envision whole scenes but cannot form a picture of the details.

Sometimes, when I am helping a person learn to visualize, I will say, "Lets start with something simple, and then we will 'chunk up'. Lets make the picture of a ball." Once he or she can imagine the ball or some other simple object, then we will add another ball and then another, until he or she is able to make a stack of balls in the shape of a pyramid or some such composite. Other times, I might have a person start with just a vague image or outline of a person, and then look for details like the buttons on his or her shirt.

I will then continue pacing and leading, either adding more complexity or detail to the picture. I might say, "Well, if you saw this ball in front of you, where would the shadow be? Where is the light source?" To "see" something in external reality we need light.

The same principle holds true for our internal images. In my own internal images, I always make sure I have light and a light source. To try to picture mental images without an internal light source is like complaining because one cannot see an object in a dark room. Since, light casts shadows, I often have people first look for the shadow cast by an object in their mind. When they are able to find where the shadow would be, it makes it much easier to see the object.

Reducing Interference from the Other Senses

One common problem people experience, when they are attempting to learn to visualize, is interferences from the other sensory representational systems. This often happens when a person is trying so hard to visualize that the person gets in his or her own way. For instance, a person may have a critical internal voice that says, "What's wrong with me? I can't do anything right. Why can't I see this image?" Rather than helping the situation, the voice produces interference to the imaging process because it is clogging up the person's representational channels.

Another source of interference is from external stimuli. In fact, one of the purposes of 'accessing cues' is to help reduce the interference coming from external sensory input. As a woman once expressed to me during a conversation, "I really feel that I can see what you are saying better when I don't look at you as I listen."

Encouraging Positive Overlap with Other Senses

This does not necessarily mean that the other senses and the external world need to be completely disconnected. The overlap and support of other senses can in fact be valuable resources if they are aligned to the task of visualizing. For instance, if a person is having difficulty visualizing an object, I will often ask the person to reach out his or her hands and 'sculpt' the space the object would take up; as if the person were tracing the edges of the object with his or her hands. By doing so, the person will often be able to 'sense' the space of the object, even if they can't yet consciously visualize it.

If the person is very verbal, I might ask him or her to describe the object in detail while looking at it in his or her mind's eye. To use the sense of hearing, you can imagine you are a bat, and send out a sound that you can hear echoing off of the object like a little inner radar. This can help to get a better sense of the object you are trying to visualize.

Rather than have it be a distraction, one can use one's interaction with the outside world to help develop mental visualization. One suggestion I often make to people who want to learn to visualize better is to practice drawing. Similarly, I often suggest to people who want to develop their internal auditory ability that they should take up learning a musical instrument. Awareness of the kinesthetic sense can be developed through dance, sports or body work.

I know a woman who is doing some fascinating work that involves teaching 'learning disabled' children how to develop the ability to visualize. One of the things that she found was that many learning tasks presuppose cognitive micro-strategies that are tacitly assumed but never directly taught. Most of us have learned from experience that when an object is moved farther away from us, it appears to get smaller and less distinct. But it is not guaranteed that everyone will learn such fundamental perceptual principles simply through their life experiences. Remember that it was only a few hundred years ago that renaissance artists, like Leonardo, figured out three-dimensional visual perspective. This teacher, for instance, found that many learning disabled children have not acquired some of these fundamental cognitive micro skills. This makes it even more difficult to form the mental representations required for classroom learning.

So she starts with real objects and has the children first learn these basic micro skills. She might say, "Look at this block of wood that I am holding. I am moving it farther away, what do you see? What happens as it gets farther from you?" Then she might say, "Now if I keep it the same distance, but turn it what do you see?" The size stays the same but the shape seems to change as it is rotated. She may even have them overlap their senses by putting their fingers on the object as it moves. The children begin to understand the interactions between various visual characteristics, or 'submodalities'. Once the children are able to experience the perceptual relationships in the external world, they are more able to do it in their own minds.

Obviously, by teaching them basic perceptual principles she is not attempting to teach them about the object, but about their own minds. Once the capacity to use one of our senses is unleashed, it can be applied to many different situations. You can change a person's life by teaching them how to take a box in their minds and rotate it so that they can see it from different angles, because it is not about the content, it is about the capability.

Clearing Personal History and Limiting Beliefs

Another possible interference to the development of a cognitive capacity such as visualization, has to do with blocks relating to one's personal history or beliefs. Some people may believe that if they really let their dreamer loose they will spend the rest of their lives in a dream world, dreaming instead of doing. It may be that a person has such a belief because he or she had a parent that was like that. I remember working with somebone who had a very difficult time hearing anything in her mind. It turned out that she had a brother who heard voices all the time and was put in a mental institution. So she was afraid of hearing anything internally. It was important for her to first accept that the capability of hearing something in the mind's ear was simply a skill and not the cause of her brother's condition.

I have also worked with several people who had trouble remembering visual images because they had been children during the second World War. They had been given very explicit messages, "If you remember what you have seen, or tell anyone about it, someone will be killed or hurt." They also may have seen many things that they do not wish to remember.

Usually, the issue in these types of interference is, "If I turn on these images, will I be able to turn them off?" Thus, paradoxically, sometimes the best way to help somebody turn on a capability is to teach the person how to turn it off. Then the person knows that he or she is in charge of the process and is not afraid of losing control.

Exploring Perceptual Filters

The following are some examples of exercises that we have people do in our NLP training programs in order to more fully develop their sensory capabilities.

Visual

1. Find a phenomenon that you can see in your external environment that is either stable or repetitive. Look at it for about 10 seconds.

2. Stop looking at the phenomenon and make a drawing of what you saw.

3. Find a partner and compare your drawings.

4. Take turns asking each other about the internal representation you used to make your drawing. i.e., Is your drawing exactly the same as your internal representation? If not, how are they different?

5. Especially check for any key features of the drawing that seem to be different from the external phenomenon.

6. Referring to the table of "submodalities" provided below, Go down the list of VISUAL submodalities with your partner. For each submodality distinction, look at the phenomenon focusing on that particular filter.

7. Compare your perceptions of where the phenomenon fits along the range of qualities defined by each submodality distinction using a scale of 1 to 10 (e.g., dim =1, bright =10).

8. Explore with your partner what reference point you assumed or presupposed in order to determine the scaling of the submodality distinction. (e.g., "Brighter than what?" "Bright compared with what?" The room? Other objects nearby in the environment? The light outside?)

9. Once again, stop looking at the phenomenon and make a drawing of what you saw.

10. Compare your new drawing with your partner and note what has changed.

11. Explore any changes in the internal representations you used to make your drawings by examining which submodality distinctions had the most impact and influence on your perception (internal cognitive map).

> **VISUAL SUBMODALITIES**
> BRIGHTNESS: dim—bright
> SIZE: large—small
> COLOR: black & white—*color*
> MOVEMENT: *fast*—slow—still
> DISTANCE: near—far
> FOCUS: clear—*fuzzy*
> LOCATION

Auditory

1. Find a phenomenon that you can hear in your external environment that is either stable or repetitive. Listen to it for about 10 seconds.

2. Stop listening to the phenomenon and find a way to auditorily reproduce what you heard using your own voice.

3. Find a partner and compare your reproductions.

4. Take turns asking each other about the internal representation you used to generate your reproductions. i.e., Is your voicing exactly the same as your internal representation? If not, how are they different?

5. Especially check for any key features of the reproduction that seem to be different from the external phenomenon.

6. Referring to the table of "submodalities" provided earlier, Go down the list of AUDITORY submodalities with your partner. For each submodality distinction, listen again to the phenomenon paying attention to that particular filter.

7. Compare your perceptions of where the phenomenon fits along the range of qualities defined by each submodality distinction using a scale of 1 to 10 (e.g., quiet =1, loud =10).

8. Explore with your partner what reference point you assumed or presupposed in order to determine the scaling of the submodality distinction. (e.g., "Louder than what?" "Loud compared with what?" The other sounds in the room? Another memory you have of that sound?)

9. Once again, stop listening to the phenomenon and make a reproduction of what you heard using your own voice.

10. Compare your new voicing with your partner and note what has changed.

11. Explore any changes in the internal representations you used to make your reproduction by examining which submodality distinctions had the most impact and influence on your perception (internal cognitive map).

AUDITORY SUBMODALITIES
VOLUME: loud—quiet
TONE: **bass**—*treble*
PITCH: high—low
TEMPO: *fast*—slow
DISTANCE: close—far
RHYTHM
LOCATION

Kinesthetic

1. Find an object that you can touch in your external environment that is either stable or repetitive. Physically feel it for about 10 seconds.

2. Stop touching the object. Reproduce the physical sensations associated with what you touched, using parts of your hands or arms such that another person could experience the sensations by touching the reproduction(s) you have created using your hands or arms. (You may reproduce different features separately and guide your partner's hands.)

3. Find a partner and compare your physical reproductions.

4. Take turns asking each other about the internal representation you used to create your reproduction with your hands or arms. i.e., Is your reproduction exactly the same as your internal representation? If not, how are they different?

5. Especially check for any key features of the reproduction that are the most different from the external object.

6. Referring to the table of "submodalities" provided earlier, Go down the list of KINESTHETIC submodalities with your partner. For each submodality distinction, touch the object focusing on that particular filter.

7. Compare your perceptions of where the object fits along the range of qualities defined by each submodality distinction using a scale of 1 to 10 (e.g., smooth =1, rough =10).

8. Explore with your partner what reference point you assumed or presupposed in order to determine the scaling of the submodality distinction. (e.g., "Smoother than what?" "Smooth compared with what?" The skin on your hand? Other objects nearby in the environment?)

9. Once again, stop touching the object and make another reproduction with your hands or arms.

10. Compare your new reproduction with your partner and note what has changed.

11. Explore any changes in the internal representations you used to make your reproductions by examining which submodality distinctions had the most impact and influence on your perception (internal cognitive map).

KINESTHETIC SUBMODALITIES
INTENSITY: **strong**—weak
AREA: large—small
TEXTURE: rough—smooth
DURATION: constant—intermittent
TEMPERATURE: *hot*—cold
WEIGHT: **heavy**—light
LOCATION

Chapter 5

Cooperative
Learning and
The T.O.T.E.

Overview of Chapter 5

- 'Telephone' Strategy Game
- Self Organization and 'Attractors'
- The T.O.T.E. Model
  Exploring the Structure of a Learning Strategy
- Feedback and Cooperative Learning
- Cooperative Learning Exercise

Cooperative Learning and The T.O.T.E.

In the previous chapter we explored several ways of developing our sensory representational systems. Yet, we also know from the memory strategy exercises, that it's the way the information is passed between representational systems that often determines the effectiveness of a strategy. If you are presented something orally, the way you process it internally and transfer it to other senses determines a great deal about how well you will be able to recall and communicate about that experience. I think one of the best ways to illustrate this point is to demonstrate it and explore it through a physical metaphor.

'Telephone' Strategy Game

When you were a child did you ever play the game "telephone?" In our Dynamic Learning seminars we play a multiple representational system version of telephone which demonstrates some important features of cognitive strategies. The simplest version involves four people (**A, B, C, & D**).

1. Person **A** demonstrates a particular action or posture to Person **B**.

2. Person **B** draws a picture of Person **A**'s posture or behavior. Persons **B** & **C** do not get to see Person **A**'s original posture.

3. Person **B** shows his or her picture to Person **C**. Person **C** verbally describes the picture to Person **D**. Person C may only use words; he or she is not allowed to show the picture to Person D or demonstrate anything with his or her body.

4. Person **D** enacts person **C**'s description with his or her body.

5. Person **A** then reshows his or her initial posture and compares it with the posture of Person **D**.

RD: Marsha, Mary Beth, Diane and Jean will be our group of four. 1) Marsha, you will demonstrate a particular action or posture to Mary Beth. 2) Mary Beth you will look at Marsha and then draw a picture of the posture or behavior. Diane and Jean, you do not get to see Marsha's original posture. You will have to close your eyes or turn away during this first phase. 3) Mary Beth, you will then show your picture to Diane, who will look at that picture and describe to Jean what she sees in the picture. Diane can only use words; she can't show the picture to Jean or demonstrate anything with her body. 4) Jean, you are to try to enact Diane's description with your body. 5) Marsha will then reshow her original posture or action and we'll see if Jean's posture or behavior looks anything like what Marsha originally did.

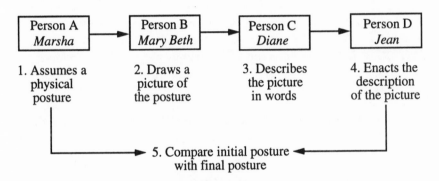

Diagram of 'Telephone' Strategy Game

So, Marsha acts, Mary Beth draws, and Diane describes. OK, Diane and Jean you two look away for a moment. Marsha, strike a pose. Put your body in a particular posture and freeze it. [*Marsha makes a pose.*] Mary Beth, draw a picture of Marsha's posture. This part is a little like the game "Pictionary." [*Mary Beth makes a sketch of Marsha's posture.*] Now, Diane you take Mary Beth's picture and describe it to Jean. Diane, you don't actually get to look at Jean while you are making the description. Otherwise you will operate off the feedback you are receiving from Jean and change your description. At this stage you can only describe what you see in the drawing.

Diane: Stand perfectly erect with a stoic expression on the face. Both hands are stretched out at shoulder height. Point your right forefinger toward the audience or straight out. Spread your feet and legs apart about three inches. That's all I see in the picture. [*Jean assumes a posture.*]

RD: Fine. Jean, hold that posture. Now Marsha, you show the posture you had initially chosen. (Laughter)

TE: As you can see, Jean's and Marsha's postures are quite different from one another.

RD: By the way, this is the kind of thing that will happen inside of a student's brain. You input some experience like Marsha's posture. It goes through these visual and auditory transformations represented by Mary Beth and Diane, and comes back out in a form that might be quite different than the original input.

It is important to notice, however, that we did not allow any corrective feedback between the various steps in the 'telephone' process. If we had, our end product may have been more like the original input.

TE: With feedback, you can have a self-correcting mechanism. Without feedback, you can see what happens.

RD: Incidentally, you can create a number of variations of this exercise. One typical structure is that the input and the output be the same representational system - i.e., visual in/visual out or auditory in/auditory out or physical in/physical out, movement in/ movement out. In between the input and the output, you pass the information through one or two of the other representational systems. For instance, you could make a variation of this game in which Mary Beth would draw a picture of Marsha's posture and Diane would also have to draw a picture from looking at Mary Beth's picture. So that you would have one picture being transformed into a second picture. Instead of describing it, Diane would give her drawing to Jean, and Jean would have to figure out how to enact that picture.

TE: You could change the relationships between the steps by changing their order. For example, we could have had Diane and

Mary Beth switch places, so that Diane would describe Marsha's posture to Mary Beth, who would then have to draw a picture from Diane's description and show it to Jean.

RD: Think of how much more challenging it would become if we allowed Marsha to move. The input would then be much more multi-faceted. Or, what if Marsha had to start with a verbal description, Mary Beth had to represent those words in pictures, Diane had to act out what she saw in the picture and Jean had to put that action into words? This would be a similar structure to giving somebody a written test; you have words coming in and words going out. The strategy is what happens to those words in between.

It is also challenging to start with something purely tonal, like a quacking sound, and translate it through visual, kinesthetic or verbal representations. As Todd was saying earlier, we don't generally have much language to describe tone and timbre. So that if you were to try to describe that sound in words, how would do it?

TE: Of course, some people cheat with this exercise and input obscene gestures or dirty words. Those always seem to come across clear as a bell. They're a universal language.

RD: As I pointed out earlier, this exercise is a basic metaphor for a strategy and can help you build intuitions about what makes a good strategy. If the group of people represented a brain, the sequence of transformations might be a learning strategy.

TE: Each person in the group is like a step in somebody's strategy for learning something.

RD: The principles that you will discover through finding an effective way to transfer information between the people are the same principles behind an effective strategy. For instance, strategies are not just simply a reflexive chain of responses. They require feedback loops in various places. If we had let Marsha look at Mary Beth's picture and ask, "What about this part of my posture? You might want to do it this way," we might have ended up with something that was a more accurate representation of the original posture.

TE: Often the most important factor involves just adding feedback loops between the steps without changing or altering anything else about the sequence.

RD: Sometimes we use this type of exercise to try to externalize and 'model' a particular mental strategy so that we can study it. For instance, what type of 'telephone' game would we make if we were attempting to replicate the mental processes behind spelling? Marsha might write down a particular spelling word and Mary Beth would pronounce it aloud. But then would Diane draw a picture of what the word meant and show it to Jean? If she did, Jean might end up outputting a word that is quite different from the original word that Marsha wrote down.

I have actually worked with kids that do that. They create a meaning from the word and then what they actually write down is a reflection of their comprehension, as opposed to a replica of the actual visual representation of the word that was input at the beginning of the strategy.

Another interesting way to use this 'telephone' process is to attempt to construct a 'learning disabled' group.

TE: That's easy. You take away the feedback between the people, tell them there's only one right way to do it, and then have a person representing an internal dialogue that stands off to the side yelling at everyone all the time about how stupid they are. (Laughter)

RD: Part of what we want to accomplish by having people act out these types of sequences is to demonstrate that, in a way, cooperative learning or team learning is also a type of strategy. It's just that the representations and feedback takes place on the outside between several people instead of on the inside of a single person's mind. Similarly, a mental strategy is a cooperative learning or team learning process which takes place between your different representational systems. And, as Todd's comment implies, you will sometimes have different 'parts' of you that are involved in learning. Cooperation may not only be required between different sensory representations, but also between different beliefs and value systems.

Self Organization and 'Attractors'

RD: We have already discussed the processes of 'chunking' and 'pattern finding' during the Memory Strategy exercises. Chunking and pattern finding is also something that happens between people that are forming a 'team' strategy. In fact, one interesting use of this type of 'telephone' game is to find what are called 'perceptual attractors' in the field of self organization theory. Perceptual attractors tell us more about how our nervous system works in general than they do about any particular individual. For example, one interesting version of this 'game' involves giving pieces of blank paper to about a dozen people in a group. You then instruct the first person to draw a dot somewhere on his or her paper. That person is then supposed to briefly show the paper to individual #2. This second person is instructed to draw the dot on his or her paper in the same location that he or she saw it on person #1's paper. (Person #2 does not get to look at person #1's paper while he or she is drawing the dot or after he or she has drawn the dot.) Person #2 is then instructed to briefly show his or her paper to person #3, and the process is repeated for all twelve people. Each person in the group only gets to see the paper of the person next to him or her. That is, person #11 can only see person #10's paper, and person #12 can only see person #11's paper. Thus, there is no real opportunity for corrective feedback.

Regardless of where the dot starts, it almost invariably ends up in one of the corners of the paper by the time it gets to person #12. The following figure shows a typical example of what happens to the dot.

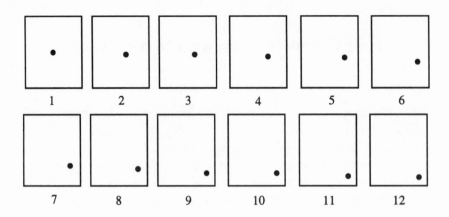

Typical Progression of Dot in a Group of 12 People

The dot follows a kind of 'path' leading to the corner of the paper as shown in the following figure.

Depending on its starting state, the dot might 'gravitate' to one of the other corners in a similar path.

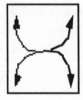

Once it reaches a corner, however, the dot typically stabilizes and would not move around as much if more people were added to the 'telephone' chain. This same type of pattern will occur even if you change the order of all of the individuals in the group.

The corners of the paper are called perceptual 'attractors' because we perceive locations with respect to edges or some other fixed reference point. In the absence of any other feedback or direction, we will tend to orient toward the area that gives the best feedback for accomplishing the task of reproducing the dot. These types of perceptual 'attractors' can tell us a lot about how we perceive and learn.*

What is important to keep in mind with respect to the learning process is that the kinds of 'attractors', miscommunications and conflicts that happen between people in a group process will happen inside a person's mind as well. In other words, a habitual mental strategy has many similarities to people communicating and interacting.

The main point of this discussion, however, is that 'attractors', miscommunications and conflicts—whether they are between people or inside of a person—all occur in the absence of feedback. So, one very important element of an effective learning strategy is the presence of feedback loops. In addition to the sequence of representational systems followed in the strategy, feedback loops are the most essential element of an effective learning process.

---

* An interesting study was done at the University of Bremen in which a member of a group of AIDs patients and a member of a group of heroin addicts were each told the same story. They were then instructed to tell one of their fellow group members the same story. The second person was then instructed to tell another group member and so on. Not only were the stories at the end of this 'telephone' chain quite different than the original, but the AIDs group had emphasized quite different aspects of the story than the heroin addicts. It would seem that different 'archetypic' elements or emotional 'attractors' characterized the two different types of groups.

The T.O.T.E. Model

In NLP, the fundamental feedback loops that form our mental strategies are described in terms of a structure called the T.O.T.E. (Miller, et al, 1960).   The letters **T.O.T.E.** stand for *Test-Operate-Test-Exit*.   The T.O.T.E. concept maintains that all mental and behavioral programs revolve around having a *fixed goal* and a *variable means to achieve that goal*.   This model indicates that, as we think, we set goals in our mind (consciously or unconsciously) and develop a TEST for when that goal has been achieved. If that goal is not achieved we OPERATE to change something or do something to get closer to our goal. When our TEST criteria have been satisfied we then EXIT on to the next step. So the function of any particular part of a behavioral program could be to (**T**)est information from the senses in order to check progress towards the goal or to (**O**)perate to change some part of the ongoing experience so that it can satisfy the (**T**)est and (**E**)xit on to the next part of the program.

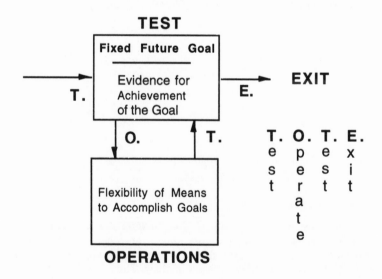

T.O.T.E. Diagram

Exploring The Structure of A Learning Strategy

To explore an example of the T.O.T.E. from your own experience, take a few moments and answer the following questions as completely as you can.

1. What is a subject that you are able to learn easily and effectively?

2. What are the learning goals or objectives that you are attempting to accomplish with respect to this subject?

3. What do you use as evidence to know you are accomplishing those learning goals?

4. What do you do to get to the goals - what are some specific steps and activities that you use to achieve your learning goals with respect to this subject?

5. When you experience unexpected problems or difficulties in achieving your learning goals with this subject, what is your response to them? What specific activities or steps do you take to correct them?

Look back over your answers to the questions and see which R.O.L.E. Model elements you can identify.

1. Context:

What perceptual aspects of the context or subject were most involved in stimulating you to learn effectively?

Something you saw?
Something you heard?
Something you felt?
Something someone said?
Something you said to yourself?

2. Goals:

How did you cognitively represent your goals in this context?

Visualized them in imagination?
Remembered them visually?
Drew them?
Verbalized them to someone else?
Verbalized them to yourself?
Recalled something verbally?
Felt them?

3. Evidence:

What cognitive or sensory processes did you use to assess your progress toward your goals?

Something you saw?
Something you imagined?
Something you heard?
How you felt?
Something someone said?
Something you said to yourself?

4. Operations:

Which cognitive or perceptual processes did you use in relation to achieving your goals?

Fantasizing?   Self talk (inner dialogue)?

Intuitive Feelings? Visual memory?   Emotions?

Drawing?   Discussing?   Touching?

Watching?   Listening?   Moving/Doing?

Recalled words or instructions?

5. Response to Problems:

Which cognitive or perceptual processes did you activate in response to problems?

Imagining options? Self talk (inner dialogue)?

Intuitive Feelings? Visually remembering options?

Recalled words or instructions?   Emotions?

Drawing?   Discussing?   Touching?

Watching?   Listening?   Changing Actions?

These are only some of the questions you might ask yourself. Take a moment and explore your answers for anything else that might be a clue to your learning strategy for this subject.

As you consider your answers, think about where there is flexibility and where there is not. For instance, if you changed the representational systems you used to represent your goals would it significantly change the result of the process? If you substituted words for images, say, as evidence, what impact would that have on the way the process functions? If you watched instead of acted, what difference would it have made?

Feedback and Cooperative Learning

RD: The T.O.T.E. model maintains that in order to learn something effectively —or engage in any effective behavior for that matter— you need:

1) some kind of representation of the goal

2) some kind of evidence to know if you are moving in the direction of that goal, and

3) some set of operations that will help you move toward the goal under various conditions.

Thus, rather than have a 'stimulus', a reflexive 'response' and a 'reinforcement', you have an 'input' a 'test' that lets you know how close you are to some desired goal, and a selection of operations to choose from based on the feedback that you've received from your test. Take our 'telephone' game for example. If I'm trying to get somebody else to represent my body posture through a picture or some verbal description, it helps for me to be able to tell that person, "Yes, you are getting closer" or "No, you're not."

In the context of our 'telephone' game, for instance, we could have set up a T.O.T.E. loop between Diane and Jean. In our original version, Diane did not get to look at Jean. She was only allowed to look at Mary Beth's drawing of Marsha's posture and describe it. If we had made a T.O.T.E. loop, Diane would have been able to vary her verbal descriptions in response to the feedback that she would receive by looking at Jean's posture and comparing it with the picture. Thus, Mary Beth's drawing would have been the representation of the goal. The comparison of Jean's posture with that picture would be the 'TEST'. Diane's words would become the 'OPERATIONS' to attempt to get Jean's posture to match Mary Beth's picture. Diane would describe something to Jean, Jean would try it and ask, "Like this?" Diane might respond with "Yes, right" or "No, wrong." We would have a feedback loop oriented toward achieving a particular goal which would have probably led to a much more effective result than what we achieved initially.

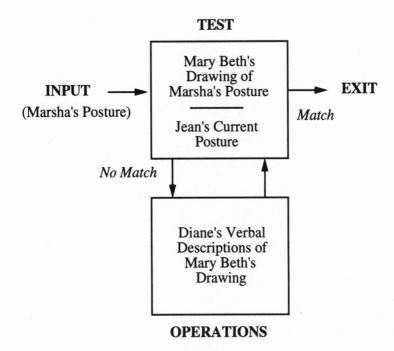

TEST

INPUT ⟶
(Marsha's Posture)

Mary Beth's
Drawing of
Marsha's Posture
————
Jean's Current
Posture

⟶ **EXIT**

Match

No Match

Diane's Verbal
Descriptions of
Mary Beth's
Drawing

OPERATIONS

T.O.T.E. Loop for 'Telephone' Strategy Game

TE: The T.O.T.E. is the basis of effective communication as well as learning. For instance, let's say I have a communication goal of establishing rapport with a particular student (a novel idea, I know). I may try out a first set of behavior and see if I get some kind of rapport. If, instead of rapport, the student gets angry, the T.O.T.E. model tells me to keep my goal of rapport—rather than giving up like many people do. So, I maintain the outcome to establish rapport or trust. Since I've already done behavior X, I have to find another choice. I try that choice; and check, "Do I get trust?" Maybe I get fear this time. OK, fine. I still want to get trust, now I have to try something else. I have to do something different each time. That is the basis of the T.O.T.E. That's how you would finally get to the point where you get trust. In NLP we say that is it the responsibility of the communicator to find the way to communicate in order to reach his or her goals. So good communicators need to be flexible in the way they communicate. The other person may not even know what your goal is.

RD: According to the T.O.T.E. model, effective behavior comes from having a fixed goal, sensory evidence that indicates whether or not you're achieving that goal, and a lot of different ways of getting to that goal. So if one doesn't work, you can try another. Unfortunately, most of the way we do things in our educational systems are the reverse of the T.O.T.E. We have a single fixed, standardized procedure or operation—i.e., the 'correct' way to do it. We have no clear ongoing evidence as to how or whether the student is actually learning (the test is always at the end of the term). As a result, we end up with variable outcomes—a few students do well and the rest do either average or poorly.

I think this is a very important point to consider with respect to both learning and teaching—whenever you use a standardized or fixed operation, you're going to get varying results. If, on the other hand, you want to consistently reach a particular learning goal or result for a whole variety of learners, you have to allow for a flexibility of operations to account for varying learning styles and circumstances. In the NLP view, the traditional 'bell curve' associated with learning and intelligence is actually more of a measure of how a particular test or procedure matches an array of different learning strategies and styles than it is an actual measure of intelligence.

If you standardize a particular procedure with the belief that all students 'should' learn with this procedure, then you start selecting out the students whose performance varies because their strategies don't fit that procedure. The belief becomes, "These students can't make it so we're going to have to separate them out." Or, "We're going to group them together because they can't do this particular procedure." In other words, the evaluation of students is based on how well their learning style fits that particular procedure.

If your goal, on the other hand, is to teach a group of different students how to learn something, then in order to hold that goal constant you need to vary all of the strategies you use to teach them until you find the ones that achieve that goal. This is a different approach than separating out or sorting the students according to their performance on standard procedures. If you take something like "good spelling," as an outcome, you can't just teach a single procedure for spelling. What you do is hold the goal and evidence of "good spelling" constant, and you vary the processes that students can use in order to learn the words. You have a variety of strategies that somebody can use in order to reach the goal of consistent spelling. Thus, if the student can't succeed one way, you can offer another way. This is very different than believing, "There's only one right way to accomplish this task."

We have many new learning tools available today that can be used to fit and encourage individual learning styles. 'Standardization' may have been appropriate when the production line and telephone switchboard were our leading edge technologies. But nowadays we have 'hypertext' and 'multi media'. Our businesses and technologies are not geared toward standardization but rather toward adaptation to individual needs. This is one of the revolutions that the personal computer has brought about.

TE: Your beliefs can really effect your ability to use different choices—and not only with respect to learning. We used to see this issue of limiting beliefs come up a lot in the early days of NLP when our trainings emphasized therapeutic applications. We'd get some pretty stodgy folks in those programs who did therapy behind walnut desks. They had real difficulty with the idea that they were supposed to change their actions in response to their clients. They had a mental image and set of beliefs of how a therapist is 'supposed to be'. Although we would teach them a multitude of different choices that they could use in order to be more flexible, they had a belief that went something like, "Being a psychotherapist restricts me to engaging in a certain set of behaviors. If I go outside these behaviors, I'm not staying within the code of how I believe a 'therapist' is supposed to act."

The same thing can happen with teachers. They build the belief that "as a teacher, I need to have this position at the front of the room. I can only act this way, and I can only have these kinds of interactions. If I do anything outside of these prescribed behaviors, then I'm not being a 'teacher'." If you're given a lot of choices about how to interact with somebody, but those choices are restricted by your beliefs about what teachers are allowed to do, it's those beliefs that tie your hands. It's not that you actually run out of choices with students, it's that your beliefs tell you, "That door can't open. You're not allowed in that door because teachers aren't allowed to act that way."

RD: Incidentally, operating from a T.O.T.E. also requires having effective evidence for achieving the goal—which sometimes requires a reevaluation of our beliefs about what provides 'effective evidence'. For example, is a written comprehension test really evidence that someone is achieving the goal of reading; or is it a more of a measurement of how similar the student's strategy and values are to that of the person who made up the test? Is getting an 'A' on a test an effective evidence that a student has achieved the goal of learning how to read or learning how to apply math? The question, in terms of the T.O.T.E., is, "What kinds of evidences actually provide effective corrective feedback?

In the analogy of our 'telephone' game, starting with Marsha's posture and going all the way to the end of the group without any feedback is similar to taking a math test or spelling test and getting the results a week later. You get your test back with red X's by the answers that were incorrect. By that time, you have absolutely no idea what you were doing mentally at the time you produced the incorrect answer. In other words, it gives you no feedback at all about how to change the mental process that happened during the ten seconds that you were trying to spell that word or solve that math problem.

TE: By that time, the mental process has become separated from the feedback. You take the math test on Wednesday, and the following Tuesday you get the results back. A week has past. You may have corrections, or red marks. You may even have the answers. You might even have little notes that say, "Here's how you should have carried this number here..." The teacher might even come into class and go over the some of the problems that were most commonly wrong. But that doesn't tell the students what is the most important thing that they need to know—which is, how to change the thinking process they were using at the time they came up with the incorrect answer. There is an important difference between the declaration, "You should have carried the number," and the question, "How did you or did you not carry that number?" 'Carrying a number' is actually a procedure, done on paper, which is a function of an internal mental strategy. To edit that strategy, you'd have to go back and determine what your thought process was a week earlier when you were actually taking the test.

RD: To actually learn something from the feedback, the student has to try to determine, "What happened in those 30 seconds a week ago when I was doing that problem and didn't carry that number?" Not only that, just knowing what you did wrong doesn't tell you what to do to do it right. I think we often tend to overemphasize the effectiveness of negative feedback. In fact, I remember some of my teachers who were so caught up in negative feedback that, even if you got all the answers correct on a test, instead of scoring it as '100% right', they would put 'minus zero'. It can lead to a rather depressing outlook on life.

TE: Sometimes, when I was going to school, I'd get back papers with red checks on them and I'd have to sort through to figure out whether the red checks were for those that were wrong or right. For some teachers the checks meant "OK." For others, they indicated "incorrect." It was very confusing.

RD: Part of what we're saying is that a test score gives you feedback on the level of behavior rather than at the level of 'capability'. It gives you feedback about your behavioral performance, but may tell you little or nothing about how to develop the strategy or capability that is required to perform well. I know that many teachers will be thinking, "OK I understand the concept, but I have 40 kids in my class. I can't possibly give that feedback for those 30 seconds to all of those children." My reply is, teachers don't have to do it. Your students can provide it for each other. That is what 'cooperative learning' is all about. Cooperative learning involves getting students to share learning strategies and to monitor each other. With the kinds of tools provided by NLP, you can get the students to teach each other effective strategies and give each other feedback. The teacher doesn't have to sit there and be in charge of all forty students—that's one of those beliefs that Todd was mentioning earlier. Students can be as good a teacher as the one in the front of the classroom when you provide them with the appropriate resources and the permission.

TE: I think it also helps to better prepare them for interacting in the 'real world' outside of the classroom. Some of these kids that perform well in a classroom context are extremely competitive and independent. And when they get out of school they can't cooperate with other people.

RD: This is another issue relating to beliefs and values. What kinds of beliefs and values does the typical approach to testing install in students? Hide the test so that the other students don't see anything about what you're doing because they're going to cheat. It is a different approach to actually encourage the students to cooperate with one another rather than constantly trying to outperform one another. In the Pajaro Valley school system, students teach each other and monitor the learning process so that they can provide each other with feedback during those critical 30 seconds when the actual strategy is being applied.

TE: Success in education isn't simply a function of what school books you have, what the building is like or whether the bus is warm. Those things are important—pencils, pieces of paper,and so forth—those are all very important; but I've seen kids learn in places where none of that was available. For example, I know a person who is the teacher in a one-room school in a small town in Georgia. She has 60 kids who range from Kindergarten to the 8th grade. Kids have to share pencils, they have to share a book between 5 kids, and yet the success that she has in that classroom is incredible. One of the things she does is to set up cooperative learning groups among her students. By the time these children are 12 or 13 years old, they know as much about NLP in education as you would if you had taken a 15 or 20 day course. That's how much she has trained them; a little bit at a time. Each year she has a group of students that keep passing the most effective strategies on to each other. They have developed the reputation that if you go to that school, you'll get smart. The job of the older students is to see that the younger students get the strategies they need. She focuses on the youngest and the oldest kids in the school—the ones in between get the benefits through the cooperative learning process.

RD: The following is an example of a cooperative learning exercise based on the T.O.T.E. that helps people to compare and widen their strategies for effectively addressing a particular task or situation.

Cooperative Learning Exercise

Effective strategies may be transferred between two people. For example two teachers, or two musicians, or two spellers may have different strategies for accomplishing the same kind of task in the same context. Eliciting and sharing goals, evidence procedures and operations can help to widen and enrich the range and scope of your creative abilities.

Find a partner and choose a common task or a situation that requires learning. Each fill in the T.O.T.E. information on the chart below and compare your answers for the similarities and differences. Imagine what it would be like to add your partners operations, evidence procedures, goals or 'responses to problems' into your own strategy. How might it change or enrich the way you approach the task or situation.

Context: _____

	Person #1	Person #2
What are your goals?		
How do you know you are achieving your goals?		
What do you do in order to reach your goals? What do you do if you are not satisfactorily reaching your goals?		

In the next chapter we will show how the principles of cooperative learning and the other processes that we have explored thus far in this book can be applied toward a standard, although for some quite challenging, classroom activity—spelling.

Chapter 6

Spelling

Overview of Chapter 6

- Modeling Spelling Strategies
- Patterns of Effective Spelling
- Strategies for Learning New Words
- The Spelling Strategy
- Applying The Spelling Strategy
- Using The Spelling Strategy with Children Who Have Learning Problems
- Practicing The Spelling Strategy
- Teaching The Spelling Strategy in the Classroom

Spelling

Spelling is an important and fundamental language skill that does not come "naturally" to everyone. In fact, intelligent people who otherwise excel in the classroom, even in language abilities, may experience strong and even debilitating difficulties in spelling. According to NLP, spelling ability is not a function of some kind of 'spelling gene' but rather the structure of the internal cognitive strategy one is using as one spells. Thus, if people experience difficulty with spelling, it is not because they are *'stupid,' 'lazy'* or *'learning disabled'* but rather because they are trying to use an ineffective mental program.

RD: I myself had difficulties spelling throughout my school years, even though I didn't experience problems in other subjects. Using the tools of NLP, I eventually discovered an effective strategy that not only improved my own spelling but has been able to produce extremely effective results with people of all ages who have experienced difficulty spelling.

TE: I think its important to point out that Robert's spelling strategy isn't really just one strategy. When you do the spelling strategy with different students, you can't do it the same way with every person. You have to vary it and adapt it to fit the needs of various individuals.

RD: The point Todd is making is important, because people will take the spelling strategy and teach it as if it was a standardized process. If you do, you're going to get variable results. The spelling strategy is not intended to be used as a 'cookie cutter' type of approach. Like all NLP techniques, the strategy itself is just a skeleton. The life and the flesh that makes it work comes from you, your creativity, your rapport with people, and the kind of empathy and contact that you make with people.

TE: There are basic components that need to be there; but the way in which you order those components needs to match the learning process of the student. If we define "spelling" as the achievement of a particular behavioral result, then what is the capability that the child needs to engage in in order to accomplish that behavioral result? That's where the essential structure of the strategy comes from. A fundamental underlying structure needs to be there to make it effective and appropriate. But, because each person is different, the strategy has to be flexible enough to deal with the many differences between people.

RD: The Dynamic Learning approach to spelling is an interesting combination of cooperative learning, adaptation to individual learning styles and modeling. *"Modeling"* is one of the core processes of Dynamic Learning (and of all applications of NLP for that matter). One of the most fundamental forms of modeling involves identifying the mental processes of people that excel at a particular task, and then comparing them with the mental process of people who have difficulty with that same task. Optimally you would select people that are the same basic age, with the same educational background, a similar cultural heritage, etc., but who differ in their performance of a particular task—such as spelling.

The following is an example of how we incorporate the process of modeling in our Dynamic Learning seminars.

Modeling Spelling Strategies

RD: Is there anyone in here who has trouble spelling? You do Kate and Patty? Then why don't you come up and take these seats right here. Do we have any good spellers? Lisa and Jean? OK, both of you come up and sit in these chairs here. We're going to start by examining and comparing the structure of your current strategies for spelling. For instance, Patty, can you spell 'accommodate'?

Patty: (*Looks down and left.*) Yeah, but not the way everyone else does. (*Laughter*)

RD: OK, what Patty did is to look down and to the left, and said "Yes, I can spell it but not the way everyone else does." Which is an interesting belief.

Patty: I could, but I haven't the appropriate way to spell the word.

RD: Notice that words like "appropriate" indicate judgment, which relate more to beliefs and values than to capabilities. I think this might be as important a factor influencing how Patty spells than anything else. What would you do if I asked you to go ahead and spell it for us Patty?

Patty: I'd like to check the hearing. "Accommodate", is that what you said? I can try to spell it.

RD: Patty says, "I can try." That's really interesting. Patty's starting state is, "I can try to spell it, but I don't know if it would be in the traditionally acceptable way." This is before she engages her strategy or anything. Let's compare her starting state to that of our good spellers. Can you spell "accommodate" Lisa?

Lisa: Uh huh.

RD: She just goes, "Uh huh." Can you spell it Jean?

Jean: Yes.

RD: She says, "Yeah, OK." And all this is before any actual spelling is done at all. It has to do with their beliefs about their ability to spell. How about you Kate? Can you spell 'accommodate'?

Kate: Well, I have a process by which I could come up with a spelling. Do you want me to write it on anything?

RD: Just spell it out loud.

Kate: (*Eyes move down and the left, then shift to a lateral left position. Her mouth moves as if speaking silently to herself.*) AC-C-OM-O-DATE.

RD: Is that correct?

Kate: I don't know. (*Laughter*)

RD: First of all, let's review for a moment what Kate did. She said "I have a process," a strategy. You could see that the strategy was kind of sounding it out, breaking it into letters. She got to the end of the process, producing a bunch of letters, and then I asked, "Is that correct?" Her response was, "I don't know." In other words, in the language of the T.O.T.E. model, she has a standardized operation with no clear evidence of success. Going through the operation ended up with something, but is it the correct spelling? "I don't know." The result could vary each time.

TE: We are happy to report that the operation was a success, even though the patient died. (Laughter)

RD: Let's compare Kate's strategy with that of one of our good spellers. Lisa, would you spell accommodate?

Lisa: (*Looks up and to the left*) A-C-C-O-M-M-O-D-A-T-E.

RD: OK, is that right?

Lisa: I would have to write it out and check it. But, I have a feeling that it is right.

RD: Lisa says, "I have a feeling that it is right, but I'd have to write it out to check it." Notice that she just described two evidence procedures—an internal feeling and the physical process of writing it out. What I hear is Lisa is saying is, "I have one internal evidence and a way of getting an external evidence. My internal feeling check indicates that it is correct, but when I get the external evidence I'll know for sure."

Also, notice that Lisa's mental 'operation', as reflected in her eye movement, was different from Kate's. Lisa also ended up with a group of letters, but I don't think she used the same process Kate did. Kate's eyes moved around her lower left hand side the whole time she was spelling, and her mouth was moving too. Lisa looked up and to the left, kept her eyes glued to that spot and said the letters as if she were just reading them off the ceiling.

Kate, when you were spelling, what mental strategy were you using? Were you aware of one?

Kate: The only thing I'm aware of is, when I'm spelling, I say the word to myself, and then I try and figure out the sounds.

RD: So, you have the sound, and you try to find letters that represent that sound.

How do you do it, Lisa?

Lisa: I see it.

RD: You see it. Where do you see it? (*Lisa gestures in front of herself and slightly to the left.*) Sort of right there? Which of course is something quite different than what Kate was doing.

Let's check Patty's strategy. Patty could you spell 'chrysanthemum'?

Patty: Yes, but...

RD: I know, "Yes, but not like everyone else would." Why don't you spell 'chrysanthemum' anyway?

Patty: CR-IS-AN-TE-MUM.

RD: OK, is that correct?

Patty: You tell me.

RD: She says, "You tell me. It could be." Alright. How were you just spelling that? What were you just doing in your mind?

Patty: I was trying to sound it out.

RD: OK, so like Kate, you go for the sound and you try to represent the letters that would fit with that sound.

Patty: That might fit that sound.

RD: That *might* fit with that sound. Again, I think we see a commonality in the T.O.T.E.s (or shall I say lack of T.O.T.E.s) of our 'not-so-good' spellers. We have a single fixed operation but no clear evidence as to whether or not the goal was reached.

Let's compare that with our other 'good speller'. Jean, can you spell 'chrysanthemum'?

Jean: I'm not sure. (*Looks down and to the left and then up and to the right and left.*) CH-RYS-ANT-H-E-MUM?

RD: Is that correct?

Jean: Ah, it sounds right.

RD: Now this is interesting. Because Jean initially said, "I'm not sure I know how to spell it." And actually what her eyes did looked more like the strategy Kate and Patty were using.

Let's try Lisa. Lisa, can you spell it?

Lisa: I'm pretty sure I can do it. (*Moves eyes up and to the left.*) CHRYSANT (*Eyes shift down briefly and then back up left*)-H-EMUM.

RD: Is that correct?

Lisa: I'm not sure, I'd have to write it out.

RD: You're not sure.

Lisa: I'm 99% positive.

RD: You're 99% positive. I'll bet I even know which one you're not positive about. Did any one watch her? I know what letter she is unsure of, because her eyes shifted down slightly when she came to that letter.

Lisa: Is there an 'h' in it?

RD: There is an 'h' in it, that's correct. But, that's an interesting thing about these words; the sound will not tell you the answer. Another interesting thing is why Lisa would have to write it out to be sure. What does that do for Lisa? So far, our spellers have talked about either sounding out the words or seeing them, but the kinesthetic aspect of writing it might be another important evidence procedure. So that when you have an overlap of sound, picture, and feeling, if they all fit, it must be the correct spelling. Whereas, if it only sounds right but I don't know if it looks or feels right, how can I be sure if it is really correct? Furthermore, if I am going to check my answer visually, it is harder to do so if I am holding one mental picture in short term memory and trying to compare it with another image from long term memory. If I write down the images of the letters I am holding in short term memory, my visual representational system is then free to focus only on my longer term memory of the correct spelling.

Now, I have used spelling as an example of a simple and easily testable mental strategy for years. I have brought up many good and poor spellers in front of the class in order to observe and demonstrate the differences in their mental strategies. It soon became quite obvious that good spellers have a very consistent strategy and accompanying set of accessing cues. The vast majority of them tend to look up and to their left while searching for the spelling. According to NLP this indicates an accessing strategy of remembered visual imagery (notated V^r in NLP). When asked how they know that their spelling is correct, many of them, as expected, do not know consciously how but say something like, *"I just **feel** that it **looks** right."* This indicates a relationship between the kinesthetic and visual representational systems. Furthermore, if shown a page of writing containing a number of incorrectly spelled words, good spellers often claim, *"It makes me **feel uncomfortable** to **see** all of those misspellings,"* again indicating a visual and kinesthetic overlap. The fact that they mention that seeing the misspelling makes them feel uncomfortable suggests that the image causes the feeling and thus comes first in the sequence (notated $V{\longrightarrow}K^i$).

As good spellers do become more conscious of their internal strategy, they report seeing a mental image of the word accompanied by feeling of familiarity. The availability and clarity of the image along with the strength of the feeling determines their degree of confidence about the correctness of the spelling.

The typical overall strategy of a good speller is that 1) they repeat the word as a whole, not in syllables. They'll repeat the word as a whole, and then 2) look up and visualize it. 3) The way they know if it's the right image is that it'll feel familiar. In other words, because you see words printed and written all the time, the one that you see the most is the most familiar; and that hopefully should be the correct one. So they make a comparison that goes something like, "Does this one feel more familiar than the others?"

Poor spellers, on the other hand, have a variety of strategies - although none are the same as the strategy of the good spellers. In fact sometimes poor spellers will even change those strategies in the middle of trying to spell a word. This often leads to inconsistency, extra effort, and frustration. Furthermore, as I discovered as a child, creative spelling is not rewarded like creative writing is.

The particular strategy that our 'not-so-good' spellers, Kate and Patty, were using was trying to sound out the correct spelling through breaking the sound of the word down into small enough pieces that they each sounded like letters (this would be notated as $A_d{}^r—>A_d{}^c$). This is called "phonics" (pronounced *"puh-hon-iks"* if you sound it out phonically). While phonics has a number of important features (for example, making a guess at the spelling of word one has never seen before), it is not the best strategy for spelling words in English since many words are not written like they sound, and the exceptions do not follow consistent verbal rules.

This was, in fact, the strategy that was ingrained in me when I was in grammar school. I was taught to spell by sounding out words. I have to admit I was a bit concerned when I first discovered one could not correctly spell the name of the method using the method (my first try came out *"fonix"*). My consternation grew, however, as we began with basics - such as the names of the first ten numbers. Instead of *"wun"* the first number was spelled 'one' (that looked like it should be pronounced *"oh-nee"*). There was no 'W' and an extra "silent E." The second number, instead of being spelled *"tu"* like it sounded, was spelled 'two' (As the comedian Gallagher points out, perhaps that was where the missing "W" from 'one' had gone). After 'three' (*"tuh-ree"*), 'four' (*"fow-er"*) and 'five' (*"fi-vee"*) I knew something was wrong, but being young, I figured it was probably just something wrong with me. In fact, when 'six' and 'seven' came along I started to build back some hope. But then they struck with 'eight' (*"ee-yi-guh-hut"*) and I felt like the next number looked as if it should sound - 'nine' (a *"ninny"*).

When I discovered years later that good spellers simply remembered how the word looked, I actually thought it was cheating. It didn't involve any effort, you didn't have to start from scratch each time you spelled - it seemed too easy.

The point I want to make is that excellence in spelling is not a function of "spelling genes."

TE: Didn't Frank Lloyd Wright have designer genes? Or was that Calvin Klein?

RD: We believe that good spelling is the result of a strategy that is so obvious that you can watch it happening in front of you over and over again, as in our demonstration. We could easily see the difference between Lisa's eye pattern and that of Patty and Kate. It was even possible to see the difference in Lisa's and Jean's eye movements when they were unsure. For instance, rather than looking up and to her left, Jean's eyes started down and left and then moved around to her upper right hand side.

Jean: I was writing it up there.

RD: You were writing it up there—which is a kind of visual strategy, but you still weren't sure. In the end, you said, "It sounds right. I can't say for certain that it is right, all I can say is it sounds right." In fact, a very common strategy, that makes for about "C" or "B-" spelling, is sounding out the word, constructing a mental picture based on the sound, and then comparing the pronunciation you get from reading the mental construction with the way the word is supposed to sound (notated $A_d{}^r\!\!-\!\!>\!V^c\!\!-\!\!>\!A_d{}^c$). So the person is visualizing, but the eyes are up to the right (the area for constructed rather than remembered visual imagery). You see the person looking for a mental picture, but he or she is constructing it from the sound and comparing it to a sound rather than recalling a visual memory of the letters.

My guess is, Jean, that you use a different strategy when you know that you do know a word. For instance, can you spell 'phenomenon'?

Jean: Sure. (*Looks up to the left*) PHE-NOMENON.

RD: Is that the correct spelling?

Jean: Yes.

RD: How do you know that?

Jean: (*Gestures up and to her left*) I can see it easily. I've written it a lot of times.

RD: Do you hear that? She said, "I've written it a lot of times. I can see it here and it matches something I'm familiar with." She's essentially saying, "I've got an evidence procedure. I've got a goal and I've got an evidence procedure. I can see it." Jean didn't say anything about sounding it out and the letters matching the sounds. Jean, when you know that you know a word what makes you sure?

Jean: Because I see it. When you said "chrysanthemum," I didn't get a clear picture of it, just parts of it.

RD: Jean says, with the word 'chrysanthemum', "I didn't see the whole thing, just parts of it." So even good spellers might use different strategies for words they are not so familiar with.

Now, I have a question for both of you 'not-so-good' spellers. I'm certain that there are words that you *do* know how to spell. For example, do you know how to spell 'beautiful', Patty? Can you spell it for me—the way that everybody spells it?

Patty: Well I could.

RD: Ah, you could. Would you choose to at this moment? I think that might be as much the issue for Patty as anything else. Patty, please go ahead and spell it if you can.

Patty: (*Eyes move briefly up and to the left*) B-E-A-U-T-I-F-U-L.

RD: Alright. Is that correct?

Patty: Yes.

RD: Now this is something new. How do you know that it's correct? How do you know for sure that's the way to spell it?

Patty: Ah, I remember seeing it before. (*Laughter*)

RD: Now, notice, here is a person who is supposedly not a good speller. Yet the way that she knows a word that she can spell correctly has the same structure as our good spellers. Kate, how about you. Would you be able to spell telephone?

Kate: Yes. You want me to spell it? (*Looks down to the left*) T-E-L-E-F Wait a minute. (*Kate's eyes move up and to her left*) P-H-O-N-E. (*Laughter, Applause*)

RD: Now, wow, we saw a different strategy here than before. You even caught yourself. It was like, "Whoa there!" What did you do in your mind? How did you know that you had to change directions?

Kate: I know that I'm not meant to spell it with an 'f'.

RD: Now listen to that. This brings up a very important point about mental processes and communication. If I say to you all, "Don't think about spelling 'telephone' with an 'f'," what happens? There's a funny thing about negations; they often plant the very idea they are trying to avoid. If I say, "Don't be nervous now, Kate. Don't notice that all these people are watching you right now," what happens? You start to notice that they are watching you. Kate essentially said, "I've been told so many times not to spell 'telephone' with an 'f', that that's the first thing that comes to my mind— the 'f'." So even though Kate is trying to respond in an appropriate way, she is unintentionally setting herself up for error. That's one of the problems with negative feedback.

Now how did you catch it, Kate? Even though you heard these voices about what not to do, how did you know how to spell it?

Kate: I remember that it's written with a 'p'.

RD: Notice how this strategy begins to resemble that of the 'good spellers'; writing it out as an evidence procedure. She said, "I know I was meant to write it with a 'p', but I heard, "Don't spell it with an 'f.'" My guess is that Kate associates 'spelling' with 'saying it out loud'. 'Writing' is something different. Because she was verbalizing the spelling out loud, the 'f' issue came up as an interference. I think if she wrote it, the issue of the 'f' probably wouldn't have ever been there.

Woman: My students have developed a strategy called "o-a." When they can't sound it out, they write the letter in such a way that it can look like either an 'o' or an 'a'.

RD: Yeah, I know that one. I call it 'doctored' handwriting, because it's similar to the way a doctor writes a prescription. You kind of squiggle it out so no one can really tell what the letters are. They can only tell by the context what the word is supposed to be.

TE: That's when they move from task orientation to relationship oriented strategy. When you ask them, "Did you mean that to be an 'o' or an 'a'?" They watch your non-verbal response in order to tell you which one it was supposed to be.

Patterns of Effective Spelling

RD: Let's begin to summarize some of the things we've discovered so far. To make an effective spelling strategy, you need to stabilize some things; because the purpose of spelling is to produce a standardized version of a word. There is a result that is produced which can be judged as either 'correct' or 'not correct' according to some socially accepted standard (although this standard sometimes varies; for instance, between American English and British English). In order to produce a consistent result we have to keep some things stable and allow other things to vary. If I hold the operation constant (i.e., a 'sounding out' strategy) I will probably produce varying spellings. When I was a kid I could spell 'chrysanthemum' at least three different ways; even though I used exactly the same 'sounding out' process each time. I believe it was the American president Andrew Jackson who said, "I just can't trust a person who only knows how to spell a word one way."

Of course in my case, I wasn't intentionally trying to spell these words differently all the time. I didn't even know the spellings were different until I looked at my paper later on. I would come up with something that 'sounded' right at the moment and write it down. As far as I was concerned, I was doing the operation I had been taught correctly. It seemed to me that as long as you could figure out what the sound of the word was, that was good enough to communicate the ideas. I even got angry at people who complained about people's spelling and didn't appreciate their ideas.

I remember when I first went to the British Museum in London, I got a kind of smug satisfaction from seeing a deed that William Shakespeare's father had taken out on their property—and they spelled the name four different ways. They included all four spellings so you'd be sure to know who it was. So, the father of the person considered the 'master of the English language' was not a stickler for spelling. Of course, this was before the average person had books and newspapers and learned to read. Shakespeare wrote plays, not books. Consistency in written spelling was not such a high priority. That's why I like to humorously point out that English spelling was created by 'the greatest minds of the

13th century'. You've got to keep in mind that these were people who thought the world was flat. Even though we've changed a few other things since that time, we're still using the same language system and spelling rules.

TE: When I was a kid and couldn't spell something and would ask how to spell it, I was always told, "Look it up!" But how do you look up something you don't know how to spell? They'd say, "Sound it out." Yeah, I tried sounding it out. The problem is, I could never find 'phenomenon' under 'F' or 'pneumonia' under 'N'.

In fact, when Robert was talking about Shakespeare I remembered something I read recently about how indexing was initially done by first sound instead of first letter. Now in Italian and Latin, as articulated by Italian speakers, the letter H is not pronounced. So, for example, in Latin works published as late as 1506 in Rome, any word starting with the letter H and followed by the letter A would be listed among words under the letter A.

RD: That all changed with the spread of the great technological innovation of their time: the personal book. Before printing presses, people didn't have their own books. The emphasis was always on spoken language. Spelling was not the everyday concern with respect to communication that it is today.

In fact, it was a technological innovation of our time that was responsible for my developing the spelling strategy. It wasn't until I got my first personal computer and started programing that I finally began to have feelings for people who were good spellers. Because I realized if I spelled a command wrong to my computer, it didn't understand it, literally. My computer wasn't some conceited uncreative jerk trying to force its belief system on me. It really didn't know what I was saying. I realized that I had to be consistent with the way I was communicating to it.

To become consistent, I had to find the answer to some important questions: (1) How will I know that I have reached the goal of spelling a word correctly? (2) What kind of learning strategy will give me the most consistent results? (3) What can I do to come up with the correct spelling if I'm unsure, or have never been exposed to the word before? To me these are all essential for good spelling. For instance, if I wasn't sure how to spell chrysanthemum, how would I go about trying to come up with a spelling? And then, what process would I go through to commit it to memory so that I would be sure the next time?   As we have observed in our demonstration, some strategies work better than others. For example, even though Jean she wasn't sure how to spell 'chrysanthemum', she went through a different process to make a guess than Patty did. Patty stayed exclusively in the auditory system. Jean tried to construct a mental picture of the sounds.

TE: It's not that we're against the auditory representational system mind you. For instance, it is certainly important to have the sound of the word connected to the pictures of the letters, so should I get called on in class and told to spell a word, I'd know which letters went with the spoken word they had given me. Usually the teacher says the word and you spell it. It's not like math problems which you could conceivably do totally visually. So, I would want have the sound of the word "cat" connected to the letters C-A-T, which I would want connected to a feeling that those are the right letters.

RD: I personally think phonics is an essential back up strategy for effective spelling, especially if you've never seen a word before. The main problem is when phonics is used as the primary strategy for spelling and it is taken to the kind of extreme that Patty and Kate took it; in which you always attempt to move from the sound of the word to the sound of the individual letters. It's a problem because (a) it's inefficient and (b) it'll lead you to error. I know that from my own experience. When sounding out is your only strategy, it leads to confusion because, with a word like 'pharaoh' for example, the way it sounds and looks are at odds with each other. Then you've got to decide which one you are going to go with; the way it's supposed to look or the way it's supposed to sound.

Incidentally, even if the English language was completely phonetically based and phonics was 100% accurate, a visual strategy would still be easier and more effective since vision functions much more rapidly for visual material. In fact, I have interviewed a number of copy editors - people who are professional spellers - and have never encountered a single one who claimed to begin at the top of the page and sound out all of the words in order to know if they are correct.   Rather, every one of them claims that they simply look down the page and the misspellings *"jump out"* at them. We don't program the spell checkers on our computers to do it phonetically.

The main arguments in favor of phonics as a primary strategy for spelling, as far as I can tell, are that either a) it is not possible for some people to learn to visualize words easily, or b) it is easier to teach people phonics since they first learn language by speaking it. I would like to address both of these issues in the next demonstrations.

What I would like to do is to find a word that none of our group of spellers already knows how to spell. Then let's see how Jean and Lisa would learn it. We'll model their strategy and see if we can transfer some of the elements to Kate and Patty.

Strategies for Learning New Words

RD: Do any of you know how to spell 'pteridophytes'?   No? Naturally, Patty is going to say, "I can spell it. Whether it would look like the way anyone else would spell it, I don't know, but I can spell it." (Laughter) OK I'm going to write it down. Let's model how Jean and Lisa would learn it. And we'll do some cooperative learning. We'll have Lisa coach Kate and Jean can coach Patty.

Kate: What are they?

Lisa: Something from biology or botany. I don't know how to spell it but I know it's Greek.

RD: Now listen because you will hear their strategies popping up already. Kate begins by asking, "What are they?" Why should I learn to spell it to begin with?   When Lisa says, "It is from biology or botany and its Greek," she is already starting to think about common language elements. If you listen you'll hear how people code information, how they make it important, what chunk they go to first and how they store it in there. With a word like "pteridophytes," do you store it under Greek words? Do you store it under Biology? Do you store it by sound? These issues are really important in terms of strategies. And if you listen you're going to hear it happening all the time. (Incidentally, to answer your question Kate, 'pteridophytes' are ferns that have no seeds.)

TE: I just want to point out, however, that you don't need to know what it is, or how to pronounce it, in order to learn to spell it. Spelling is a separate skill from comprehension (which we will explore later on) or pronunciation.

RD: That's right. In fact, Lisa, we'd like to ask you to do whatever you need to do right now to learn this word, and then let us know when you have it.

Lisa: *(Glances at the beginning of the word, the end of the word and then to middle.)* OK. I've learned it.

RD: You got it? Alright. Now, did anyone see or notice at all what she did? Based on what I observed her doing, I think that she had already made a guess about how the word was spelled and just looked at it to confirm her guess. Is that correct Lisa?

Lisa: Right.

RD: See, once you know a little bit about accessing cues and observation, it's as if you can watch thoughts happen. Its as good as mind reading. Lisa, was your guess completely correct, or did you have to make any adjustments in your mind for any of the letters that you saw there?

Lisa: I guessed the first part that started with a P-T. And it sounded like a science word so I figured out the last part from my knowledge of other scientific words.

RD: So, your whole guess had been correct?

Lisa: I didn't make any guesses about the middle part. I hadn't thought about it yet.

RD: Notice how it's much easier if you already have made a guess and have a picture of the word in your mind. Then all you have to do is just have to refine it a little bit. It's quite different than going "Oh, gosh, I have to start from scratch—and this is a big, long word." Instead, Lisa makes a good guess and just updates the guess. She's not having to learn something new. She's already got most of it in there and is just going to change it around a little bit.

Lisa: That word is a suffix and a prefix, with a little tiny part in between.

RD: Listen to that. She's chunked it already. The only new part is just the little tiny part in between.

TE: Lisa, when you see the word, do you use your auditory system at all?

RD: By the way, notice that Lisa's squinting her eyes as she's considering her answer. I'm not quite sure she sees what you're saying. (*Laughter*)

Lisa: I don't say the letters, I say the word.

RD: Lisa says, "I say the word." Her auditory comes in at the level of the whole word, so she can identify it.

Lisa: Some words I always say wrong. Like 'friends', I always say "fry-ends," so I don't forget to spell it right. Or 'Wednesday', I pronounce as "Wed-ness-day."

RD: You say it the way that helps you remember to spell it, whether it makes sense or not in the world. So, you vary the pronunciation as a function of the written spelling. This is especially interesting because it is the opposite of the 'sounding out' strategy, in which you vary the written spelling as a function of the sound.

Jean, show us how you would learn to spell the word 'pteridophytes'. Learn it, and signal us when you know it.

Jean: *(Scans eyes back and forth several times over the word.)* OK, I got it.

RD: Good. When you just looked at it here, what did you do? I noticed that Jean looked at it a little bit more than Lisa did. I saw her eyes going back and forth, as if she were wondering, "Should I put it together in two pieces or chunk it some other way?"

Jean: I ended up dividing 'pterid' into one chunk and 'phytes' into another. Then I had to remember to connect them with the 'o'.

RD: So, Lisa already had a guess about the beginning and the end of the word. She just verified those and then she only really had to look at the little part in the middle and pop it in. Jean had to work out her chunking as she was actually looking at the word.

Now, the question is, Lisa and Jean, would you be able to spell that word now, without looking at it?

Lisa: Sure.

RD: How do you know that? How do you know that you know that word in your mind now?

Lisa: I can see it.

Jean: Yeah, the same for me.

RD: You can see it now Lisa? And Jean you can see it too. What about feelings?

Lisa: I have a kind of feeling but its hard to describe.

RD: Lisa says, "I have some feelings, but they're not really like describable feelings." What are they like?

Lisa: Its almost more like I have the smell of the word.

RD: Interesting. Lisa says it is almost like a smell actually. How about you Jean?

Jean: Maybe just a feeling that I can spell it now. A sort of feeling of confidence.

RD: Jean's feeling has to do with a confidence in herself that she can spell it now. Which I think is also very important. It's not like this is just some 'stupid spelling word', it actually builds her self-esteem to learn a new word. Kate and Patty, what happens when you try to learn a new word—either of you? Do you feel good about yourself when you're done?

Kate: If I'm honest, I think it's a meaningless waste of time.

RD: So Kate starts with the belief that it's a meaningless waste of time.

TE: And if it's a meaningless waste of time, why do it? Why bother to spell correctly? You can look it up in the dictionary or use a 'spell checker'.

Kate: My answer to you is, I only bother to learn it correctly if I'm going to get the 'A' grade at the end of it. But if it is just for personal use, and I don't get any benefit in the classroom, then it doesn't make any difference.

RD: If you do decide that its worth it, how do you go about learning it?

Kate: If I really want to be sure I know it? I write it out fifty times.

RD: How about you, Patty. What happens when you're learning a new word, what do you typically do?

Patty: Typically?

RD: Patty goes, "You ask, 'typically'? There's nothing 'typical' about my spelling." (*Laughter*) I mean, if you were going to learn this word what would you do?

Patty: Well, you know, I'm tone deaf and was told that a lot when I was a child. Being good at following instructions, I bought into the notion that there was something wrong with me and I became a bad speller. By doing as I was told.

RD: What Patty is saying in essence is, "It's not that I learned to spell badly, it's that I learned to be a bad speller." This is something at the level of identity rather than capability. So, by the way, if Patty spelled this word correctly right now, I can almost guarantee that she would say, "OK I can spell that word, but it doesn't change anything. It doesn't make me a good speller. Because I'm a bad speller, and even bad spellers can spell some words right. So just learning how to spell this word would not make me a good speller. It could be an exception to the rule." I've heard that kind of remark frequently: "I learned this one word, but it doesn't make me a good speller, any more than swimming one lap makes me a good swimmer". Because identity is a different level than capability. And of course, for Kate, "Spelling this word right doesn't make spelling any less of a meaningless waste of time." So, notice we have the capability nested inside of issues relating to beliefs, values and identity.

In fact, there is another important belief issue I want to explore. Lisa and Jean, how much effort did you put into learning the word 'pteridophytes'?

Lisa: Hardly any.

Jean: Negligible.

RD: Do you worry a lot about being able to spell well?

Jean: No.

Lisa: I don't really think about it.

TE: Doesn't keep you up late at night, huh? You don't spend all your time thinking about being good spellers? Then how did you get to be so good at it? If you didn't spend all this time worrying about it , how did you get to be so good at it?

Jean: I've always liked spelling.

TE: You've always liked spelling. How did that come about? How does one get to like spelling? Wouldn't it be great if all the kids liked spelling?

RD: How about you Lisa?

Lisa: Well, I never liked spelling, but I liked reading. I've been reading since I was four. I always had my nose in a book, and I think that's why I'm a good speller.

RD: Are you a good reader, Kate?

Kate: I like reading.

RD: You like reading. But spelling is something different that is a waste of time. This is another one of those interesting belief issues. Lisa seems to be implying, "If I read a lot, I can't help but learn to spell the words, because I'm seeing them all the time. It's impossible to not learn them." For Kate, however, spelling and reading are two different things. But if Kate could learn to spell while she were reading, without investing any time in it, that would be quite different wouldn't it? That wouldn't be such a meaningless waste of time.

TE: It's the differences in their strategies that allows one of them to be able to look at the words while she's reading and learn to spell because her "nose is in a book," while the other reads a book and doesn't see anything on the page. For example, I have a question for both of you: How do you get the information while you are reading? Do you get it from looking at the words or do you get it from saying the words for yourself? Where does the meaning come from in the novel when you're reading it? Do you look at the words and get the meaning or do you have to say the words? What about you Lisa?

Lisa: From looking at the words, and hearing them.

TE: How about you Kate?

Kate: I say them. It drives my father crazy because I mouth everything.

TE: You can almost predict that that would be Kate's response. Given the way she spells. It would be very difficult for her to spell auditorily and read visually. The way she spells is the same way she reads—auditorily. For Kate, the meaning of the word doesn't come from the way it's spelled visually, it comes from the way it sounds. Therefore, you can read any number of misspelled words, but if they sound like a word you can recognize you can always get the meaning.

There is another thing I want to check out. Lisa, you said that you look at the words and you hear them. Is it that you mouth every word on the page like Kate does?

Lisa: No. I don't say it, I just hear it—like someone's telling me the story.

TE: What about you Kate?

Kate: It's my voice; but my father says, "Then read it with your mouth closed."

RD: So it might be an interesting thing for Kate to learn how to hear a voice saying the words, like Lisa does, without having to move her own mouth. This is why cooperative learning can be so powerful. People can compare and share strategies. And these strategies are coming from peers, not a teacher who will punish you if you do it 'wrong'. For instance, if Kate had Lisa's strategy, she would be practicing spelling all the time without even knowing it. And there might be other aspects of Lisa's strategy that could benefit Kate.

Lisa: I was thinking back on the question of whether or not I liked spelling. I remembered that I didn't like spelling but I always loved words. Like when you said, 'pteridophyte', I said to myself, "Aha. Like pterodactyl, must be Greek.

TE: So you had fun with it.

Lisa: Yeah, I love looking for relationships.

RD: Lisa says, "I love looking for relationships." This is another thing she could help coach Kate to do.

Let's turn back to Patty for a moment and see what kind of coaching could be of value to her. Patty, what would you need in order to be able to believe that you were a good speller? Would somebody have to tell you?

Patty: No, I generally don't believe what people tell me.

RD: If you really have a strategy that you don't believe what people tell you, then why did you believe it when people told you that being tone deaf made you a bad speller?

Patty: Because as a little girl, I didn't know that I could believe otherwise.

TE: But you know differently now?

Patty: Yes.

RD: What if you went back in your mind to that little girl that didn't know she could believe anything different and told her that she could believe otherwise?

Patty: (*Becomes very quiet.*)

TE: It's alright to do that, it's OK to believe that it can be different.

RD: What would that little girl do? If you went back in time to that place for a moment and were like a big sister to her, and told her that she could believe otherwise? Would she trust you?

Patty: I think so.

RD: What Patty was just dealing with here is something that we call an 'imprint'. Imprints relate to events that occurred at the time a person was first learning something; events that set the stage for later beliefs. Often we will build a belief about learning during a time when we don't know any better. It is sometimes important to become aware of those earlier formative experiences and then revisit and update them, like Patty just did.

Now Patty, there is something else I wanted to ask you about. Do you think that it's dangerous to be sure of things? For instance, are you concerned that either (a) if you become too sure of yourself, or of an answer, you can screw something up, or (b) being sure will make you into a kind of person you don't like? The reason I'm checking is that it seems that every time we ask Patty something, it is really important for her to equivocate about it a little bit. Its as if she always needs to add, "I think" to the end. This could become a kind of interference to spelling if you feel that you will lose the choice of being unsure. You might want to think about that Patty. Do you have any hesitations about being sure?

Patty: Yes.

RD: What would they be?

Patty: I'm not the kind of person who thinks things are only one way. I like to see things from many perspectives.

RD: That's important. Of course, the question is, does spelling go against that kind of person?

TE: Patty might have the belief that, "If I to learn how to spell, things will always have to be the same way. I can never make them be any different. Then, where do I get my creativity from? I've got to do it the same way every time? Great, sounds like a lot of fun, man."

Patty: I feel like I might lose choices.

RD: So, Patty, you might want to consider whether there is anything that you can be sure of, that doesn't take away from this really important choice to see things from different perspectives? We might also ask Jean how she manages to not lose choice even through she is able to learn to spell a word.

Jean: Well for me its not so much about being 'sure' as it is about being 'confident'. The issue for me is not being sure that I have the right word, but rather being confident in my own ability to learn. When I'm confident, I have more choices, not less.

RD: So, Patty, that might be a perspective that you would want to have the choice to take. It might be nice to try out the perspective that the goal is not to be sure of your spelling but rather to be confident about your ability to learn.

Patty: Sounds interesting.

RD: Again the purpose of cooperative learning is to add perspectives that help create choices and widen our maps of a particular task. It can be quite surprising what you can learn from a peer that has a good strategy for something.

I think you will also find that good spelling paradoxically requires a healthy amount of creativity. In fact, I'd like to lead both Kate and Patty through the basic version of the spelling strategy. As you will see, it incorporates principles of spelling that both Lisa and Jean were using. It puts them into the form of a feedback loop, or T.O.T.E., rather than a rigid procedure.

The Spelling Strategy

RD: According to the Spelling Strategy, in order to learn a new word, or a word you are having trouble with, you would basically look at the correct spelling, move your eyes up and to the left and visualize it in your mind's eye. In order to associate the spelling with the feeling of familiarity, it is useful to first think of something else that you are already confident about and familiar with in order to access a positive feeling state. Then when you look at the word, it will become anchored to the positive feeling instead of the feeling of effort or frustration (as often becomes associated with spelling). People tend to automatically remember things that make them feel good.

Of course, this basic process is not always enough. Adults, in fact, often have a fair amount of 'unlearning' to do. Often they will habitually and unconsciously try to use the old 'sounding out' strategy, which can lead to confusion and conflict in trying to spell. To combat that tendency, and to provide a convincing evidence that the image of the word is indeed in their mind, I have people spell the word **backwards** as well as frontwards. It is very difficult to sound things out backwards (for example, try to figure out what '*Albuquerque*" sounds like backwards). The auditory representational system is very time dependent for perception, and sound tends to propagate in a particular sequence. The visual system, on the other hand, is more simultaneous.

For example, think of which letter comes three letters after "**P**" in the alphabet. Now think of which letter comes three letters before "**P**" in the alphabet. If you primarily remember the letters of the alphabet utilizing the "**ABC**" song most English speakers learned as children, you probably experienced much more difficulty identifying that "**M**" is the letter that comes three letters before "**P**". People that use an auditory strategy such as this, sometimes even have to go all the way to the beginning of the alphabet and come forward in order to find the answer. Something visual maintains it shape whether we look at it *left-to-right* or *right-to-left*. Thus, if someone could read the letters of a word off backwards (i.e., from right-to-left) one could be pretty certain that that person had a reasonably clear image of it in his or her mind.

The spelling strategy is essentially a **T.O.T.E.** with three operations. The Test phase of the **T.O.T.E.** involves checking one's visual and kinesthetic representations ($V^r => K^r$) associated with the word. This test involves verifying both the **clarity** of image and **intensity** of a feeling of familiarity. The fundamental sequence of operations in this T.O.T.E. include:

(1) thinking of something positive and easy to remember and anchoring that feeling to the correct spelling by simply looking at the correct spelling;

(2) looking up and left and visualizing the correct spelling in your mind's eye; and

(3) looking up and left and reading off the letters both frontwards and backwards.

With long words, people often experience difficulty in being able to initially visualize the entire word easily (especially people new to the process of visualizing). Frequently what happens is that some letters are clear but the rest get out of focus or become hazy. In such a situation one needs some operations in order to make the unclear letters stand out. In this case there are several sub-operations that may be used including:

(a) breaking the word down into groups of letters (typically groups of three). These groups or 'chunks' do not need to be in the form of syllables, phonological units, or logical relations. The purpose of these chunks is simply to help build the image of smaller pieces.

(b) changing some of the sub-modality quality of the letters that have been difficult to visualize in such a way that makes them stand out. For instance, the letters can be made brighter, put in one's favorite color, put on a familiar background, made bigger, etc.

(**c**) tracing the letters with your finger. This helps to anchor in the remembered image of letters that are not clear by creating an overlap to the kinesthetic system.

The following T.O.T.E. diagram summarizes the basic elements of the overall strategy.

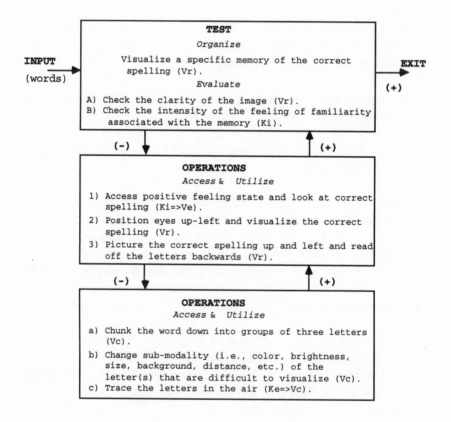

TEST

Organize

Visualize a specific memory of the correct spelling (Vr).

Evaluate

A) Check the clarity of the image (Vr).
B) Check the intensity of the feeling of familiarity associated with the memory (Ki).

INPUT (words)

EXIT (+)

(−)   (+)

OPERATIONS

Access & Utilize

1) Access positive feeling state and look at correct spelling (Ki=>Ve).
2) Position eyes up-left and visualize the correct spelling (Vr).
3) Picture the correct spelling up and left and read off the letters backwards (Vr).

(−)   (+)

OPERATIONS

Access & Utilize

a) Chunk the word down into groups of three letters (Vc).
b) Change sub-modality (i.e., color, brightness, size, background, distance, etc.) of the letter(s) that are difficult to visualize (Vc).
c) Trace the letters in the air (Ke=>Vc).

T.O.T.E. For Effective Spelling

These functions may be put into a simple step-by-step format for instruction as follows.

BASIC SPELLING STRATEGY

1. Place the correct spelling of the word to be learned either:

    a. directly in front of you at about eye level; or
    b. above eye level and to your upper left (or right if you are left handed).

2. Close your eyes and think of something that feels *confident, familiar and relaxing*. When the feeling is strong, open your eyes and look at the correct spelling.

    a. If you placed the correct spelling in front of you, move your eyes up and to the left (or right) and picture the correct spelling in your mind's eye.

    b. If you placed the correct spelling to your upper left, remove the correct spelling, but keep your eyes up and to the left and continue to see the correct spelling in your mind's eye. *(If you have difficulty use the **Helpful Hints** on the next page.)*

3. Look up at your mental image and verbalize (or write) the letters you see. Check what you have verbalized or written with the correct spelling. If any letters are missing or incorrect, return to *step #1* and use the Helpful Hints to help clarify your mental image.

4. Look up at your mental image and spell the word backwards *(i.e., verbalize or write the letters down from right to left)*. Compare what you have verbalized or written with the correct spelling. If you have difficulty or any letters are missing or incorrect, go back to *step #2* and use the Helpful Hints to assist in clarifying your mental image.

HELPFUL HINTS

A. Picture the word in your *favorite color*.

B. *Make any unclear letters stand out* by making them look different than the others in some way - e.g. *bigger, brighter, closer, a different color, etc.*

C. Break the word into *groups of three letters* and build your picture three letters at a time.

D. Put the letters on a *familiar background*. Picture something like a familiar object or movie scene then put the letters you want to remember on top of it.

E. If it is a long word, make the letters small enough so that you can *see the whole word easily*.

F. *Trace the letters in the air* with your finger and picture in your mind the letters that you are writing.

It is important to remember that there is a difference between a strategy and a mnemonic technique. A strategy involves setting a fixed outcome with a variable means to achieve it (such as the "Helpful Hints"). One continues varying these mental operations until the image is fixed in the mind's eye. Memory techniques tend to be fixed means, or processes that produce variable outcomes. People end up concentrating more on what to do in order to remember the information than on the information itself. The NLP strategy involves the variation of fundamental sensory processes that require no training to learn. People often have to learn to *remember the memory techniques* before they can use them to remember what they have learned them for in the first place.

Applying the Spelling Strategy

RD: Let's demonstrate how to teach someone this strategy using the word 'pteridophytes'. I'll write it down for Patty and Kate. You each get to choose where you want to put the word, either placing it in front of you or holding it up to your left. Then, according to the spelling strategy, you want to get into a positive state, a state of confidence. Spelling is similar to sharpshooting in this respect; you go through the three stages 'ready, aim, fire'. Rather than just 'fire' or 'aim and fire', you get into a state of readiness first. I think both Lisa and Jean got themselves ready. For example, Lisa was already prepared with a guess.

It is similar to the way Todd did the first memory exercise. He said, "I want to be in this state while I'm learning. And I'll just keep varying my process until I can stay in this state, and have those letters pop into my mind."

TE: And it's a lot different if you start from comfort and confidence, as opposed to fear or stress.

RD: Now, with both Patty and Kate, we did find that there were some words that they both were confident that they already knew. You two might want to think of that sense of confidence that you have about words that you are familiar with. Find that state that is confident, familiar and relaxing. Then close your eyes and really get into that feeling. And in your mind, make a place for the word. Remember how Todd made a place for his characters? When you have that place, gently open your eyes and look at the letters on the paper you are holding in front of you. You don't need to spend a long time with it. Just open your eyes briefly and then close them again. Then look in your mind's eye. What's stuck in your mind?

TE: What has stayed there naturally? What parts of the word are in there? Notice what you did get.

RD: Notice what stays there more clearly. You can also notice if there are any fuzzy spots. Get ready, so that when you open your eyes again, you're going to confirm what you already saw, so that it will get clearer. You can then look at the parts that you don't have so clearly yet. If you want you can make those stand out in some way. For instance you can make those letters be in a different color, perhaps your favorite color.

Once again, open your eyes, look at the word, and check what you see in front of you against what is stuck in your mind. Is it what you thought it was? Identify any of the letters that did not naturally stick in your image or weren't clear. Look at those letters and imagine them in a different color, or underline them, or make them bigger. Do something to them to make them stand out—to make them seem special. What you do to make them stand out is your choice. That's a function of your own creativity.

Now close your eyes again. Notice that there are more letters that seem to naturally stay in your mind now. Notice how that strengthens your feeling of confidence. You can relax even more because the letters are becoming clearer and easier to remember. If you need to adjust the color of the letters or make them larger or smaller so that you strengthen that good feeling, that's OK, too.

Again, open your eyes and look at the word. If there is a certain part that you want to trace with your finger, you can do that if you want. Now, just keep opening and closing your eyes, until when you close your eyes, you see the word as clearly as when you're actually looking at the word.

Do you have it Patty?

Patty: Uh huh.

RD: OK. Do you have it Kate?

Kate: I'm not sure. I don't really *see* it.

RD: Just close your eyes, and notice what is there. Relax your forehead. You're putting in too much effort. What do you see in your mind's eye?

Kate: I can't see the P-H-Y, but I know P-H-Y is there.

RD: By the way, I notice that you reached out in front of you, pointed to a particular spot and said, "I know the P-H-Y is there." Even with your eyes closed, you said I know it's there.

Kate: Well I know that the word on the paper doesn't actually disappear just because I close my eyes.

RD: And even if you don't 'see' it with your eyes closed, you 'remember' where it is on the paper.

Kate: Well, yes.

RD: With your eyes closed, can you tell me what is the beginning of that word?

Kate: P-T.

RD: Uh huh. What comes next?

Kate: E-R

RD: OK, good. Now, instead of 'seeing' them, all you need to do is remember what comes next on the paper. How would you know that you could remember where all those letters were on the paper?

Kate: (*Pauses for a moment with her eyes closed.*) OK, I can spell it now.

RD: Now that's interesting. How do you know that you can spell it now?

Kate: Because I can repeat the sequence in my head by saying P-T-E-R-I-D-O-P-H-Y-T-E-S.

RD: So you need to be able to say it to yourself to confirm that you know it. Well, let me ask you this, then, can you start with the S and repeat the sequence backward? Just give it a try.

Kate: S-E-T—Y—H-P—O-D-I—R-E—T-P (*Applause*)

RD: Very nice!! Bravo. And you didn't even write it fifty times. You didn't even write it three times. Now let's have Patty do it. Close your eyes, Patty. Can you see the letters in your mind's eye?

Patty: Yes, easily.

RD: Then maybe you can just start off by spelling it backwards.

Patty: SETYHP-O-D-I-RETP *(Applause)*

RD: Alright. Did you hear how fast she does it? I think that she really has a clear picture of that word. What is interesting to me about someone like Patty, is that she obviously could do it in a snap. She has had the capability all these years. It is more a matter of giving herself the permission to do it. I think with you Kate, it is a matter of learning to trust some of your other senses. For instance, when you were spelling the word, did you have to sound it out?

Kate: I'm not sure.

TE: Did you sound it out backwards?

Kate: I think I was sort of writing it, actually.

RD: And this is something I want you to realize, Kate; you can know how to write something, without having written it fifty times. You already have that connection in there. And when you make that kind of connection you have done something even more important than learning a word—you have learned how to learn.

To show what I mean, let's put up another word. One of my personal favorites is 'Albuquerque' (it's one of the first words I myself learned how to spell backwards). I'll write it on the board. *(Kate begins to lean forward and tense her face.)*

TE: Now Kate and Patty, don't bother with what's on the board just yet. Close your eyes for a second, and relax. Think about something that's enjoyable for you; something that's fun, that makes you feel good, that's easy and that has to do with looking at things. In other words, an important part of this good experience is that you open your eyes and you look at things. I don't care if it's cars going by, boys walking down the hall in school, it doesn't matter to me. It just needs to be something where you use your eyes to take in information, and it's fun. It doesn't need to have anything to do with learning or school. It may not even be something that you remember visually. Just pay attention to the feeling that goes along with this experience of looking at something and enjoying it. Notice where the image that you are looking at is located.

RD: And even if you don't see it perfectly, Kate, you know that it's there. You know that you have seen it. And when you've got that state, open your eyes and look at this word on the board. Close your eyes and put it in the same place as that experience that you really enjoy. The place that is right there in front of you.

TE: You're not really trying to remember what all the letters are; just imagine that you were putting those letters in that same place as that enjoyable visual experience.

RD: Now Kate, if you were to write the first four letters of that word, what would you write?

Kate: A-L-B-U?

RD: OK, that's correct. And you didn't even have to write it a bunch of times on your leg.

Kate: No, but they look nice.

RD: Well, close your eyes again then. And keeping your eyes closed, can you spell that word backward?

Kate: You want me to spell it backwards? E-U-Q-R-E-U-Q-U-B-L-A (*Applause*)

RD: That's right. Bravo. And the amazing thing is, Kate, that if you did this with a few more words, you'd probably get even faster at it, until it becomes second nature to you like it is to Lisa. Then you'd be able to look at words, as you read them, and be learning to spell them without even having to invest any energy into it.

TE: I thought it was interesting that Kate said the letters "looked nice," given the starting state we chose. When Robert started writing the word up on the board, I noticed that the first thing Kate did was to tighten her forehead and go into this 'concentration' state. So what I did was ask her to find a state where things are fun, have nothing to do with school, but where you use your eyes. Afterwards, when Kate opened her eyes to look at the word, her whole face was completely different as well as her muscle tone, the way she was breathing, and even the location of the image. She had actually moved it up a little bit. The point is that you want to begin with a state that attaches seeing to having fun. You start from that state—even if you have to go back to that state each time you're getting ready to learn a new word.

RD: And I think another important thing for you to realize, Kate, is that you already have that positive feeling when you're reading. All you have to do is let your brain know that you can automatically write things that you see without having to consciously write them out multiple times. (To group) Notice how a particular experience can also be a confirmation for a new belief, as well as an example of a strategy.

Now, Patty, let's check in with you. Do you know how to spell Albuquerque?

Patty: Sure.

RD: OK, close your eyes. Can you spell it backwards?

Patty: E-U-Q-R-E-U-Q-U-B-L-A (*Applause*)

RD: Patty, I think something that might be important for you to consider is, since it doesn't take that much effort or time, what would happen if you continued to spell as well as you've just done?

Patty: People might start thinking I'm a good speller.

TE: And what do people think about good spellers? Some people don't think about it at all. They don't walk up and go, "Gee, I was wondering whether or not I would like to go out with you on a date. Can you spell?" (Laughter) Although there are those who might say, "If you can't spell then I'll go out with you. But if you can spell, forget it; because you're liable to figure out that I don't know what I'm talking about."

Using the Spelling Strategy with Children Who Have Learning Problems

RD: As you can see, the spelling strategy, done in a framework of cooperative learning, was quite effective for Kate (a junior in high school) and Patty (a young woman in her early twenties). One question that many people have, however, is whether the strategy is able to help children with learning disabilities improve their ability to spell as well. In fact, we have found this strategy (and the overall NLP approach) to be remarkably effective with people who have been diagnosed with learning handicaps. Our initial work with the Pajaro Valley School District was focused entirely on special education for children who had been diagnosed with some type of learning problems. It was because that program was so effective that the approach was generalized to the regular classroom.

The following is a transcript from one of our very first Dynamic Learning Seminars illustrating how effective the spelling strategy can be with children who have learning problems. Christopher, a 10 year old boy, was brought to the seminar by his father, Hans. Christopher had been diagnosed as dyslexic and was experiencing many learning difficulties in school.

RD: Now, Christopher, are you learning to spell or have you been learning to spell?

Christopher: Yes.

RD: Are you a good speller?

Christopher: No. I'm lousy.

RD: Well, when you spell, what do you do in your brain?

Christopher: Think.

RD: (*To group*) Most of the time people don't really know what they do in their mind when they're doing something. You ask, "How do you do that?" And they reply, "Well I just 'think' about it." But that doesn't mean that they might not be able to learn to do it better.

TE: (*To Christopher*) For instance, could you tell someone how to ride a bicycle?

Christopher: No. It would be hard to do that.

RD: You couldn't tell them what to do to ride a bike?

Christopher: I could teach them but I couldn't really tell them.

RD: How did you learn to ride your bike?

Christopher: I just got on it and kept trying until I could do it.

RD: So instead of thinking about it or talking about it, you just got on your bicycle and tried to go somewhere. And even though you fell down, you kept getting back up and trying until you could do it. I think the same thing is true with spelling. You get good at it in the same way you learned to ride your bike. The thing about spelling, though, is that you've got to know where you're trying to go, and where the pedals in your brain are. For instance, do you remember what the front of your house looks like?

Christopher: Sure.

TE: How do you know what the front of your house looks like?

Christopher: Because I play with my dog around the house.

RD: So you didn't have to try to remember it. Just by being around it while you are playing with your dog, you remember it naturally.

TE: What color is the front of your house, do you know?

Christopher: Gray—or bluish.

TE: A bluish color.

RD: Do you think about spelling in the same way you think about the outside color of your house?

Christopher: Um...I don't know.

RD: It would be nice if you could do it that way, wouldn't it? If you could just naturally remember the spelling of the words.

Christopher: Yeah.

RD: Do you know how to spell 'geography'?

Christopher: No. That's a hard word.

RD: Well, let me ask you to try something. I'm going to write out the word 'geography' on the blackboard, and I'd like you to look at it and make a picture of the word in your mind. Look at the word and then sort of look beyond it, maybe to the ceiling above it. See if you can still picture that word in your mind as if it were written on the ceiling. Can you do that?

Christopher: It disappears when I put my eyes up there. (*Christopher's eyes begin to move down to the left.*)

RD: Just keep your eyes up there for a second. There's no need to try to sound it out. I can tell that you're trying to say it.

TE: Just make a picture of it like the front of your house, Christopher.

RD: You can visualize the front of your house, right?

Christopher: Yeah.

RD: See if you can visualize those letters written on your door. Look up and see your memory of your front door.

Christopher: (*Christopher looks up and to his left.*) OK.

RD: Now put the "G" on your door, just the "G." Can you do that?

Christopher: Uh huh.

RD: Now can you put the "GE" on the door of your house?

Christopher: Yeah.

RD: OK, can you go back and forth in doing that until you get all of the letters?

TE: (To group) This is one of the ways that we help people develop the ability to visualize. We already know that Christopher can visually remember the front of his house. Now all we're doing is asking him to take that visual image we already know he can make, and place these letters on the front of that door. This way, we're ensuring that he's making a picture of the letters. Because he was having a difficult time making a picture of the letters on their own, just floating in space, we tagged them onto something familiar.

RD: (To Christopher) Now I notice that your eyes are moving down a bit again. You don't need to sound them out, just see them on the door. OK. So right now just read off what you see on your door.

Christopher: "G E O G R"

RD: Great. Now put the "A" up there. Can you see that clearly? Now put up the "PH."

Christopher: "GEOGRAPH"

RD: OK. Keep going until you can put all the letters on your door.
 (Christopher starts to look down and to his left.)

TE: And you can stop talking to yourself. See, we can read your mind, so you better watch out.
 (Christopher moves his eyes back and forth from the board to his upper left.)

RD: Do you have the whole picture?

Christopher: Uh huh.

RD: Good. Now I'd like you to turn around for a minute so that you can't see the word. (To group) Since Christopher was having a difficult time visualizing the letters we took something that he could see easily already—his front door—and had him put the letters on that door.
 (To Christopher) Can you put your eyes up and still see them all on the door now?

Christopher: Yeah.

RD: OK, would you read off what letters you see on your door right now?

Christopher: "G E O G R A P H Y"

RD: Very good. Now look at those letters on your door and starting at the "Y"—go backwards. Start with the "Y."

Christopher: "Y" (*Begins to lift his hand to his forehead.*)

RD: There's no need to put your hand there. It's not going to help.

TE: You're covering up the door.

RD: OK, do it frontwards again first.

Christopher: "G E O G R E P..."

RD: Is it an "E?"

Christopher: Um—I guess not.

RD: Now remember about learning to ride your bicycle. You have to fall down a few times before you get the hang of it. Go ahead and look back at the word and keep going back and forth from the board to your mental picture until the ones that you see on your front door look the same as the ones on the board.

Christopher: OK, I got it. (*Turns away from the board*) "G E O G R A P H Y?"

RD: So do you have them pictured all clearly? Are there any of them that you're not sure about?

Christopher: The last couple.

RD: OK. Look back at the last couple. Now look back up here at the door in your mind. Now can you see them all clearly now? OK, now read them forewards first.

Christopher: G E O G A R...

RD: Is that right?

Christopher: No. It's R A

RD: (To group) Now what Christopher just did here is not a mistake, but rather a tremendous success. He stopped because he knew he had switched the two letters. Clearly he must already have at least an unconscious image of that word in his mind so that when he sees or hears an inappropriate spelling he automatically knows it. He didn't know consciously at first what it was, but there was a hesitation. It's like starting to get your balance on the bicycle Christopher. So, go ahead and try it again from the beginning— forewards.

Christopher: G E O G...

RD: OK, is that one not clear? Make sure that you've got it right on the door now. Maybe you could trace it with your finger, make it bigger or even put it on your door in silver letters. Can you see it?

Christopher: G E O G R A P H Y

RD: OK, do it one more time.

Christopher: G E O G R A P H Y (*Applause*)

RD: OK, now can you spell it backwards? Just look at the door. See the "Y." What comes before the "Y?"

Christopher: Y G H P...

RD: That's right, you knew something was out of place. Just look at the word on your door and read the letters off.

Christopher: Y H P A R G O E G? (*Applause*)

RD: Very good! Now do it frontwards one more time.

Christopher: G E O G R A P H Y

TE: All right!

Woman: He'll never forget that one.

RD: Right, but see that's the point. What does it mean to say you'll 'never forget' something. If you have something that you're never going to forget, what do you have? You have a strategy for getting to it whenever you want it. But this strategy is not just about that particular word. For instance, do you know how to spell 'receive' Christopher?

Christopher: Not yet.

RD: What I'm going to do now is to ask Christopher to learn to spell the word "receive." I think that we're going to find that the time it takes him to learn "receive" will be much less than it was for 'geography'. In other words, once you learn the *process* of visualization, visualizing anything becomes easier.

Our goal was not really to teach Christopher to spell one word, but rather to install the ability to spell. Spelling ability is not about learning one word at a time. That's the thing about spelling. If you learn your ten words for the week, 'sure enough if the next week they don't give you ten more'.

TE: And you've got to go through it all over again.

RD: It's that notion that if you give someone a fish you've fed them for a day. If you teach them how to fish, you've fed them for the rest of their life. What we want to do is to give Christopher a strategy so that the process of learning to spell becomes easier and easier. So that when he gets his ten words next week, instead of having to laboriously go over each one, he can just take them, pop them all up there in his mind, and be done with it.

Man: Will he have to put each one of those words onto a door?

TE: Well, he may or may not continue to use the door. The reason for using the door came from the fact that we knew that he could already visualize it. So by having him look at the door in the first place, it got him to access his visual memory. So we used it as a 'doorway' to visual information. At some point, though, Christopher may say, "Oh, I don't need to use door any more. I can just put the letters up on whatever I want to put them up on."

RD: What we want to show here is the process of 'learning to learn'. In other words, you saw how long it took for Christopher to do the first word. Let's go to a different one and see if that process gets any faster and easier—like learning to ride a bike.

OK Christopher, I've written the word "receive" under "geography." Just put it in an image in your mind and when you've got it, turn around. (*Christopher looks at the word and moves his eyes up several times then turns away from the blackboard.*) OK, so notice

Christopher has turned around already. Do you have a picture of it, Christopher?

Christopher: Uh huh.

RD: OK, can you spell that word?

Christopher: R E C E I V E (*Applause*)

RD: OK, now can you do it backwards? Just look at the picture and read the letters off starting with the 'e'.

Christopher: E V I E C R

RD: OK. Is that right?

Christopher: I think I missed the last two letters.

RD: OK, no problem. Look back and make them clearer. (To group) This time he almost got the whole thing on right his first try backwards. And he got it forewards right away. (*Christopher looks at the word on the blackboard then turns back around.*) OK, you got it?

TE: Tune that thing in.

Christopher: (*Looks up and left*) E V I E C E R (*Applause*)

RD: Wonderful. Now I want to ask you another thing. Can you spell "geography" backwards? Start by looking at it frontwards.

Christopher: Oh, OK. Y H P A R G E O G (*Applause*)

Hans: (*In amazement*) I've got to go home.

TE: You're next, Hans. Don't leave.

RD: Again, the thing I wanted to demonstrate here is the process of 'learning to learn'. Once Christopher knows how to make a picture in his mind, spelling becomes a progressively easier task for him—like riding a bicycle.

TE: Incidentally, Christopher, are the letters still up on the door? Or do you have some other picture of them?

Christopher: I forgot about the door, it's just up in my mind.

RD: By the way, I understand that Christopher was supposedly dyslexic. Is that right Hans?

Hans: That's right.

RD: Obviously anyone can see that his spelling gene is hopelessly broken, right?

Hans: Huh?

TE: He's got a broken spelling gene.

Hans: So we were told.

TE: So much for that diagnosis.

Practicing the Spelling Strategy

RD: We'd now like to give you an opportunity to practice the spelling strategy. As you know, the goal of NLP is not to interpret people as robots but to be curious about what they do. Start by pairing up with someone and asking that person to spell a few words. Find out what your partner's current spelling strategy is. Then, have your partner go through the spelling strategy that we've demonstrated here, whether that person's current spelling strategy works well or not. Remember, our whole approach to strategies is this—we want to add resources, not take them away. If you have a phonetic strategy for spelling, that's fine, but what we want to do is to add some other choices to that T.O.T.E. You can always go back to phonetic spelling if you want to. What we want you to do is to simply add the ability to visualize.

Identify something that you would like to remember, but that you sometimes have difficulty recalling accurately. It could be a telephone number, a social security number, or it could be spelling 'chrysanthemum'. Even if you are a good speller, there might be some words that you have difficulty remembering, like Jean. You can always take the word "orthographer" if you want—an expert speller.

First try to remember the word or characters naturally using your own strategy. Then try it using the spelling strategy that we demonstrated here. The basic strategy involves moving your eyes up to your left and forming a visual image in your mind's eye. Hold the spelling of the word up and put it up in your mind's eye until you have a clear enough picture that you can read off the letters both forewards or backwards.

The simplest version would be to just look at the word, look away from it, and see what sticks in your mind. Then you look back at the paper and notice if what sticks is the same as what is on the paper. If it is, great; if not, then I need to ask, "What can I do to make them stick?" Perhaps I can make them in my favorite color. Or I can visualize them twice as big—or closer. Or I can trace them out with my finger. So, what you're doing is one of these T.O.T.E. feedback loops. The whole purpose is to see how quickly you can make the letters stick. Maybe 90% of the time the characters will just automatically stick.

If you have difficulty, you can try out some of the 'Helpful Hints'. But for many words or memory tasks you probably won't need them, because the letters or characters will naturally stick in your mind. Remember to start with a good feeling, or a positive state.

The purpose of chunking, tracing, changing the colors, changing the size, are simply to get the letters to stick in your mind's eye.

TE: If all else fails, attach it to something that already sticks there. That was the process we used with Christopher. Find something that's already there and see if you can place the letters or characters you want to remember on top of it.

RD: Connect the letters or characters to something you already know. That's a version of what we call 'pacing and leading' in NLP. I think it is one of the most fundamental principles for learning. I think another interesting thing that you will discover about spelling is that it does sometimes involve a fair amount of creativity. I hear people say, "I hate spelling because it doesn't involve any creativity. Yet, all the people I know who have good memories are really creative when it comes to making what they're trying to remember stick in their minds. They're creative about how they reach that goal.

TE: The 'Helpful Hints' are the variable choices, the fixed goal is to get that visual image in place.

RD: Memory is basically a function of one thing and one thing only—how to make something stick in your mind. If it sticks in your mind, that's it. The rest of the stuff is only to help make it stick.

TE: It's the goo. The spelling strategy then becomes another choice. As Robert said, it's not that we want to take anything out once it's in there.

RD: You can't physically remove someone's internal dialogue as— far as I know.

TE: You can just rearrange that inner voice or give a person more options, but you can't take it out. That way, you can spell using a number of methods; you can sound the word out or you can make pictures of it. We just want you to do it visually one time and find out if it's the same or different from yours. Then you can use it or throw it out. But of course, remember, that once it's in there, it stays there and you can use it whenever you want—you can turn it off and on.

RD: The goal of the exercise is to give you the opportunity to develop your capability to be able to visualize the words clearly enough that you can them spell forewards and backwards. And remember, once you have that skill, it gets easier. It's like riding a bike or running a track course. If you run around a track four times every day, it's going to start to get easier and easier. Similarly, when you start to learn to visualize, it only gets easier.

Keep in mind, by the way, that a key part of your task in being someone's partner is to be an observer. You will want to watch the person who's trying to spell so you can see if they're unconsciously slipping into another strategy—like we were doing with Kate, Patty and Christopher. Todd noticed that Kate was furrowing her brow and helped her to find a more appropriate learning state. We could tell when Christopher was trying too hard and was going to lose his image because his eyes began to move down and to his left or his hand would start coming up. You want to make sure that the person is in the appropriate accessing posture, because a person's posture is going to influence the way that he or she is thinking.

●●●●●●●

After the Exercise

RD: Are there any questions or comments about the spelling exercise?

Barbara: Would you say that you should give children very simple words for a long time so that they have many positive experiences in being successful?

RD: Well, I think that an approach that emphasizes incremental improvement is an effective use of 'pacing and leading'. But I also think that what constitutes 'simple' words depends on the strategy you are using with the children. When you use a visual strategy, it's not so much a matter of 'simple' words or 'difficult' words—which usually relate to how close the sound of the word matches its spelling. If you are visualizing its just a matter of how many letters there are.

TE: We believe that if you take children and spend a little bit of time developing their visual, auditory and kinesthetic abilities—so they can use all their senses—then when you start teaching them words, you could just as easily start with words like "encyclopedia." You don't have to limit yourself to starting with words like "cat" because, if they have the ability to make a picture of the word, it's just a matter of how many letters can they hold in their mind's eye at any given time.

RD: Think of how complicated a process it is for a child to recognize his or her mother. I mean there are all these other people that have eyes and noses and hair, and things like that. As soon as they have the capability to make those discriminations, they potentially have the capability to recognize the difference between "encyclopedia" and some other word.

Barbara: But isn't it easier to build that capability if you start with easier words?

RD: Can you give us an example of what you mean by an 'easy' word?

Barbara: Like "happy." You start with something that's easier and maybe shorter to visualize and then move on to the longer ones. I mean I can spell "happy" easier backwards now that I can "encyclopedia."

RD: I understand that it is easier for you to spell 'happy' backwards, but that's probably because you don't have a clear picture of "encyclopedia" yet. If you had a clear picture, it would be like reading the two of them off of a piece of paper.

Barbara: But maybe if you start with a shorter word it would be easier to get a clear picture.

RD: Yes, of course it would be. And that's the whole idea behind 'chunking'. A ten letter word is just two three letter words and a four letter word. Or, as Lisa maintained, many words are a prefix, a suffix and a little bit in between.

TE: Notice, Barbara, that you may be speaking more about yourself than about children in general. My point is that if you take a kid at a young enough age and you teach him ten letter words, he's going to know how to do ten letter words. If you always teach him three and four letter words, then when it comes to the ten letter word, its going to seem like bigger a jump.

RD: I guess we're just asking you to think carefully before you tell children, "You're not old enough to do that yet. Sorry, you can't spell these words. They're too hard for you. This is a third grade word and you're only in second grade." Those may be unnecessary limitations.

However, I strongly agree that if a person is having difficulty visualizing a longer word then you go back one step and chunk the word into pieces so that the task is simpler for the person to do.

Barbara: What I just realized was that when I try to write the word 'encyclopedia' up in my mind, the letters seem so big that I can't see them all at once. When I look at the end of the word I can't see the beginning of the word anymore, like I can with 'happy'.

TE: Well can you make 'encyclopedia' take up as much space as "happy?" Can you just shrink the size of the word and see "encyclopedia" in smaller letters?

I've worked with a number of students who regardless of the chunk size, their TV-screen, so to speak, isn't big enough for the word. In other words, rather than the front of a door, it's as if what they see in their mind's eye is a television screen or computer screen. And maybe their TV or computer monitor at home has a little twelve inch screen; and on that twelve inch screen they can only get four or five letters across. So, they do fine spelling words with five letters, but then they get one with eight. They can see the first five letter letters, but those remaining letters are kind of squished in. And you ask them to make the screen bigger and suddenly they say, "Oh, yeah, I can get all eight. They fit now." I think that there is an important relationship between chunk size and screen size.

Stephanie: A similar thing happened for me. I found that this worked better for me when I went back and found out how many chunks of information I was making room for on my mental screen. Before I looked at chunk size, I looked at screen size. I hadn't done that before. I didn't really know if I could fit 5 or more on one screen; so some things would have been difficult to chunk in a certain way if I hadn't made my screen bigger.

RD: The number of chunks you can put in depends upon how large your screen is. To use another computer metaphor, it would be like suddenly jumping from an 8-bit computer processor to a 16 bit processor. You suddenly have another level of capacity which allows you to handle exponentially more information. So, rather than simply try to teach content, you find out what kind of things would help the person to expand their neurological processor one more bit.

Linda: I think I have a good example of that. I always had difficulty spelling 'separate', because I couldn't tell if it was supposed to be an 'a' or an 'e'. I would normally chunk it sep-a-rate. Lisa told me to chunk it "se-para'—"See pair a".

RD: That's a really powerful comment. Sometimes the reason that you consistently spell something incorrectly is because of how you're chunking it and if you rechunked it, you'd have a completely differently perception of it.

TE: Any other questions or comments?

Christine: I can see that using this strategy and the cooperative learning approach could save a lot of time for teachers. Because in most classroom situations you have three or four spelling groups; and, at least in our situation, we seem to spend a lot of time going from one spelling group to another in order to get to all of them. You can eliminate that if you teach them all the "how".

TE: Right. Once they all have the basic strategy it's just a matter of fine tuning. Then if you get one kid who does well with four letter words but not with seven letter words, you've just got to find out, 'what does that particular individual need in order to be able to visualize a seven letter word as opposed to a five letter word?' It's just a matter of fine tuning based on what that individual needs.

Teaching the Spelling Strategy
in the Classroom

RD: Incidentally, the way I would do the spelling strategy with a whole class is to put one of the lists of words up in the left hand corner of the room and one up in the right hand corner. Then, all the children who are right handed can look over at the words on the left hand side of the room; so that they were looking up to their left. The other children can look at the words that have been placed up and right. I would instruct the whole class to just keep looking up at the words and closing their eyes until they can close their eyes and still see them. At that point, cooperative learning can be used to help with the 'fine tuning' as Todd was saying. The students can help each other with different strategies and hints for making the words 'stick'. It doesn't really matter what level they are—whether they were in the 'Rockets' or the 'Trucks'—all that is necessary is to make sure that they can make a visual image of the words. It helps you bypass the stigma created by separating people with different learning styles into different groups.

The essential goal is to make sure that all of the children in the class develop the skills of visualizing. In fact, you can even tell them they can 'cheat' during the spelling test by looking up and over to where the words were placed and copy the answer down from what they see in their head—in their mind's eye.

TE: Those of you who are teachers have probably had the experience of having written something on the board and then erased it. Forty five minutes after it's been erased you're still pointing at the place on the board where it was and talking about it, and the students are going, "Oh, yeah" and they're looking at the board too, as if its still there. It's a type of anchoring.

Laura: What about some left handed people, or ambidextrous people, whose eye movements may or may not be switched? How do you know where to tell them to look?

RD: That's actually a matter of a simple 'calibration'. What I'd do is to start off by asking everybody to remember some picture that was really easy for them to remember and they really enjoyed looking at. Then I'd watch to see where their eyes went. I'd instruct the people I saw going up to their left to look at the words I put up on the left hand side of the room. The one's who looked off to the right, I'd instruct to look at the words on the right hand side of the room. In other words, I'd use experience rather than theory. I'd say "perform this visual task." Then, I'd instruct them to look where their eyes moved naturally.

Incidentally, once they have a good visual reference experience you can use it as their 'doorway' to visualization. So, if some students like airplanes and can visualize them easily, you can have them put words on an airplane wing as decals. Others might like cars, so you can have them see their spelling words as license plates. If they like ballet, you can have them see each letter as a person doing a different ballet step or position. This way, you would already have something that has a positive association and is something that's easily visualized. It helps streamline your ability to teach.

Also, since you will have calibrated which way the various students look when they are remembering something easily, you can observe them during spelling tests or exercises, notice if they are having trouble, and remind them of where to look to be most effective.

TE: This brings us back to the notion of feedback. In addition to giving feedback to students, it's important to realize that you are always getting feedback from the students that you're working with. If you ask a kid to do something and you notice his eyes go one way or the other, that's immediate feedback for you that is letting you know what to do next. People move their eyes all the time. Whether you tell them to or not, they'll be doing it. Now that you know about it, you might be surprised when you go out to restaurants, hotels, bars, or your office, and see that people are moving their eyes all over the place and you haven't asked them to do anything. They're just moving their eyes all on their own. They did it long before NLP discovered accessing cues.

RD: In conclusion, the Spelling Strategy is an important resource for classroom learning. In fact, it is probably one of the few spelling methods thats general effectiveness has been confirmed by university research studies (see Appendix C). Appendix B contains a more detailed description of all of the specific steps of the strategy.

I have also developed a strategy for learning basic math equations based on the spelling strategy (see Appendix D) that employs the visualization of fundamental mathematical relationships.

Chapter 7

Learning Language

Overview of Chapter 7

- Modeling Effective Language Learning
- 'Second Position' Modeling
- Developing Vocabulary
- Objects and Actions
- Adverbs and Adjectives
- Obstacle Course
- Nominalizations, Abstractions and Unspecified Verbs
- Idioms
- Simple Syntax
- Role Playing

Learning Language

RD: As we get ready to move on to some other strategies, we want to remind you of the point we made earlier that spelling is a separate skill from comprehension, composition, grammar, pronunciation and so forth. I think sometimes it is important to separate these various tasks. For instance, I know a lot people that get in trouble when they are trying to write. They have a difficult time expressing themselves on paper. They're the kind of people that say "Hey, I can talk up a storm but when it comes to writing it down it's really difficult". One of the things that I noticed about these people is that as soon as they start writing something out they immediately begin correcting the grammar and the spelling. By the time they're done correcting the spelling they've forgotten what they were going to say next. When I'm writing I frequently begin by doing it totally auditorily, as if I'm speaking. I'm basically transcribing my internal dialogue. Then I make a second pass for the spelling. I don't care what the grammar or the spelling looks like on the first draft. I want to get the ideas down. I can check the grammar and spelling on the next pass.

TE: That's why we have spell checkers and copy editors.

RD: My point is that being able to spell is a separate task from writing, and I do them at different times. Spelling is different than understanding or generating verbal language. When I'm working on a book or an article I just write down whatever comes into my mind at the time. I might not even write out the whole word. Shorthand, of course, is a great example of that. It's at a later stage that I think about how am I going to put the words together so that they fit the conventions of the English language.

Spelling a word is just a matter of getting the right letters in the right order, in order to make that particular standardized or conventional representation. Deriving meaning from a word is a very different process. Spelling is a building block in the process of comprehension. For example, the word "cat" is an arbitrary set of letters that have been passed down through the ages—a set of symbols. There's no indication within the structure of the word itself as to the actual meaning of the word. The meaning of "cat" comes, not from the structure of the word, but from the representations that you anchor to it—that is the sights, sounds and feelings that that particular set of letters or that sound sequence triggers up in your mind. So for instance, if you think of the meaning of the word "cat," how many of you see a visual image of a cat?

TE: How many of you hear a cat?

RD: Does anyone feel the cat's fur?

TE: Does anybody smell the cat box out by the washing machine? Hey, we give equal time to all representational systems here, you know.

RD: The point is that the meaning of that word doesn't have anything to do with the way it's spelled or the way it sounds. "Cat" is a three letter word but a four legged animal. There are some words in English, like "hiss" or "boom", where the sound of the word is somehow associated with the meaning. But these are the exceptions. For the most part the sound and the meaning of a word are unrelated.

TE: Imagine a child that was raised in an environment where he was taught to form perfect sentences in English. In other words, the child was taught enough grammar so that he could form perfect sentences and perfect paragraphs. The child could even write pages upon pages using this formula. But he had absolutely no experience connected to those sound sequences. In other words, this child would just be babbling sound sequences. This kid would have gown up being able to form all these perfect sentences and paragraphs but would have no reference experiences for the words. He wouldn't have the slightest idea what "door" or "window" meant, because there would be no experience connected to the words. He would be able to say the word "window" and even put it into a sentence with other words, but it wouldn't have any meaning.

RD: Sounds like my high school French class.

TE: Similarly, I could say or write, "Medu fure upquink..." and you'd probably have no idea what I meant. Yet, if we grew up in an environment such that those sound sequences were related to something in our experience, those sound sequences would make sense to you. In a way, it's incredible that you can even make sense out of these noises that I'm making right now (or the little squiggly marks on the paper that you are looking at) but our culture provides us with the opportunities to make links between these noises or squiggles and certain experiences. All cultures provide these links for the native speakers of their respective languages.

For example, you can take a little kid to the grocery store who can't read, but he knows which box is the Sugar Smacks, and he knows which box is the granola or the wheat flakes that he doesn't want. And if he wants Sugar Smacks and you point to a box of something else and go "Sugar Smacks"— thinking he can't read it—he'll go "Uh uh" and point to the red and blue box with the white writing with "Sugar Smacks" on it. Yet he can't read. The child doesn't have the slightest idea what it says on the box, but he knows by the association of those sound sequences with that matched visual experience in the outside world, what it is that he wants—and he's letting you know in no uncertain terms that those boxes of wheat flakes or granola are not Sugar Smacks.

RD: When my daughter was two and half years old, one of her favorite books was called *Aardvarks Disembark*. It was a variation on the story of Noah's ark in which, as he is emptying the ark, Noah calls out all of the names of all the common animals that he knows in order to get them to leave the ark. When he is done, there are still many animals left on the ark. So he just tells all the rest of them to leave, and the book is about the names of those animals. My daughter knew the names of all of those animals just by looking at the pictures. She knew the 'servals' and the 'jaguarundis', the 'numbats' and the 'onagers', the 'hyrax' and 'pangolins'. There were over a hundred and thirty animals and she knew all of their names. All you had to do was point to one of them and she could tell you its name. I am not exaggerating. Even two years later she could still remember a surprising number of them. I couldn't have done it.

It was incredible. With other books that I had read to her before, I would sometimes try to take a short cut and summarize a page or skip over words. But she would remind me of the words that were supposed to go on the page.

Our point is that there was a time when we were all children and we didn't know what words meant. In order to acquire language, we had to use our consciousness to make the associations that would give meaning to our native language. By the time you are an adult, those processes have become to a large extent unconscious. Most of us have no real idea about how we know how to put the nouns and verbs in the right order and how we decide to choose this word as opposed to that word— and with language it's very easy to make a mistake. "Mistake a make to easy very is it language with."

TE: Sometimes always but I keep moving.

RD: Yet, for the most part, we speak our native language effortlessly and error free. So our ability to use language is quite remarkable and, to a large extent, quite mysterious. For instance, people will consistently say things like, "Well, I don't quite see what you're saying, but if we could focus on it a little bit more perhaps you could begin to see it from my perspective." People use that kind of language all the time, but they're not consciously thinking, "Oh, I'm making a visual image in my mind so I'd better use visual language." Our meaning-making processes, like the rest of our strategies are to a large extent unconscious. In fact, many of the things that have the most impact upon communication are to a large extent the things that are not in our consciousness.

Anybody that's ever been to a foreign country knows that you pick up more of the language in a week than you do in years of trying to learn it in school because you get direct experience. In other words, people will give you feedback, they respond right away and you're not learning to translate. There's less opportunity for you to translate it back into your native language, which is just substituting one set of words for another set of words. Instead, you are attaching words to the experiences that they refer to and the culture from which they emerged.

I know a man that had to move to Latin America for a few years for business. He brought his family with him, but he was worried because they didn't know Spanish. The first day after they arrived, the man was out meeting with some associates and there was a bunch of kids out playing soccer. His son went over to play with them. After a while the man looked over and saw his son playing with the other boys, shouting, "Arriba, arriba," and the other kids passed him the ball. When his son come back after the game, the man said to him, "That was great. I didn't realize that you spoke Spanish. Did you take lessons at home?" The boy said, "Heck, I had no idea what I was saying, but it sure got me the ball fast." The point is that he didn't have to know what the word was in order to know how to use it. Similarly, if you are in a foreign country and you have to go to the bathroom or you want to order something from a waiter that doesn't speak English, you learn very quickly; because if you say the wrong thing they bring you the wrong food.

TE: Or they send you to the library instead of to the toilet.

RD: You're in a situation where there's an immediate consequence of your words and actions. You get immediate feedback. If you're ordering from a waiter and you say the wrong thing you're going to find out very quickly.

There's no question that feedback is an integral part of learning. In the spelling exercise, for instance, if someone had difficulty spelling a word there were a number of things that you could do immediately to help the person while he or she was still involved in the process. We mentioned some of the difficulties that occur if you don't find out until three days later which ones you got wrong. So if you misspell a word, and you don't find out until two or three days later, you don't know what you did at the time that made it come out wrong. I think the same thing is true in learning a language. Getting immediate feedback is really important because you have to know what it was that you were doing when you were producing that behavior that got a particular result.

Unfortunately, in classrooms, instead of getting experiences, you typically get more words. The meaning of one word is provided as another set of words, and the meaning of each of *those* words is another set of words.

TE: People think, "If you don't understand this word we'd better use more words to explain it," rather than finding some behavior that would be a representation of the word. There is an old story about an American who goes on a safari in Africa. At some point they stop at a bar in a small village. The American asks for a martini, and the waiter, who does not understand English, just stares at him kind of blankly. So the American begins to shout, "I SAID I WANT A MARTINI" as if saying it louder will make the waiter understand it more clearly. Now if he reached over the bar and pulled out the gin, mixed the drink, pointed to it and said, "martini," then the waiter might have been able to make the association.

Richard Bandler used to tell the story of how he had taken Spanish as a required class in public grammar school. One of the things that they had then were what were called 'language labs', where they'd have you sit in front of a peg board and listen to a recording of the language on audio tape. He says that all Spanish words now mean 'pegboard' to him. So, if you start speaking Spanish to him he'll get a vivid image of pegboards.

Modeling Effective Language Learning

RD: We'd like to provide an alternative to this in the form of a basic language learning comprehension strategy, for both written and spoken language. As you know, a key aspect of the Dynamic Learning approach to learning is to find people who are good at what they do and model them. Much of this strategy was drawn from a fellow from Vancouver, Canada that I modeled named Powell Janulus. He could speak 42 different languages; and he was only 38 years old at the time I modeled him. He was a certified court translator for 28 of those languages. Someone brought him to a seminar that I was conducting there to see if I could figure out how he did it.

Believe me, he didn't learn a language the way that I was taught in the California school systems. He had a completely different way of going about it. Which was much more alive and active and involved some very different assumptions and presuppositions about language and language learning.

When I was studying French in High School, they taught us grammar first. This man didn't learn it that way at all. Rather than translate from whatever language he was learning into his native language (which happened to be English), he would attach the words (or sound sequences) in that language to living moving actions, objects, colors, etc. He was going directly between language and experience, just like a child does.

To learn pronunciation, he did not practice trying to repeat words and say them right. Since he had not grown up in that culture, he knew that he did not have the auditory intuitions to know if he was indeed pronouncing a word correctly. Often people think that they are pronouncing a word from another language correctly because it 'sounds right' to them, even though it would sound ridiculous or atrocious to a native speaker. This is because they don't have the neurological templates—developed from years of exposure to a language—that would even allow them to make the discriminations necessary for the appropriate pronunciation of a word in a particular language.

As an example of these differences, even the sounds of animals are represented quite differently in different languages. In my travels, I often acquire books for my children in other languages. I was surprised to discover that, in Scandinavia, the sound of a frog was represented as "quack" and the sound of a duck was written "croak." This is the inverse of how these animal sounds would be represented in English. At first I thought the books had a typographical error until I checked with my friends in Denmark. When I asked them what sound a frog made, they all immediately responded, "quack quack," amazed that anyone could think that it would be any different.

So, instead of trying to listen carefully to the pronunciation of a word and repeat it as he thought he heard it, this man Powell Janulus would watch the native speaker carefully and then put himself into that person's skin, reproducing their facial expressions, movements and gestures. His belief was that, if he could identify well enough with the person kinesthetically, the words would come out sounding right automatically. So, he would just keep going to second position until he got a positive response from the native speaker. Then he would memorize the feeling that went with saying those words.

It was like he wanted to learn to play the instrument before he tried making music. And you don't just play the instrument of your voice through the muscles in your throat. You play it with your stomach, your diaphragm and your heart as well as playing it with your glottis and your tongue.

Once he got the feedback that he had pronounced something correctly, he would also put it into a special notation system in his mind. He had his own special code for pronunciation—based entirely on sound. Whenever he wanted to know how to pronounce something he'd look at how he had mentally written it in his own notation. When he sounded that out, he would be right. This same code worked for all languages.

The location and type of coding for pronunciation was different than what he used for the spelling of the word. It looked different from the spelling for the words, so that he didn't get the two confused. He visualized pronunciation written in one type of language—the phonetic language—and he visualized the spellings in a different kind of language.

Interestingly, even though this was an important part of his strategy, he didn't know that he was doing it at first. But I kept seeing his eyes looking up when he learned a new word. I'd ask what he was picturing. He'd say, "I'm not aware of picturing anything." After a while he became aware of his own mental strategy and was surprised to make a new discovery about his own process.

Since then, I've checked this strategy out with several other multi-lingual people. They also claim to be aware that they write it out for themselves in a kind of phonetic alphabet. These 'alphabets' are not necessarily made up of letters as we know them. They could be color codes, or letters with little lines under them, to make the sounds stretch out a little bit. They could be metaphorical symbols as well. It doesn't have to be letters. It is something that fits with their personal intuitions.

TE: If you know anything about audio engineering you are probably familiar with the kind of notations they use for different kinds of sound frequencies. Visual images like that can be used to reproduce the sound frequencies as opposed to the word.

RD: One of the other things that fascinated me about this man's language ability was how was it possible for him to keep the vocabularies of these different languages separate. Since he knew 42 languages, how did he keep them from getting all mixed-up? If some particular object has at least 42 names, how did he determine which name went with which language? This is where issues relating to internal state and identity became significant. When he would speak a certain language, for instance, he would go into a particular state, and only certain words go with that feeling or sense of identity. One of the first things he would do was to identify with the culture and identity of the language he was speaking. It was another reason why it was really important for him to learn from a native speaker. It was not just in order to hear the words spoken correctly, but so that he could observe the person, and begin to absorb aspects of that person's identity, their state and their way of being.

Incidentally, speaking of modeling, there is a group of people who are consistently able to learn languages rapidly and are almost 100% successful. Out of millions, even billions, there's only a few that are not very successful. Of course the experts in learning languages that I am referring to are children between the ages of two and six. I've watched both of my children acquire language, and what they are able to do is awesome. As every parent knows, one of a child's biggest learning tools is imitation. That is, if children want to learn something, they watch somebody else (like their parents or siblings) do it and pretend they can do it too. In NLP we call this 'mirroring' or taking 'second position' with another person. This provides a lot of powerful and immediate feedback, both conscious and unconscious.

TE: When you are a little kid, between one and five, you get lots of immediate feedback. If you grab the wrong thing or put your hands near the light socket or you're in the refrigerator, you immediately get feedback, because somebody's constantly monitoring your behavior. Somebody's going to respond to it, immediately. When you get older, you get less and less of that in your everyday life. Your best friends won't usually come to you and tell you when you're screwing up. They'll watch you do it and let it go by because they don't want to hurt your feelings.

RD: This brings up the notion of positive versus negative feedback, and what we call in NLP, the 'feedback frame' versus the 'failure frame'. We often give people 'feedback, by telling them what they are doing wrong, what we don't like or what they should not do. Rather than being given a more effective strategy, students are told, "You're not working hard enough."

TE: Or if a student asks, "How can I understand this better," he or she is told, "Go back over your work and find out where you went wrong." Of course, the student is thinking, "Well, if I knew where I went wrong I would have done it the other way." Telling somebody to "Study your mistakes to get better," is a bit like studying schizophrenics to find out how to not think like a schizophrenic.

RD: A failure frame emphasizes what someone has done wrong. A feedback frame emphasizes what to do in order to be effective. Effective feedback gives you something you can go towards. You can't go toward the negation of an experience.

TE: If you're going to prepare dinner for somebody, and you ask, "What do you want for dinner?" and they respond, "Well, I don't want steak," that doesn't tell you what to make yet. So you ask again, "Well what do you want for dinner?" "I don't want chicken."

"What do you want then?" "I don't want spaghetti ." "Well what the heck do you want?" "Well I don't know but I don't want any of those things." "I guess you're not hungry." "No, I want a hamburger. That's what I want." Then the problem has finally been stated in a way that it can be solved.

RD: In the failure frame you find out what went wrong, why it went wrong and whose fault it is. In the feedback frame, you ask "What do I need to do to make it work?" And the way that it didn't work is going to give me information about what I need to do next. So if I have somebody try to visualize a word and they still are unable to spell it, does that mean there's something wrong with them, with me, or with the technique? Or does it mean that there's something else that I need to find and incorporate or to do differently? Our belief is that, if what you're doing isn't working, do something different. Do anything different. Because anything is better than what you're doing now. If you've already proved to yourself that what you're doing isn't working, then you might as well try something else. If what you're doing isn't working then instead of trying it again or feeling bad—do something different. Try something new. It's an opportunity.

TE: The feedback frame is something natural, the failure frame is something learned. In other words, you've got to learn to feel bad when you don't spell a word right. You have to learn to feel bad if you don't do the math problem right. It's not something you're born with. You don't genetically feel bad if you don't get a spelling word or math problem right, it's a learned behavior.

'Second Position' Modeling

RD: One purpose of this next exercise is to emphasize the 'feedback frame'. In the exercise you are going to go to 'second position' with a person who is a native speaker of a language that you are unfamiliar with. The native speaker is going to utter a complete phrase, question or greeting in his or her native tongue. You are going to use your whole body to model that person. For instance, let's say Todd was unfamiliar with French, and I said, "Comment allez vous?" Todd would attempt to step into my shoes, take my place and try to do exactly what I did; gestures and everything. A third person is going to be an observer who makes sure that Todd's tone and gestures match mine. Once he's been able to match it reasonably well, then Todd would make a guess about what he had just said.

TE: Based on the non-verbal experience I get from just saying it—even though I may not know what it means—I would guess what it was that I just said.

RD: You're not going to be trying to figure out what the individual words mean. It will be one complete communication. Children learn many things by phrases initially, rather than by individual words. In fact, if you thought about what words meant individually, many phrases would be quite confusing. To say that it's "raining cats and dogs" would seem strange if you actually made a picture of what each word meant. You learn many things as a whole unit.

   In this exercise then, you are going to recapitulate a whole behavior instead of breaking it down into pieces. Unlike spelling, in which you chunk a word in smaller pieces in order to learn it, we're going to move to 'chunk up' to a whole phrase, question or greeting in order to get the sense of a language.

   Let's do a demonstration. Joelle, you are a native speaker of French, right?

Joelle: Yes.

RD: Is there anybody here who doesn't know French at all? Alright, Patrick and Joelle why don't you come up for a moment. Joelle, I want you to stand here, and Patrick stand over here where people can see you. Joelle, say something to me, or ask me a question in French.

Joelle: Avez-vouz un bon livre de PNL?

RD: Now Patrick, I want you to sort of step into Joelle's shoes for a moment and pretend that you are Joelle saying that. You don't have to say it right, just imitate her like a child might do.

TE: Just try and make the sounds and movements that Joelle did.

Patrick: [Patrick imitates Joelle.]

RD: That's a good start. Let's practice it again. Joelle, ask the same question again.

Joelle: Avez-vouz un bon livre de PNL?

RD: Now, just try to say that being as much like Joelle as you can.

Patrick: [Patrick imitates Joelle.] (Laughter)

RD: Alright. Now, I want you all to notice that, as Patrick was doing this, he got all the non-verbal rather than verbal aspects first. This is the opposite of how speech recognition and comprehension is typically approached. For instance, in order to get computers to understand words, they try to remove all the changes in pitch or volume so that the computer inputs words only. The problem that results from that approach is that the computer cannot hear continuous speech. It can only hear one word at a time. It is as if they have made computers completely into what you would call the "left brain"—which only hears words. It cannot utilize pitch, tempo and all the things that Patrick was pouring out. Thus, the computer cannot listen to you speaking naturally and figure out what you're saying. You have to speak one-word-at-a-time. One of the things they are beginning to realize, is that the reason we have two hemispheres— two parts of the brain— is because one part of the brain listens to all of the aspects of language that Patrick was engaging in. These non-verbal aspects of language are called *'meta messages'*—because they are messages *about* the verbal message being spoken. Meta messages are necessary to tell what *kind* of communication you are being given. Is the speaker angry, asking a question or pausing because he or she is about to say something important? The answers are provided by the meta message that comes from all the non-verbal signals that accompany the words. The message itself may be verbal, but to understand the message you need the accompanying meta messages. Those of you who have struggled to learn a language may have had the experience that when you start speaking to people who are native speakers, they don't understand you even though you are saying all the right words. Often it's because you don't have the appropriate meta messages. On the other hand (or shall I say, on the other hemisphere) if you are able to provide all the non-verbal cues, they can often understand you better, even if you are not speaking their language, because they can figure it out from the context and non-verbal cues.

TE: So remember Patrick, the goal is not to try and figure out exactly what Joelle is saying. What is important is to say it as if you were Joelle, standing like her and making the sounds like she does, in order to get the gist of it.

RD: Let's do it one more time. Then we'll have Patrick guess what it is he thinks he's saying.

Joelle: Avez-vouz un bon livre de PNL?

Patrick: [Patrick imitates Joelle.]

RD: That's getting much better. Now, Patrick do you have any idea what you're doing? Just guess what you would be asking me. For example, would you be asking me to do something for you? To show you something? What is your guess?

Patrick: It's an information question. I don't know what she asked, but I would just guess that it was something like, "Can you give me some more information about what we're doing today?"

RD: OK, so, Joelle, you were actually asking if I had a good book on NLP.

Joelle: Yes.

RD: So Joelle was asking whether I had a good book on NLP and Patrick's sense was that he was asking for some more information about what we're doing today; which is actually pretty close, if you don't focus on the content. Let's try another example. Say something else to me Joelle.

Joelle: Pourriez-vouz ouvrir la porte?

Patrick: [Patrick imitates Joelle.]

RD: All right. One more time.

Joelle: Pourriez-vouz ouvrir la porte?

Patrick: [Patrick imitates Joelle.] (Laughter) I don't mean that in rudeness.

RD: I'm sure no offense was taken. In fact, part of the reason that children learn languages so effectively is because they will do exactly what Patrick is doing, but without feeling embarrassed about it. They don't know any better. They don't think, "Oh, this is disrespectful," or "I'm embarrassed." They just do it. They'll do exactly what you're doing Patrick. That's the way that they learn. They build intuition about the language first, through imitation, before they go and try and actually learn all the bits and pieces. If you don't have the intuition or the dynamics for it, all the rest is just dry and spiritless. So, let's try it again.

Joelle: Pourriez-vouz ouvrir la porte?

Patrick: [Patrick imitates Joelle.]

RD: OK, now it's getting better. This time, Patrick, what kind of thing would you be asking me? Would it be for information, as in her previous question?

Patrick: I'm hearing more of a request of you to do something. Something like would you go to the port, like a harbor, to leave; or a port could be like a glass of wine, "Would you have a glass of wine?"

RD: Actually what she was doing was requesting me to go open the door. In French, "porte" is a door. Notice that the ambiguity you experienced came because you were trying to map over a particular word into what it sounded like in English. But, your interpretation of her 'meta message' was quite accurate. This was a request for action, whereas the previous question was more of a request for information.

By the way, Patrick, how did you feel as you were asking this question?

Patrick: I actually tried to feel French. I tried to take on the feeling of being a Frenchman.

RD: I think that's important because if you feel (and the term 'feel' is quite appropriate) French, all those words get attached to that kind of feeling. And feeling Spanish or Italian, at least in my experience, is quite different than feeling French or feeling German or Japanese.

TE: There are certain words for which there are no translations, not because there isn't any literal or grammatical translation, but because there is no experience that matches the word; there is no feeling. For instance, there are certain Spanish terms that do not translate into English. Even if you could find similar words, it wouldn't translate across. I know that in Hebrew there are some words that just won't translate, at all.

RD: Incidentally, this exercise has some similarities to the Lazenov method of language learning. One of the things they have people do is to take on a different identity during class. So if you're a doctor, you might become a maintenance technician on holiday. If you're a teacher, you might become a receptionist. This helps people to drop some of their typical filters. When you take on a different identity it gives you a sense of freedom to choose new beliefs and behaviors. It is similar to being like a child.

So the point we want to make here is that learning language involves a lot more than just learning the vocabulary.

TE: Take some time now and do this exercise. Find a person who is a native speaker of a language that you do not already know. This person is to speak a phrase, question or greeting, engaging whatever cultural nonverbal communication goes along naturally with that phrase. A second person in the group is to 'step into the native speaker's shoes' and imitate the non-verbal and verbal communication. A third person will be watching to make sure that the imitation is a good match. After the second person has done this type of 'second position modeling' a few times, then he or she gets to guess what it is that he or she has been saying. The native speaker will then tell person number two whether or not he or she was accurate. Accuracy is not to be judged solely on guessing the content of the statement, but also on the 'meta message' of the statement. Give it a try.

Developing Vocabulary

RD: While there is more to language acquisition than vocabulary, learning vocabulary is certainly an important part of learning a language. Even as native speakers of a language we continue to add to our vocabulary as adults. For example, in a way, learning about NLP is a kind of second language acquisition—"anchoring," "accessing cues." What is all that stuff? Neuro-Linguistic? Its a foreign language. So, we'd like to explore some principles and strategies for learning vocabulary, and how we acquire the comprehension of words, that can be applied to both written and spoken language.

It has been said that almost anyone can easily learn languages up to the age of 16, just by exposure them, but that then you lose the ability. Yet this man, Powell Janulus, didn't know any other language besides English until he was 18 or 19. Then the first language he acquired was Pakistani, which is supposedly a difficult one for English speakers. He learned it by living with a Pakistani family in Canada. They had a bunch of friends, so he was constantly exposed to the interactions of these native speakers. Everyone kept telling him how difficult it was going be for him to learn this language. Then, one day, he saw a Pakistani fellow who was supposedly mentally retarded. He looked at this guy who supposedly had all these learning handicaps, and asked if this person could speak Pakistani. He was told, "Why yes, it's his native language." So he thought to himself, "If this person who supposedly is supposedly mentally disabled can learn to speak the language, then I ought to be able to speak the language, because I'm probably no more learning disabled than that guy." That was the belief he started with.

TE: I've worked with quite a few Vietnam veterans. A lot of these guys had little more than a high school education, and certainly they never took any foreign languages. Most of the guys I worked with took metal shop or whatever else they could get away with. But you'd be amazed how many of these guys speak Vietnamese fluently. It isn't because they went over there and saw it as an opportunity to improve their language skills. It was more like, "If I learn Vietnamese, I might get back home to San Francisco." They definitely didn't learn it by translating it to English. As a matter of fact, if you asked them to translate Vietnamese, they wouldn't be able to tell you what it meant in English, but they would demonstrate what it was that the sounds were telling them. It's amazing how quickly you can learn when you need to survive.

With children, I don't think it is the same survival issue, but I think that it is a survival issue. That is they know that they need to be able to figure out this thing with sound in order to be able to have some control over their world.

The point I want to make, though, is that intelligence as measured at school has little or nothing to do with learning a foreign language.

RD: I recently read an article about a brain study that had some interesting implications with respect to language learning. It involved a brain imaging technique called a 'PET scan' in which parts of the brain are shown in different colors according to their degree of activity. It has been traditionally thought that when people are reading they have to look at the word and then transfer the image through the auditory center of the brain. The assumption was that you have to take what you see and translate it into spoken language before you can understand it. This new research showed that this is not necessarily true. Their brain scans showed that people can actually look at words and the information can be transmitted directly to the frontal lobe (or association area) of the brain where they can make meaning out of it without actually saying the word to themselves. Of course, this is something that people who are speed readers have known all along. You don't necessarily have to translate what you see into spoken language. You can get meaning directly from either the sight or sound of the word.

Again, the implication of the examples we have been giving is that the comprehension of a word, either spoken or written, comes from connecting that word to the relevant reference experiences.

TE: For instance, let's say you wanted to teach a child the meaning of the word "fragile". What experience might you provide for the child that would let him or her know what "fragile" meant? What would you have to do to provide that experience for someone so that when they saw or heard the word "fragile" they would understand what it's meaning was? For example, you could drop a wine glass, or an egg.

RD: Or you could show them something flimsy and say the word or point to the word. These would be ways to connect words to reference experiences.

Speaking of reference experience, I'd like to demonstrate some of the principles we've been talking about here. I'd like to show that you can learn to understand a word without having to know what it sounds like. To do that, I'd like Christopher to help us out again.

Christopher, I'm going to put up two words (writes the words "cat" and "transderivational" on the chalk board). This second word is from the 'foreign language' of NLP. Now, which one of these two words is a harder word?

Christopher: The second.

RD: OK, I figured you would say that. Now my question is, is it really? What makes this word harder—because it's got more letters? Because it seems like it should be more complicated to understand? Why is this a harder word? I'd like to demonstrate that this word is as easy to understand as "cat". And I'm not going to tell you what that word sounds like yet, Christopher. What I want to do is to give you an experience of what that second word means. Can you make a visual image of a "cat" in your mind?

Christopher: Yes.

RD: OK. When you see that cat, do you see a particular cat or is it just sort of a general cat?

Christopher: A general cat.

RD: OK. Now, have you ever had a cat?

Christopher: No.

RD: If you were going to have a cat what color would you want it to be?

Christopher: Orange

RD: Have you ever had anything else that was orange?

Christopher: Yes.

RD: What was it?

Christopher: A gold fish.

RD: A gold fish? Did you only have one gold fish or did you have more?

Christopher: Two.

RD: OK Christopher, now in order to answer my questions, you had to do what this word means. That is, I asked you to think of a cat and then to think of other things from your past that had to do with cats and pets and colors. For instance, if I say "gold fish" what do you do in your mind?

Christopher: Start thinking about my gold fish.

RD: Start thinking about the gold fish that you've had? That's what that word means. Not gold fish, but that process of remembering past experiences related to the word. If I say the word "goldfish" and when you start thinking back about your own experiences that you associate with "goldfish" like you were just doing, that's what that word is about.

TE: For instance if I say to everybody in this room right now, including Christopher, if I use the word "trust" or if I say "a warm day when you were outside," each of you are going to find your own warm day. You're looking back through your memories.

RD: So, Christopher, do you know what this word means now—as easily as you know what the word "cat" means?

Christopher: It means looking back through the memories I have about something.

RD: Right. Now, let me ask you now, is that second word still the harder word?

Christopher: Well, not as much. I know what it means.

RD: Now if I wrote this word down somewhere and you saw it would you be able to recognize it?

Christopher: I guess so.

RD: I'm going to write out some different words and see if you can identify that word.
(Writes the following words on the board:)
Transportational
Transmigrational
Transderivational
Transgressional
Which one of those words is the word that you know?

Christopher: The third one.

RD: As you can see, in addition to knowing its meaning, Christopher can now distinguish that word from similar looking words. He doesn't have to sound it out to be able to recognize it and understand it.

OK Christopher. Now what I'm going to do is tell you the name of that word. The name is "transderivational." Can you say that? Transderivational?

Christopher: No, I can't say that.

RD: Try it. Transderivational.

Christopher: Transderivational.

RD: Good. Do you know what that word means?

Christopher: It means looking back.

RD: OK. Do you know what the name of it is?

Christopher: Transderal...transderivational.

TE: There you go—yeah with a "v."

RD: So let me ask you this, Christopher, if I asked you to make a "transderivational" search with the word "bottle," would you understand what I was asking?

Christopher: Um hum.

RD: OK, so you'd know what I was talking about. So what did you do to understand it?

Christopher: I started thinking back about bottles and things; different kinds of bottles.

RD: Now, when we started a few moments ago, Christopher said this was a 'hard' word, but it didn't take very long for him to understand it, if you can provide the experience of it. Christopher has an experience of going through what that word indicates and that has become attached to the letters and the sounds.

TE: It's like the Sugar Smacks on the shelf. Christopher didn't know what it sounded like when we started. We gave him an experience of doing it and then gave it a name, which is the natural sequence in learning.

RD: My guess is that the only thing that is different between "cat" and "transderivational" for you now, Christopher, is that you already know how to spell "cat"—but I know you can learn to spell "transderivational". Am I right?

Christopher: (Smiling) Yeah. I guess so.

RD: Well, show me. Make a picture of it in your mind.

Christopher: (Looks at word and looks up to his left a few times.) OK. TRA-NS—DER-IVA-TION-AL. (Applause)

RD: I'll bet you can even do it backwards.

Christopher: I can try. L-A-N-O-I-T

RD: Take your time.

Christopher: I-V? No A-V.

RD: Right!

Christopher: I-R-E-D—S-N-A-R-T (Applause)

RD: Fantastic Christopher. Now which is the harder word?

Christopher: They both seem pretty easy now.

Objects and Actions

RD: The following exercise is a way to develop basic vocabulary and comprehension that is based on the principles and strategies of language learning that we have been discussing and demonstrating.

1. Find a native or expert speaker of the language you want to learn to use as a model. The same strategy will work for a foreign language as well as English.

2. Have the model make a list of six specific objects *(e.g. door, chair, book, wall, etc.)* and six actions or activities *(e.g. run, jump, touch, hold, etc.)* that are in the immediate environment or are easy to act out.

[Note: Include articles, etc., if they are a necessary part of the name.]

3. Have the model show and pronounce the word and then either draw or point to it (if it is an object) or act it out (if it is an action). Repeat three times.

4. Have the model say and/or show the name of one object and one action (or vice versa depending on the syntax of the language).

   a. If the word is spoken, the student must pretend that he or she is the model and mimic the pronunciation and expression (including gestures) of the model. (NOTE: This is different than trying to pronounce the word "correctly.")

   b. If the word is shown, the student must copy the characters that make up the word. Initially you may allow the student to look at the characters as she or he is copying it. Later you can require that it be done from memory.

   c. Once the students are familiar with the words you may (1) show the words and require the students to pronounce them; or (2) say the words and require the students to write them.

5. The student must act out the indicated action to or with the indicated object. If the student makes a mistake, the model

presents the words again and demonstrates the appropriate behavior.

6. Once the student has mastered all of the combinations created by pairing single objects with single actions, the model may string together combinations of object-action pairs (adding in articles and conjunctions as needed).

7. To continue building basic vocabulary, repeat the process adding other sets of objects and actions.

TE: To demonstrate this process we need to get a couple of models. Who are native speakers of a language other than English?

RD: OK, we have French, German, and Spanish. That's pretty good. I'd like to ask our three models to each take two pieces of paper. On the first piece of paper write down six words for objects that are in this room.

TE: They need to be objects that are in this room: chairs, floor, walls, ceiling, blackboard, cups, milk, doors, lights, etc. They should also be visible objects —because you are going to need to point to them.

RD: On the second piece of paper write the names of six actions that could be done in this room: such as walking, running, sitting, standing, skipping, crawling, etc. To teach your group the words for the objects, you will show and say the words at the same time you are pointing to the objects they represent. For actions, you show and say the word as you are demonstrating the appropriate action.

Let's demonstrate an example of what this would be like. Joelle, would you be our native speaker? Who would like to learn a little French? Ella and Marsha would you be two group members? Let's just start with a couple of objects and a couple of actions. Joelle, would you write down the names of three of your objects and three of your actions on the flip chart paper?

Now, Joelle, as the native speaker, is going to point to the word, pronounce it, and then point to the object that that word represents. Marsha and Ella, you will repeat the word, modeling Joelle as we were doing in the previous exercise, and also point to the object that that word represents. OK?

Joelle: [Points to the word "tableau" on the flip chart.] Tableau. [Touches the chalk board.]

[Marsha and Ella point to chalk board and repeat "tableau."]

RD: OK, now another object.

Joelle: [Points to the word "porte" on the flip chart.] Porte. [Touches the door]

[Marsha and Ella point to the door and repeat "porte."]

RD: OK, one more object.

Joelle: [Points to the word "chaise" on the flip chart.] Chaise. [Touches the a chair.]

[Marsha and Ella point to the chair and repeat "chaise."]

RD: Just as a check, Joelle, say a word and see if Marsha knows what it is.

Joelle: Tableau.

[Marsha points to the chalk board.]

RD: Alright, good. Now let's do the first action.

Joelle: [Makes a motion with her hand as if she is writing with a pen] Écrire.

[Marsha and Ella make a writing motion and repeat "écrire."]

Joelle: [Begins walking] Marcher.

[Marsha and Ella start walking and repeat "marcher."]

Joelle: [Crawls on hands and knees] Ramper.

[Marsha and Ella start crawling and repeat "ramper."] (Laughter)

RD: Now, Joelle, choose an action and an object and put them together. You can either point to the words or say them out loud, it doesn't matter.

Joelle: Ella, écrire sont le tableau.

RD: Now Ella you repeat what Joelle said and then do what you think Joel

E: Écrire d writes on the chalk

RD: Vio d object for Marsha.

Ella: [P

RD: M and then do what yo

**Marsh ter)

RD: object and an action ing each other to do t got through a numb nd six actions. And even though we're just can add more and can increase your vocabulary very quickly. You might be surprised at how easy it is to learn a language with this kind of exercise. Now, we're starting with relatively concrete things that can be demonstrated. After this, we will shift to more abstract ideas and concepts. However, I think you'll find that once you have a basic vocabulary, learning abstractions is no more difficult than learning objects or actions.

TE: Marsha and Ella, can I ask you both a few questions? What did you do mentally as you were learning the words and putting them together? Were you making any translations to English. Were you saying to yourself, "Oh, 'tableau' means 'blackboard', or 'écrire' means 'write'?

Marsha: I've had a little French, so I had some recognition. But the interesting thing is that I was taught French when I was in kindergarten. And it didn't work then. I realize now that the emphasis was on the translation when I was a child. With Joelle and Ella, I was recalling, and gaining a feeling for the words, but not knowing what they meant in English necessarily.

RD: A 'feeling' for the words.

TE: How about you Ella? You were obviously learning the words at the same time. Were you making translations?

Ella: No. I just related the word to the picture.

TE: Very good. Again, one of the statements that Robert made earlier was to start with the 'feeling' of the language. One of the other states that I might suggest to you is one of 'not knowing'. For instance, not only do kids not make translations, they literally don't know what the connection is between the object and the word until they learn it. In other words, the child doesn't know that object is a 'blackboard'. He doesn't have any word for it in any language. So as you engage in this activity, part of being childlike is to attempt to put yourself in a state such that when somebody points to something, you really don't know what it is—like the Nerk-Nerk state we mentioned earlier. If you can get into that state, you'll have a lot less unlearning to do.

RD: Let me give you an example of this. Everybody fold your arms for a moment. Now, notice which of your arms rests on top of the other? Usually about half the class has their left arms on top and the other half has their right arms on the top. Now reverse it so that the other arm is on the top. For many people that feels very strange. Now this is a metaphor for learning language in a way. We believe that, as we get older, we lose the ability to learn language. But I think it is similar to crossing your arms. It's not like you've lost the ability to cross your arms the other way—it's a function of habit and inertia. In the same way that it feels so funny to cross your arms in a different way, it's going to feel funny to visualize a word instead of sounding it out or have a different name for some object or action. It won't "feel right"—only it's inside your brain that it doesn't feel right. That's what Todd means by "unlearning." You begin to attach a feeling of familiarity to a certain way of thinking or acting.

As you reflect over this exercise, you will probably notice that different strategies are involved in doing the different aspects of the process. Even when you can understand a word, it does not mean that you can automatically pronounce it. They required a different kind of commitment of neurology. To speak a word out loud to somebody else involves more neurology than to simply hear that word. To actually do something based on a set of words involves more neurology than just recognizing that you heard the words before. Part of what we do with Dynamic Learning is to create a context where you can use all of your neurology. The more neurology that you get involved with a learning task, the more it will sink in. The more that you can play with what you are learning in a context where you are free to enjoy yourself, the more your brain is going to want to keep doing it.

Long term learning for language is a function of strategy—certain strategies are going to engage more of your neurology than others. That's what we want you to engage in this exercise with a sense of fun, curiosity, exploration and freedom. There's no such thing as a mistake in this vocabulary game. You can't make a mistake. In fact, it's only a mistake if you try to do it right and that's not even a mistake; that's just habit. Give it a try.

Adverbs and Adjectives

RD: Adjectives and adverbs are on a different level than objects and actions. Objects and actions are concrete and directly observable. What about an adjective? How do you teach somebody what "green" or "round" or "beautiful" means? These things are qualities or properties of many different objects. Similarly how do you teach adverbs, like "faster" or "slower," or prepositions, such as "on" or "below?"

For example, if I were teaching German, and wanted to show the qualities "fast" or "slow," I might start with an action like *gehen* (Robert begins walking). This would be *gehen schnell* (Robert walks quickly). This would be *gehen langsam* (Robert walks slowly). We also had *drehen* (Robert begins to turn around). So this is *drehen schnell* (Robert turns quickly). And this would be *drehen langsam* (Robert turns slowly). This is *hüpfen schnell* (Robert hops up and down quickly). And this would be *hüpfen langsam* (Robert hops slowly). I would show how different actions are modified by the adverbs. For instance, we were also talking about *tanzen* (Robert dances). This would be *tanzen schnell* (Robert dances more quickly). This would be *tanzen langsam* (Robert dances slowly).

Adverbs and adjectives relate to what we call sub-modalities in NLP. They relate more to form and relationships rather than a specific content. Thus, the strategy for teaching them essentially involves emphasizing the relationships between various objects and actions.

Adjectives *(e.g. green, round, tall, etc.)*

1. Show 3 different objects, that the student has already learned, that share the named quality. For instance, if the adjective you are teaching is "green," you would show a "green" pencil, a "green" chair and a "green" ball.

2. Show 2 objects that are exactly the same except in the quality named. (e.g., a "green" pencil and a red pencil.)

3. Use the basic structure applied for 'objects and actions' to present the words to the student.

4. Test comprehension by having the student identify (a) a different object that shares the named quality (e.g., a "green" shirt), and (b) a similar object that differs in the named quality (e.g., a blue pencil).

Adverbs and Prepositions *(e.g. fast, up, left, over, etc.)*

1. Do 3 examples of different actions, that the student has already learned, keeping the named quality the same. For example, if the adverb is "fast," you could walk fast, crawl fast and dance fast.

2. Demonstrate 2 examples of the same action varying only the named quality. (e.g., walk fast and walk slowly).

3.   Present the new words to the student using the procedure applied for 'objects and actions'.

4. Test comprehension by having the student demonstrate (a) a different action that shares the named quality, and (b) the differences in quality by varying that quality in an action as he or she names it.

So, as another example, if I wanted to teach an adjective I might show objects that share that property. For instance, this is a *stuhl* (points to a chair). This is *braun stuhl* (points to a brown chair). This would also be a *braun stuhl* (points to another brown chair), versus this (points to a green chair) which is also a *stuhl*. Now you know that the objects are the same but there is something different about them—their color. This is a *gross braun stuhl* (points to a larger chair) and this is a *klein stuhl* (points to a smaller chair). What am I talking about? Size. Adjectives and adverbs are relational. So I have to show relations, rather than just show objects.

TE: It's a lot easier to teach someone the notion of 'small' and 'big' in relation to each other than it is to teach the idea of 'small' by itself. Big and small are always in comparison to something else.

RD: In NLP terms, language is a 'surface structure'. That is, language is a code that represents 'deeper structures'. Deep structures would be the sensory representations and internal feelings that make up our primary experiences. The English words "short" or "small" are surface structures that represent an experiential deep structure involving a comparison with something "big". They are terms relating to a comparison between objects which can be represented in many different surface structures-i.e., the words for "small" or "big" in other languages. Once such 'deep structures' have been anchored to a particular surface structure, that surface structure becomes a tool that can be used for communication.

For instance, I could now say to Ella, "Ella, *gehen gross stuhl.*" (Ella walks to the larger chair.) Or, what if I were to tell you, "Ella, *hüpfen klein stuhl.*" (Ella hops over to the smaller chair.) In other words, now I have different objects that I am distinguishing with the adjectives. I could also say, "Ella, *drehen langsam braun stuhl.*" (Ella turns in slow circles until she reaches the brown chair.) Now, *"Tanzen schnell klein stuhl."* (Ella dances quickly back to the small chair.) [Applause] So, at this stage in the game, you can begin putting qualities to the objects and actions that you know. You are reinforcing the old vocabulary plus you're getting to do new things with it. And they're relational terms.

So I'd like our native speakers to take a moment to think about which qualities you might add to your objects and actions. It adds diversity to the game and makes it more fun. It's fun to have *tanzen schnell.* (Dances quickly) [Laughter, applause] It is a good idea to pick qualities that are polarities (such as 'fast' vs. 'slow' or 'short' vs. 'tall' or 'upon' vs. 'under', which can be demonstrated easily through comparisons.

TE: You may want to start by first finding several things that have the quality you want to show or demonstrate.

RD: By the way, I think you may find that when your focus is on learning the adverbs and the adjectives, any difficulties that you may have had in trying to remember the names of the objects and actions starts to dissipate. When your attention is no longer on those words, they become presupposed. When you're focusing on the color, then the name of the object becomes more a part of the background. Often it's much easier to learn words when you're not actually focusing on them.

So, take some time now and go back into the same language groups that you were in for the previous exercise, and build on your vocabulary with three adjectives and three adverbs or prepositions.

TE: When you play this part of the game, don't worry about the syntax yet. We will get to that in a later exercise. Just have fun for now.

• • • • • •

After the Exercise

TE: One of the things that you may have noticed about this exercise is that, whether or not you understood what was being said, you had to act and interact. I think that makes it easier to stay engaged and less judgmental.

RD: Often, if you just go with your intuition, you find the understanding is actually in there unconsciously, even if you can't consciously say what each individual word meant.

TE: I don't think children run around wondering if they got the words just right, asking themselves, "Did I miss a word there?" They sort of go with their intuitions and sort it out through feedback.

RD: Another thing you may notice during this exercise is that you start to hear the communications in sentences as opposed to individual words. Even though the sentences don't state the words exactly the same way that you learned them, they actually become easier to understand when used in context with other words. I think this is partially because you have more opportunity for meta messages.

Language is an interactive process. If you're trying to learn an interactive process through a method that is non-interactive, it could be very difficult and take a lot longer. I think in the future of education we're going to be seeing the development of many interactive tools for learning. You'll have interactive classrooms as opposed to passive learning environments. There will be a whole technology of interactive processes.

For example, I am working on a computer program that would teach you language by interacting with the computer. The idea is to record people who speak a particular language but whose voice tones are different. The computer would match up your voice with the recorded voice that sounds like yours and teach you how to speak in that language   For instance, it could tell you if your pronunciation matches the model 75%, 50% or 98%, and could coach you in the pronunciation. The computer would also animate things that you have named or described. So you could tell a little character *"tanzen schnell"* or *"hüpfen klein stuhl,"* and the character would act out what you said. One of the games would be a little obstacle course that you would have to guide the character through, using only words in the language you are attempting to learn.

Obstacle Course

RD: In fact, we'd like you to play a similar game in your language groups. To play the game, the native speakers will provide the group members with basic directional signals; such as 'left', 'right', 'foreward', 'backward', 'fast', 'slow', 'stop', etc. The group members will set up an obstacle course with the chairs or other objects. Then each group member is to choose a partner. One member of the pair is to close his or her eyes or be blindfolded. The other is to be a kind of guide or guardian angel who can only speak in the other language that you've been learning.

As a demonstration, let's say I was going to guide Ellis through this simple obstacle course that I've set up here in German. First, I want to make sure that Ellis knows the basic directions. Ellis, this is *"rechts"* (Robert turns to the right and guides Ellis to turn to his right). This is *"links"* (Robert turns to the left and guides Ellis to turn to his left). This is *"vorwärts"* (Robert and Ellis walk forward). This is *"rückwärts"* (Robert and Ellis walk backward). And this is *"halt"* (Robert and Ellis come to a stop.) You also want to remember that this is *"langsam"* (Robert walks slowly) and this is *"schnell"* (Robert walks quickly).

OK Ellis, now close your eyes. *Gehen langsam vorwärts.* OK. *Links, gehen. Gehen rechts langsam. Gehen rechts. Langsam. Linx. Schneller. Schneller. Gehen schneller. Halt.* [Applause] You can open you eyes now. Thank you.

What you'll find is that when this is the only information you have to go on, you tend to remember it more quickly, because your safety is based on learning those words and being able to respond to those words.

In summary, first build an obstacle course. Number two, review and demonstrate the basic directions in the other language; i.e., 'fast', 'slow', 'stop', 'go', 'forewards', 'backwards', 'left', 'right'. You may want to add some others like 'upwards' or 'over' if you want to be able to go over objects in the middle of the floor. Make sure the explorer is able to demonstrate the actions associated with each directional word. Then the 'guardian angel' is to guide the 'explorer' through the obstacle course. The explorer should be blindfolded or keep his or her eyes closed, so that there is no visual feedback. The explorer should have only the auditory feedback in the other language. I think that you will notice how quickly you incorporate the language, whether you are the guide or the explorer.

It is best to have one obstacle course per group and then send people two at a time through the obstacle course. With each new person that goes through you might want to change it around a little bit after their eyes are closed, so they can't just memorize the course. Go try it out.

Nominalizations, Abstractions and Unspecified Verbs

RD: The next step in our language learning process involves vocabulary related to nominalizations, abstractions and unspecified verbs. These types of words indicate a) classes or compounds of the more simple objects and actions, b) processes involving groups of objects or actions or c) relationships between objects or actions. Nominalizations, for instance, are words like 'communication', 'love' or 'relationship', which are more general and less concrete than words like 'chair', 'chalk board' or 'wheelbarrow'. Nominalizations and abstractions are more about relationships between people and objects. The word *'transderivational'* that Christopher learned earlier is a good example of a word that is more abstract than 'hopping' or 'dancing'. 'Transderivational' involves a mental process that you cannot observe directly and that can be applied to a lot of different objects or actions.

Unspecified Verbs include words like 'help', 'find', 'hurt', 'go', etc. These words stand for very general processes that are not easy to demonstrate in a single action. They often refer to a whole class of actions.

People often consider these types of words more 'difficult' to learn, but as Christopher discovered, it is simply a matter of having an effective strategy and an experience of what the word indicates. In fact, nominalizations, abstractions and unspecified verbs may be treated similarly to adverbs and adjectives.

1. Give at least 3 examples that fall into the category, compound, process or relationship named.

2. Give 2 examples that are similar except that they differ in the type of category, process, compound or relationship.

3. Repeat the modeling process described earlier to present the words.

4. Test comprehension by having the student provide examples that fit and examples that do not fit the category, compound, process or relationship named.

RD: Incidentally, finding personal reference experiences for these types of words can often have a value beyond the comprehension of vocabulary. In NLP, we find that abstract words, like nominalizations and unspecified verbs, can often lead to confusion and problems for people. They can produce a lack of clarity and poor judgments that can create conflicts. For instance, people often argue about abstractions like 'beauty'. Yet, if you actually try to define what beauty is, what you find out is that there isn't really an 'objective' beauty. You realize that it is often related to personal experiences and cultural values. Sometimes beauty is related to an internal state that you attach to your experience of something external—like a beautiful sunset. When you have to search for the deeper shared experiences related to an abstraction or nominalization, I think it helps you better understand your own model of the world. For instance, how would you provide multiple examples of love?

TE: What would have to be there to call an experience 'love'? If you want to teach that kind of a concept, you really need to think about what's the experience you need to provide for people so that they can get that concept. You can't just point to something.

Idioms

RD: Another important aspect of learning a language involves *idioms*—idiomatic phrases that are unique to that language.

TE: If you learn to speak a foreign language in school, native speakers can tell right away; not because you don't look like them, but because you don't know the idioms. For instance, native speakers of English often use more idioms than they do any kind of English formal expressions. If you're an American and you go to England, you'll learn that we don't even speak English over here. We have all these American idioms that British people don't understand at all.

RD: As an example of an idiom, I spent a little time in Greece, and one of the idioms they have there roughly translates into, "Oh, so that's how you're going to take the city, huh?" You say this sarcastically to someone if you think they have an unworkable idea. Now, the 'city' that they are referring to is Troy. So, this is an idiom that's been in their language since the Trojan war. In order to understand that idiom, you need to have some sense of Greek history and culture. Thus, idioms are often fascinating because they carry not only fundamental ways in which the language is used, but they also carry a little bit of the history. They also give you a feel for the sense of humor and the values of a particular culture.

In fact, one of our colleagues, Robert McDonald, has been conducting an informal study of the idioms of various languages and cultures as a means of identifying and understanding cultural differences. In the United States, for instance, there is a saying that "the squeaky wheel gets the grease." The implication is that if you make yourself stand out above the others, you will be able to get your needs met. The Japanese, on the other hand, have an saying that translates as something like, "The nail that stands the highest is hit the hardest." The cultural implications of this phrase are quite different from those of the American idiom. In Germany there is a saying that goes something like, "You only need to work as many hours as are in the day, but the day never ends." This implies another attitude altogether about getting one's needs met.

Even cultures that share the same language (or are 'divided by a common language') such as the United States, New Zealand and Australia will have different idiomatic phrases. For example, in Australia and New Zealand there is an idiom that goes something like, "The poppy that stands the tallest is cut first." This implies more cultural similarity to Japan in some ways than to the United States, even though they are using the English language.

TE: Idioms tend to be more culturally than linguistically related.

RD: So, for this exercise, I'd like to ask the native speakers to pick one or two idioms, or idiomatic phrases, that you may have only heard in your language.

TE: It may be that it is difficult to translate it into English words. The English translation, "So that's how you're going to take the city," doesn't necessarily make much sense without the accompanying cultural context and assumptions.

RD: The job of the native speaker is therefore to create a context in which that idiom will get meaning. The challenge is to illustrate the meaning by creating a situation, or through the meta messages, that will give people the sense for what that idiom means. For example, the sarcastic tone of voice is essential in order to be able to convey the meaning of, "So that's how you're going to take the city."

TE: You need to get a sense for the deep structure behind the idiom and what experience you could provide for the people in your group such that they would begin to understand that idiom. In other words, you first have to decide what that idiom means to you before you can pass it on to somebody else.

RD: Initially, the goal is to convey the overall sense of the idiom. This is probably best done using the 'second position' modeling method that we did for our first language exercise. Then you can translate it or use descriptions or explanations to give people a more precise sense of the idiom if you want to. The basic question is, how could you go about conveying the deep structure first?

Simple Syntax

RD: Syntax essentially relates to the way in which words are typically ordered in a language. Of course, as you get more deeply into syntax and grammar you begin to deal with the complexities of conjugating various verb tenses, and so on, but we believe it is important to begin by building basic intuitions about the language structure.

TE: Robert and I often teach in other countries where people are not fluent in English. There is a strategy that we often find ourselves using unconsciously, which is to speak English, but to put the words in the syntactical order of the native language of the country that we're in. For example, when I'm in Sweden, instead of saying, "I'm going now," I might say, "I'm now going." That makes much more sense to people in Sweden who are trying to speak and understand English. That's how they are used to saying things and thinking it at the level of their own deep structure, so I try to make it easier for them.

RD: The next exercise is a way to help these types of basic intuitions about the syntax of the other language.

1. Introduce syntax initially in 3 part sequences (i.e. subject—predicate—object, or whatever basic order is appropriate for the particular language). Demonstrate the changes in meaning that occur as you change the order.

   (e.g. "The boy runs to the chair." "The chair runs to the boy.")
2. Distinguish between grammatical and semantic errors.

   a. It is grammatically correct to say or write *"The chair ran fast to the door,"* but grammatically incorrect to say or write *"The boy the ran chair to."*

   b. It is semantically incorrect to say or write *"The rock drank the chair,"* although it is grammatically correct.

3. Demonstrate why these are considered errors by comparing correct and incorrect sequences and have the student try to act them out.

4. Test this by having the student say (or write) and then act out the correct and incorrect sequences.

For instance, Joelle could start by saying, "Pourriez-vouz ouvrir la porte?" Someone would act it out by opening the door. She could then switch the syntax to something like, "Pourriez-la port ouvrir vouz?" "Ouvrir la porte pourriez-vouz?" or "Pourriez la vouz porte ouvrir?" Trying to act out some of these phrases could become quite comical, but also quite instructive. Even the syntactic variations leading to confusion may help to establish and solidify intuitions about French syntax.

Role Playing

RD: The next step in our dynamic language learning process would be to contextualize our verbal interactions to common situations that the learner might encounter while speaking the other language. This would involve having a native speaker, such as Joelle, pretend she is a waiter or waitress in a restaurant. The learner would sit in a 'booth' at the restaurant and Joelle would show and describe various foods. The learner would then try to order a meal from her.

TE: Is that where you get only wh~~~ ronounce?

RD: Yeah, other the menu.

Another possib give the learner directions to some would try to find that location base

We hope that w ea that there are many dynamic w ne of our basic Dynamic Learning ge has been that the more of your ne easier and more effective it will be t arning exercises have obviously focused m on strategy than on a specific program for learning a language. But we believe that these strategies are at the basis of effective language learning, regardless of the specific lessons or words that you are learning. In our next chapter, we will generalize the principles that we have been exploring for learning languages and apply them to the process of reading.

Chapter 8

Reading

Overview of Chapter 8

- **Reading Comprehension**
- **Speed Reading Strategies**
- **Reading and the T.O.T.E.**
- **Accelerated Reading**

  Calibrating Your Natural Reading Speed

  Expanding Your Vision to See Word Clusters

  Choosing and Appropriate Eye Scanning Pattern

  Reducing Sub-Vocalization and Internal Pronunciation

  Developing a Visual Comprehension Strategy

  Going Through a Preorganization Strategy

  Finding Your Optimal Physiological State for Reading

  Recalibrating Your New Natural Reading Speed

Reading

RD: Let's extrapolate from general language learning and apply what we have learned to reading. In our language learning exercises, you were actually learning to read as well as learning to speak and verbally comprehend other languages. One of the nice things about Dynamic Learning is that you don't have to learn through just one modality at a time. Your brain is fast enough to make numerous associations at one time. In fact, our belief is that if you don't give your brain lots of things to associate together, it will make its own associations—and they may not be the kinds of associations you want. So the more that you give your brain to engage and participate in, the better. There is no reason that people can't learn to speak and read at the same time. With today's technology it is possible to be speaking and showing words simultaneously.

TE: If you've done any transcribing you probably have a sense for what Robert is talking about. I did a lot of transcribing for awhile; listening to audio tapes and typing out what I was hearing onto the computer. An interesting phenomena happened as a result of that. When people would talk, I'd listen to them and see their words upon a screen at the same time. It was an automatic unconscious association between the spoken word and the written word. You should try it. You don't have to consciously do anything. Just take the words that someone was speaking and allow them to become a visual image of written words passing by in your head. It's really neat.

Reading Comprehension

RD: Like all forms of language comprehension, reading is a result of having symbols that trigger reference experiences. Reading is another form of linking surface structure to deep structure. The same principles apply. The more rich, full and pleasant associations I am able to draw up, the more I'm going to read and the better retention and comprehension I'm going to have. What comes as a surprise to many people, however, is that reading does not necessarily require sub-vocalization for comprehension. In other words, when you come up to a stop sign, you don't have to take the time to sound out "sss-t-o-p" to know what to do.

TE: Sound it out, put your foot down...and get out your insurance forms.

RD: Instead, you have immediate associations so that it is not necessary to hear the word in your head in order to know what to do.

Sue: When I'm reading a book or something, though, I don't understand what a word means until I read it out loud and then I can understand it.

TE: Do you actually read it out loud out or are you saying the words quietly in your head?

Sue: Well I try to say them to myself first, and if I still don't understand—especially in stressful situations—I'll say the words out loud. For example, when I passed my driver's test and I had to answer all those questions, it took me a long time. That was two years ago. I really couldn't understand what it meant so I had to read it out loud and then I would understand it.

RD: I'm sure there are many other people who share your experience. There are some people that are able to read quickly and easily while others experience difficulty. We have found that the people that can read quickly and effectively are those that don't need to verbalize a word in order to know what the meaning is. One of the problems that we've observed with people who have difficulty reading is that they confuse the sound of a word for its meaning. Even though they can see all the words on the page, they believe that if they don't say the words, they won't understand them.

The reason that many people use a primarily auditory strategy for reading is because they learn spoken language first. As Todd mentioned earlier, you can point to something, like a cereal box, and say its name at the same time; so that the child is able to associate the visual image of it, or the experience of it, with that unique set of sounds. It is often not until a child is two or three years old that he or she is consistently exposed to the written representation of language as a form of communication. But this does not mean that written language necessarily requires a transformation to spoken language for comprehension.

As we explored in the previous section, it's just as easy to get the meaning from the visual representation of a word as it is from it's auditory form. Written words can be directly connected to experiences in the same way that spoken words can be. It is not necessary to associate written words only with their spoken counterparts. Yet, until people learn to recognize the written expressions of words, it is often easier for them to get the meanings of those written words from their spoken form. That is why they feel the need to say the words. Because most people will have learned the vocabulary of their native language auditorily, the spoken forms of words are more familiar.

After you learn to read, however, there are many words that you may become exposed to in their written form first. It isn't necessary to sound those words out to know what their meaning is—especially if you've never even heard them before. In fact, translating written words into spoken words is redundant in many respects. If you can already see the word, why should you have to say it? Again, I think that one reason people do it is because at one point they learned that when they didn't recognize the word visually, they could probably still recognize it auditorily. The other reason is that, because people learn the auditory representation of the word first, they often have more deep and rich associations attached to the verbal form of the word. These associations may be be further strengthened and enriched by adding non-verbal qualities, such as voice tone and emphasis. Thus, people (and especially auditorily oriented people) may have fuller pathways of association with the spoken form of the word than with its visual form.

People who are taught a second language the way that I was, often have the opposite problem. When I was learning French in high school, it was all done from a book. My teacher was not a native speaker and had only been to France once for a couple of weeks. As a result, I can read French pretty well, but if someone speaks it to me it's more difficult to comprehend. I can understand them better if they write it out. It's a funny paradox of our educational system. Students in the United States will often have a more difficult time with written English than spoken English—

but have an easier time with a foreign language that's written rather than spoken.

TE: When I was first learning to read in grade school, the teacher would read out loud and we'd all read out loud with the teacher, or one of us would read out loud and then the teacher would correct his or her pronunciation. Then, at a certain point, the teacher would say, "OK, now everybody read to yourselves." And if you listened around the classroom, what you heard was "buzzmuz... ." There were a lot of kids reading aloud to themselves.

The funny thing is that we have found quite a few people who still have the strategy of unconsciously reading words to themselves in their third grade voice, because that was the voice that they used when they first learned to read. As a result, they can't read any faster than that third grader.

RD: In fact anyone that has had to read something quickly but has the strategy of sounding out words ingrained as their primary reading process, knows that it slows you way down. It's much— slower - to - say - each - word - at - a - time than it is to look at a whole paragraph and know what the meaning is.

One of the reasons that kids can learn computer languages so fast is because people don't teach them to pronounce computer instructions. They just see them. I know a successful computer game programmer who supposedly had a learning disability and couldn't spell; but this guy could look over computer code that was rapidly scrolling by on his computer monitor and immediately find the errors. This was a person who couldn't detect spelling errors but could recognize programming errors instantly because he didn't have the same strategy and presuppositions about computer language that he did about human language. He didn't try to sound computer language out as it went by, but he did try to sound out the English language.

People with the sounding out strategy will become stuck because, for them, "reading" means saying all the words to themselves. Their belief is that 'reading' necessarily involves transforming the written word into the spoken word in order to get the meaning— in other words, the written word 'means' the spoken word and you can only get the deeper meaning from the sound.

I once worked with a little girl who was having difficulties reading. As we were working, she was trying to read a particular book and kept getting stuck on the word "fragile". Every time she'd come to that word she'd go "fray-jile," "fraggle," "fray-gily," "fragilly" and so on. She was unbelievably creative about how many different ways she could pronounce those letters. Finally I said to her, "Look, don't tell me what that word sounds like, just tell me what it means." And she said, "Oh, well I think it means fragile." (Laughter)

The point is that it was not necessary for her to force the word into sounds in order to understand it. Obviously, this little girl did not have to know how to translate the written letters into the correct sounds in order to know what the word meant. She could mispronounce it and still get the meaning. In fact, sometimes sounding out gets in the way. She was struggling between two reading strategies— a sounding out strategy and a visual recognition strategy.

She had been taught that the meaning of language was in the sound of the words. Yet, the meaning of the word "fragile" is not the way it is pronounced. The sound "fragile" is the name— the *verbal correlate* —for this particular set of symbols. The meaning of the word has to do with deeper structures related to the feelings, pictures or noises that you have that are associated with that word. As Gregory Bateson used to say, "The name is not the thing named."

In fact, Bateson cited some research that has interesting implications for reading. They found that leaving out letters often makes them easier to read for people who have reading problems. For example, Sue, what is this word? (Robert writes "h_p_y.") Just guess what word that is.

Sue: Happy.

RD: That's correct. How about this one? (Robert writes "te_ch_r.")

Sue: Teacher?

RD: That's right. And you didn't have to sound them out to know what they were. In fact, I found that for this girl that had trouble with "fragile," if I took her book and crossed out certain letters so that she couldn't sound them out, she didn't get hung up on their pronunciation. She'd just look at the words and guess them through visual recognition, and end up reading a lot faster and more effectively. She wouldn't get hung up trying to figure out whether the "g" was supposed to sound like "juh" or "guh" because she was trying to recognize the whole word rather than focus on individual sounds.

People who read quickly do not sub-vocalize the words they are reading. Speed readers do not have to say every word to themselves in order to understand. They can look at a word and automatically get meaning. You may have encountered this yourself, even those of you that are staunch sub-vocalizers, if you've ever read Russian novels. You know that you don't have to say a character's whole name to know who it is. If the name is "Nicholaievitch" or something like that, instead of sitting there and struggling, you just go "that's N..."

TE: It's the one with "——ski" or "——vitch."

RD: I remember my father talking about how he'd read and enjoyed *The Three Musketeers* as a boy. When he went to college he took a literature course in which the class was discussing *The Three Musketeers* and they kept referring to this guy whose name sounded like "Dartanyan." At first, he didn't know who they were talking about. When the teacher finally wrote the name "D'Artagnan" on the board he realized who it was. He had never heard the name pronounced before then, he had always just known this character as "D'—" something or other. He had seen the word and had a picture of the person, but didn't have any sound to go with that name because it was too difficult for him to pronounce as a child. He'd just skip over the last part of it.

We believe it is important for people to realize that comprehension is different than pronunciation. People can comprehend something without knowing how to pronounce it. People can also pronounce things without any comprehension of what they are saying. You've probably all seen kids who could sound out all the words on a page and still have no idea what it meant when they were done!

TE: If you ask them what was on the page what they'll do is attempt to tell you all the words that were written on the page.

Rather than have their own representation of what happened in the story, they'll try to literally repeat every word on the page. I know people who can tell you what's on a page in a particular book but can't tell you what the book is really about. They can't really tell you what was actually going on, but they can tell you that on page 6 paragraph 4 it says these words. But if you ask, "What happens on page 6," they say, "I don't know but it's got these words on it."

RD: As an illustration of the differences between the two strategies for comprehension, I once overheard two people arguing over something I had said in a class. I had mentioned something about "making new neural connections in your brain." As these two people were discussing my lecture, one of them referred to my comment about "tunneling from one experience to the other." The other person said, "What are you talking about? Robert didn't say anything about 'tunneling'. Weren't you listening?" And they were having a big argument about what I had said. Of course, what the one person did was to make meaning of my comments through visual imagery, and the best visual image that that person could come up with regarding my comment about "making new neural connections" was a tunnel. That's what my words meant for that person. For the other person, the meaning was more closely connected with the actual set of words I had used.

This brings up some important issues about testing comprehension. Which of these people "comprehended" my words better; the person who could remember what I said specifically or the one who made his own personal representation of my meaning?

Speed Reading Strategies

RD: Clearly, "reading" involves more than just taking letters and making sounds out of them. I once modeled a fellow who could read somewhere around 10,000 words per minute. In order to read at that speed, the first thing he would do was to put himself in a special physiological state. He'd hold the book for a moment, then put it down, and start to get himself limbered up a little bit. Then he'd pick up the book again, turn it around in his hands and start feeling how big it was. One of the limitations of how fast he could read was how fast he could turn the pages. So he'd get a feel for the book as he looked at it. As he was doing that he'd start asking himself questions like, "What's the book about?" "What do I already know about this subject?" "What do I want to know about this subject?" "What do I want to get out of reading this book?"

He would consider these things first because once he began reading he wouldn't have time to think about them. After going over these questions he'd put the book down again and then he'd really get ready. You could see his breathing change and muscle tension shift. He looked like an athlete getting ready to run a 100 meter race. Finally, when he was ready, he'd practically leap on book, grab it, sit down, open it up, and start turning pages as fast as he could. (Just put yourself in that state and try to read slowly.)

He claimed that, when he really got going, he wouldn't be aware of any of the words on the pages, he'd only see a picture. The picture might get more complicated, or get larger, or it might follow a sequence like a story board. For instance, if he was reading a description of a particular character, he'd start seeing a face. As he would progress through the description, the face would take on more and more shape. Then maybe the person would acquire motion. It was all very visual. He didn't have time to say the words to himself at that rate; you can't say words that fast.

In fact as I watched his eyes I could see that his eye scanning pattern didn't go across the page from left right. It went zig-zag across the page from the upper right to the lower left, totally breaking the typical eye tracking pattern people use while reading. Thus in order to read anything, he'd have to see the paragraphs as a whole. A lot of people believe that you can only see one word at a time. But our visual sense is able to discriminate many things simultaneously. For instance, you can look at a crowd of people and see several faces at once.

Furthermore, your unconscious mind, whether you know it or not, does a lot more processing than you might think. There is an interesting story about Milton Erickson, the psychiatrist and hypnotherapist that was one of the individuals initially modeled during the foundation of NLP. When Erickson was in medical school, he had to take a class on statistics in order to qualify for his degree. He didn't know anything about statistics and wasn't particularly interested in having to take the time away from his other studies in order to take a statistics class. So he decided to try to "challenge" the course, by not attending the class and just going in to take the final exam. He didn't study statistics at all for the entire term, but during the week before the test was to be taken, he'd go through the book each night and look at every page. Then he'd put it away. Every night he'd just turn through all the pages of the text book and look at it. He did this once each night for seven nights. When the examination day arrived, he went in and took the test without thinking about what he was doing, and passed it.

The implication of this is that there are many things that we know, but that we are not aware that we know. For instance, none of us really knows how we put words together to make a sentence while we are speaking. Even linguists who have studied language for years can't describe all the rules or show how native speakers of a language put words together when they are forming a sentence. There are a lot of things that we know and do unconsciously that are pretty remarkable. I think that a very important part of reading quickly is realizing just how much we know and do unconsciously—such as seeing more than one word at a time.

In fact, there are certain details that you will actually see better if you don't look right at something. For example, it is easier to see the movement of someone's chest while they are breathing if you use peripheral rather than fovial vision. There are relationships between things that you can't see if you focus on one particular thing.

Kate: I would like to know where the majority of the details lies. Sure, I can see your breathing patterns while I am looking at someone else, but there are other things that I didn't see about you which may be more important.

TE: To know whether something is important or not you need to first answer the question, "Why am I reading this material to begin with?" "What's the purpose?" For instance, when I buy new software or a new computer, I open the manuals, just flip through them quickly and go directly to the computer. If I get stuck someplace, I will know where the detail is in the manual that I will need to look at. I don't want to initially focus on details that I am not going to need.

RD: That is why the speed reader I modeled asked all those questions to begin with.

TE: It helped him to sort for the details that were the most relevant. It's not like he just opened the book and started going, "What is the first word, what is the next word, etc." Purpose directs activity. If you have no purpose in reading a book, then whatever you get from reading that book is going to be relatively random.

RD: Remember what we said about the T.O.T.E. An effective strategy involves having a fixed goal and variable ways to get to that goal. Reading is the exact same thing.

TE: The relevance of various details depends on what your fixed goal is. 'Reading' is not a goal, it is part of the activity. Reading is an 'operation' that you do. The question is, "What are you reading for?"

RD: Let me give you an analogy. In a movie or television show, the movie camera doesn't focus on every detail of every person that is involved in a particular scene. In fact, in order to try and get across the feeling or message that the movie is attempting to convey, the filmmakers might want to deemphasize certain details. They might want to make some things a big picture where you're seeing a whole bunch of things happening and suddenly you zoom in on one piece. I read the same way that a filmmaker would make a movie.

For example, a number of years ago my mother had a reoccurrence of breast cancer. I wanted to find out all I could about cancer in order to be able to help her, so I got a lot of books on the subject. I would scan quickly through some parts of the books, and at certain places I'd stop and focus on certain details that I really needed to know. There was a lot of stuff in those books that I didn't need to know.

Kate: But, how do you know that there weren't a whole lot of other important details that you missed?

RD: I suppose the fact that she is still alive today is an indication that I must not have missed any really important details. Ultimately, however, I don't know; but I couldn't guarantee that I wouldn't miss important details even if I read every single word out loud. This is where it is necessary to trust your 'unconscious mind'. Did you ever read a book or see a movie and realize later on that you had actually got a lot more out of it than you initially realized? Perhaps somebody asked you a question about it and you were able to answer in much more detail than you expected. How does that happen? The information must be in there somewhere. "Importance" often has to do with how information is related to other information and reference experiences.

TE: By the way, I want you all to realize that we're talking more about beliefs at this moment than strategies. Kate's concern is a reflection of her beliefs about reading. She's asking if it is truly 'possible' to read that quickly and not miss important things.

RD: People's reading strategies are based on their beliefs about what their brain can do and how the mind works. If Kate believes that it is not possible for her to get all the important details if she reads more quickly, then she is not likely to pursue or develop strategies for reading that are different from the one she is already using. If Kate believes that every detail is likely to be important and that you can't know the details unless you subvocalize each word, then she will likely experience a lot of resistance to changing to a more visually oriented strategy.

I have a somewhat different set of beliefs about reading. I start with the belief that I can read quickly and still get the majority of the details. In fact, I remember a few times when I used to take reading tests in grammar school and high school, I'd look at the title of the section or article and then turn to the end and take the test without actually reading the material. I could often get at least 70% comprehension based upon what I already knew in general about the subject, and because I knew how to take multiple choice tests. Multiple choice tests often follow certain kinds of rules, and if you know those rules, you don't even have to study the material. You can figure out the answers from the way the test is structured.

When I read a book more slowly, it's not because I have a harder time transforming the little black marks on the page into sounds. Rather, it is because I'm connecting the concepts or experiences being represented to a whole bunch of other things. Let's say I'm working with a particular child who has a special learning disability. If I am reading something that may be relevant to my work with that child, I might stop 'reading' at a certain moment and then start thinking of all the different ways that I might actually use the ideas I have just read to work with that child. But that process of making connections has nothing to do with the mechanics of "reading" anymore. It has to do with my strategy for applying what I am reading. It isn't even really about comprehending particular words or concepts. In this case, my speed is not limited by how many details there are but rather by what I'm doing with those details.

Reading and the T.O.T.E.

RD: This is why it is so important to consider your goal for reading. Is the goal to be able to answer a set of multiple choice questions? Is the goal to be able to help someone solve a particular problem? Is the goal to teach somebody something? Is the goal to answer questions about the material the same way your teacher would answer them? Is the goal to simply get some enjoyment?

Some people might read in order to discover something new. This has to do with finding out something you don't already know. Rather than confirm what you already know, you may want to just look for what's new.

Kate: But until I believe that I know what I've read, I don't think I've read the book.

TE: I have no doubt that you believe that. But it is still a belief. Our question is, "What's your evidence for 'knowing' what you've read?"

RD: That evidence is going to determine as much about your strategy for reading as anything else. For example, do you use the same evidence when you read a history book as you would with a novel? Sometimes I read a book just to get a big picture; to get some general idea of what is happening. Sometimes I'm reading a book in order to put something into action myself. And that's very different than if I'm reading the book in order to please my teacher. When I read jokes in the *Reader's Digest*. I just want to have a different feeling than when I started. I don't even have to remember them. I'm just going for a particular feeling. But if I'm reading with the aim to tell that joke to somebody else, then I've got to commit more of my neurology to it.

TE: If you've just bought a piece of computer equipment or some software and you really want to use it, you will use a different evidence for comprehension than if you are reading a biography. The computer software that I just bought came with four thick instruction manuals. Four big manuals for one little teeny program. But, because I wanted to use that program, I went through those four manuals like I was in hyperspeed. I wanted to be able to use that program right away. My evidence was not whether I could remember all the words and tell somebody else what was in those manuals. Rather, it was whether I could get the program to do what I wanted it to do.

As a matter of fact, the manuals themselves tell you to skim over the places that you think you might already know about and start working the program as soon as possible. They advise you to start trying the program and find out what you don't know. If you've gone quickly through the manual at the beginning then you'll know where to go to get the answers.

RD: In other words, it's an interactive book that says, "You're not going to understand what is being said here until you get the experience that gives these words meaning."

TE: I've been interacting in this way with the particular software I was mentioning for about 2 months now. I still don't know all the details in those manuals. I haven't done everything that's possible to do with it yet. No matter how much or how slowly I read those manuals, I still wouldn't know any more. In the case of these manuals the evidence for "understanding" relates to being able to use what you're reading, not just being able to remember the words.

RD: "Understanding" details in this case has to do with whether or not you have reference experiences that give those words meaning.

TE: For instance, if the manual says, "Pull the 'handle' to the left to so many degrees to cause an arc that does X." My initial response is, "Huh?" To get a sense for the details in that description, I have to put something on the computer screen, try it and see what happens. Then I can go back to the book and understand what they were talking about. After I've tried something, I have a reference experience. Even if I didn't do exactly what the manual was saying, I at least have something to take back to the book and go, "That's what they meant by 'pull the handle'."

Unfortunately, most of the books that you are given to read in school aren't related to things that you can make happen in the world. They are just books full of information—such as the dates of battles and who was there. That is where the creativity in the classroom comes in. If you've been assigned a book to read (or you are assigning one) and you can somehow make that material more real or relevant, there will be a lot more motivation to read.

RD: For example, why do kids that can't read or do math learn to program computers (which requires both reading and math) so quickly?

TE: Because they can make something happen.

RD: The reading and math required to write the program is directly related to a goal that they have. It's interactive.

TE: They get immediate feedback. They can start to operate and if they find themselves stuck someplace, they know where to look in the manual for the details that will help them.

RD: If you have no reference experiences you will not be able to understand; regardless of how many times you've read the book or how slowly or how quickly. The words are just surface structure. Reference experiences are the deep structure. I could read every word in a German book and have no comprehension for any of it if I have no experiential deep structure attached to those words.

We've probably all had the experience of reading a book at some time and then reading it again two years later and having gotten something completely different from this second reading. Comprehension is not just based upon memory of details. Details mean nothing to you if you're not relating them to particular images and experiences that you've had. Let's say I'm going to go to Rome and I read a book about Rome before I travel. After I've been there I can come back and look at the same material that I have previously read and it's 100 times more meaningful to me. It has nothing to do with the detail with which I read it earlier. Rather, it has to do with the richness of the deep structures that I have connected to those words.

I can describe a lot of stuff about 'Neuro-Linguistic Programming' that I'm sure nobody would be able to understand, no matter how much detail I went into, because they wouldn't have the relevant reference experiences for it. Todd and I could talk about all the subtleties of "transderivational morphology" in great detail, but unless you share certain reference experiences, it won't mean much to you.

TE: However, if we give you a couple pieces of information and some reference experiences for what "transderivational morphology" is, then as we begin to talk about it you'd be using your own reference experiences to understand (as we did with Christopher earlier). What happens to people when they go into physics class, or history class, is that they have no past personal reference experiences to relate to the subject. They sit down and try and learn something, but they have nothing to relate it to—no experiences to base their understanding on.

RD: According to the T.O.T.E. model the effectiveness of a strategy is a function of your goal, your evidence, and the various operations you can mobilize to reach the outcome. Having different goals and evidences requires that we have multiple ways of reading. For example, when I used to read assignments for certain teachers, I had to read it in that teacher's voice. If I used my own voice, I'd read it and get a lot out of it, but it would have nothing to do with what the teacher was getting out of it. I'd be connecting an economic text with things that Einstein said about physics or something like that, but the teacher could care less about what it meant to me. So if I wanted to pass a test for that person, I'd read it like that person was telling it to me. It helped me to know what that person would emphasize. Certain details wouldn't be important in that teacher's voice.

This is what we are referring to when we say that there is no one single way to read. The process of "reading" is as different and individual as the personalities of the people who are reading. The strategy that you want to use and the choices that you want to select are related to what your goal and evidences are for reading that particular material.

For instance, I often read magazines backwards. I start at the back cover and I go towards the front of the magazine. If I read something on a particular page that's interesting, it gets me curious about what's going to come before. Then, I'm actually more ready for it than if I looked at the first page and decided I wasn't so interested in this.

TE: Besides all the interesting stuff in magazines is in the back anyway. They only have the first three paragraphs in the opening pages and you always have to go from page 3 to where the article is continued on page 88.

RD: If you read a publication like *The Wall Street Journal* every day, you realize that they have standard ways of presenting material. They do it the same way every time so you know where to look to get the conclusion, where to look to get the basic facts, etc. It saves you a lot of time.

TE: If you read through either the index or the table of contents before you begin reading a book, you'd be amazed at how much you already know about what to expect in that book. That's the nice thing about a table of contents. I can go through the table of contents and I already know the whole outline for the book. I know what to expect when.

RD: Also, remember that we have said that your ability to learn effectively is also a function of the state that you are in. Think about the example of the speed reader that I modeled. If I learn well from a curious excited state and I have a strategy for reading that takes me into a state in which I am tense and anxious, how can I learn?

TE: Your starting state is an important influence on reading and comprehension. Very often when people are going to read something that they think they 'need' to learn, they sit down and go, "OK, got the book, got the writing pad, I'm all ready to take notes. I'm going to have to know this now." And they go into a very uptight state. Their breathing shallows and their head and eyes are fixed down on the book. They go into a state that is not all that conducive to reading and comprehending. But when they take a novel to bed, they think, "Gee, I don't really have to know this." But they end up going into a state in which they are holding the book up higher where it will be easier to form mental pictures while they are reading.

It is interesting that many people easily remember what's in their novels when they lay down and read them, but when they sit down at that desk to read more 'serious' material, they have so much difficulty remembering what they've read. They remember everything in the novel; exactly what color the pendant was, whether there was a face on it, and all this detail. I don't think it's just a function of the subject matter. I think it's a function of the state that they're in when they're reading.

RD: An important part of quick and effective reading is aligning your state, your reading strategy and your beliefs in support of the goals you have for reading the particular material you are studying. Thus, it is important to have at least several different reading strategies to take into account different situations, states and goals.

In NLP we say that one choice is no choice at all. Two choices is a dilemma. You have to have at least three choices before you can really 'choose'. So, this is the context in which we want to have you start thinking about reading. That it's not a single 'thing'. There's not one right way to read anymore than there is one right way to spell; or only one right way to do anything. Because there are different goals and circumstances influencing reading, it is important to have multiple strategies.

What happens with a lot of people is that they don't have more than one choice of reading strategies. They finish reading something and say, "I didn't get it." So they go back through and read it again using the same strategy and say, "I still didn't get it." It's like the example we gave earlier of the American walking into a bar in a foreign country and ordering the martini more and more loudly.

TE: That's even what teachers do sometimes. If their students don't get it the first time the teachers just say it again louder. Or they make them stay after school and write it 50 times.

RD: Whether it is intentional or not, the message is, "Learning is about rigidity rather than flexibility." One of the basic principles of NLP is that if what you're doing isn't working do something different; do anything different. Anything else is going to be a better choice than something that you already know won't work.

Even if it's standing on your head. If you already proved to yourself that it isn't going to work why keep doing the same thing?

Of course, it's not always so easy to change your reading strategy. If the new strategy is too different from what you're already doing, it will seem difficult and uncomfortable. I know people who have gone to some speed reading course, get their speed way up, and then when they actually read, they forget about it. They say, "I could do it, but it was so much effort and so different from what I normally do when I am enjoying reading that it doesn't feel natural." It's like crossing your arms the opposite way than you normally do. If it is unfamiliar, you don't like it even if it is effective.

The Dynamic Learning approach to accelerated reading* is based on what is known as 'pacing and leading' in NLP. This involves starting with the person's natural reading strategy and then gently expanding it incrementally. We start where the person wants to start—where they're going to start naturally—then lead to something new.

---

* Note: The Dynamic Learning accelerated reading strategy is different from *PhotoReading*, a speed reading technique that is also based on NLP principles. Information on PhotoReading can be obtained through the Learning Strategies Corporation of Wayzata, Minnesota.

Accelerated Reading

Calibrating Your Natural Reading Speed

RD: Our Dynamic Learning exercises for accelerated reading involve working with a partner. The first step is to determine your current natural reading speed. To find your beginning reading speed, go through the following steps with your partner:

1. Read a few paragraphs of written material at the speed that seems most natural and comfortable for you. Have your partner look at a watch or clock and note your starting time.

2. When you are finished, signal your partner to check the time. Record the number of seconds it took you to read the material. Count the number of words you have read. (If you need to, you can estimate it by counting the number of words in one line, counting the number of lines and multiplying the lines by the number of words per line.)

3. Determine your reading speed by dividing the number of words you read by the number of seconds it took you to read them and then multiplying by 60: *Reading Speed* = (# of words/# of seconds) X 60.

Another strategy is to read for 30 seconds, figure out how many words you read during that time and then double it. That will give you a sense of how many words per minute you are reading.

The average adult reading speed is about 275 words per minute. In our Dynamic Learning Seminars the majority of people will read comfortably at around 200 to 275 words per minute. A few people are able to get up over 500.

Check your baseline comprehension by having your partner look over what you have read and ask you five questions about the material that you have read. Make a note about the accuracy of your answers. In other words, if I were Todd's reading partner, he would show me what material he had read. I'd read over that material, ask him 5 questions about it and note down how many of those questions he could answer.

Expanding Your Peripheral Vision to See Word Clusters

RD: To begin to accelerate your reading speed it is important to keep in mind that seeing is instantaneous, and that it is possible to recognize words and derive meaning from them without having to pronounce them verbally to yourself. It also helps to remember that the human nervous system is capable of registering much more than is available in conscious awareness.

A first step toward accelerating your reading speed is to expand your peripheral vision. To do this, you fix your eyes on a certain spot and see how many words you can see on either side of that spot, without moving your eyes. For instance, consider the following group of words. Fix your eyes on the 'X' in the middle and notice if you can see the words on either side of it as they become progressively farther apart.

		blue	**X**	ball		
	red		**X**		car	
green			**X**			sea
brown			**X**				horse

I have written a computer programs that does this with randomly combined words, so that you can't look ahead to see what the words would be. Another advantage of the computer program is that it can flash the words fast enough that it is impossible to sound them out. You must rely completely on visual recognition.

Something similar can also be done with flash cards. Words may be written on small cards which can then be held farther and farther apart. For instance, you can have your partner stand facing you at about an arm's length and focus on your nose. You then hold up a card in each of your hands, holding them on either side of your face. You can help your partner develop more peripheral vision by holding the cards progressively farther apart.

To begin to combine the expansion of peripheral vision with 'comprehension', you can write the numbers from one to ten on separate cards. Rather than try to read the names of the two numbers, your partner would simply give you the sum of the two numbers. A variation of this can be done as a game in which you hold up a number of fingers on your left hand, and a number of fingers on your right hand. Your partner is to tell you the sum of the two numbers while keeping his or her eyes focused on your nose.

Let me demonstrate this briefly with Nancy. Nancy, come up and face me, standing at about an arm's length distance from me. Focus your eyes on the tip of my nose. I'm going to hold up a certain number of fingers on each of my hands, and Nancy is going to tell me what the sum of those two numbers is without moving her eyes. (Robert holds up three fingers with his left hand, and two with his right hand.)

Nancy: Five?

RD: Right, OK. Let's try again. This time I'll hold my hands a little farther apart. (Robert holds up one fingers on each hand.)

Nancy: Two.

RD: OK I'm going to move them farther still. (Robert holds up two fingers on each hand.)

Nancy: Three? (Robert moves his hands slightly closer together.) Oh, four.

RD: Correct. Good. The point is that Nancy can see and synthesize the two visual inputs together without having to look at one and then look at the other separately. She can see both of them and come up with an answer. Effective reading involves the same process. You see several different words and you come up with one meaning for the entire cluster. The sum of the two numbers is the synthesis of the quantities they represent. The meaning of a sentence is the synthesis of the experiences the words represent.

Incidentally, you could do another variation of this exercise using colors instead of numbers. For example you can write down the names of colors such as yellow, blue, red, etc., on some cards.

You then hold two of them out and your partner has to tell you what the combination of the two colors is. This is another metaphor for reading.

For instance, I can instruct Nancy to look at my nose once again. (Robert holds out two cards with the words "red" and "yellow" on them.) What is the combination? Just guess.

Nancy: OK, orange.

RD: That's good. Let's try another. Look at my nose. (Robert holds out two cards with the words "blue" and "red" on them.) Just guess.

Nancy: Purple?

RD: Right. The words were red and blue; that would be purple.

As you can see, the goal of this exercise is not to consciously repeat what is on the cards but to come up with the answer which is some combination.

By the way, Nancy was seeing the names of numbers and colors that were several feet apart, that's a lot wider than the words on book page will ever be. So, she was doing quite well. Thank you Nancy. (Applause)

Find a partner and take some time to practice this exercise yourself now.

Choosing an Appropriate Eye Scanning Pattern

RD: In addition to peripheral vision, there are other aspects of physical sight that can influence your ability to read. For instance, your eyes function like natural bifocal lenses in a way. Whether or not you wear glasses, try the following experiment. First remove your glasses if you are wearing them. Hold this book below your eye level and push it away from you out to a point where you can't quite focus on it easily anymore. (If you have very good vision, you may want to have your partner hold the book and step back to the point where the print becomes difficult to see.) Then, keeping the book at the same distance, move it up to a position above your eye level. How many of you that normally need glasses can actually see it better if you hold it up?

According to the NLP notion of 'accessing cues', raising your eyes promotes contact with your visual representational system. Many people have the experience that it is naturally easier to see the print when the book is lifted to eye level or above. They also find that it is naturally easier to 'read' when the book is up a bit higher.

There was an interesting research study done at the University of North Florida in which they divided students into two groups and had them read. One group was instructed to hold their books down below eye level, and the second group was instructed to hold the books above eye level. Both the speed and the comprehension scores of the group that held their books above eye level, improved 25%.

In any event, it is important to notice that there are places you can hold a book that will expand your ability to see the print— it doesn't necessarily have to be above eye level. Find that spot for yourself. If you were to try to expand your peripheral vision to see word clusters, as opposed to single words, where would you hold this book? Locate the position in which you can see the most words easily. Make sure you are able to keep your arms in a comfortable position. You might find that you want to prop your book against the chair or something else so you can sit back if that helps. Spend some time to get a feel for where the point of best vision is for you.

Next, take a moment and have your partner watch your eyes while you read. The goal is to find your current eye scanning pattern. Have your partner watch you read for about 30 seconds. Read the way you normally would. Your partner will help you find your habitual eye scanning pattern. Your partner should observe both your head and your eyes.

When you read, you may move only your eyes, or you may move your head and eyes together. The most common pattern is to move the eyes, or the eyes and head, across the page from left to right, scanning each line on the page. A faster reader, may move his or her eyes in a less linear way, allowing them to drift around a paragraph or scanning it diagonally instead of looking at it line by line. You might not even have any clear set pattern of eye movement while you read. Take some time and get a good sense for your own current scanning pattern.

Next, we're going to apply the principle of 'pacing and leading' to shift your eye scanning pattern a little. If you try to change it too quickly it'll feel too unfamiliar. But if you could take your current scanning pattern and you could shift it slightly, you might be able to read just a little bit faster in a way that still feels natural. For instance, instead of looking at each word or each line, you might want to try looking at several words or several lines at once. Instead of scanning across each line, you may try looking straight down the page. You may want to try scanning straight down the page looking back and forth between two parallel points slightly in from left and right edges of the paragraph. The speed reader that I modeled moved his eyes in a diagonal pattern that went from right to left across the page, in order to prevent any attempt at sounding out.

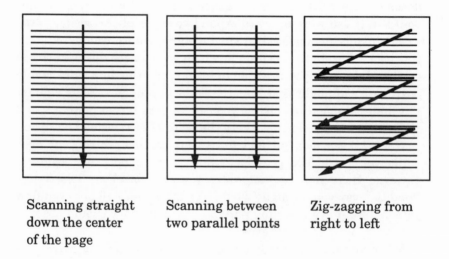

| Scanning straight down the center of the page | Scanning between two parallel points | Zig-zagging from right to left |

Some Possible Eye Scanning Patterns

Try out a few of these other patterns, or some variation of them, and find one that feels comfortable, but is stretching your typical pattern a little bit. For example, Marybeth might be able to see more word clusters than her eye scanning pattern allows her. So she might be able to speed up that pattern because she is actually capable of seeing more word clusters than her pattern of moving her eyes line by line allows her to see.

So, set a new pattern for yourself, based upon the one that you use now, but that is stretching it a little bit. You are pacing what you're doing but now leading it a little bit in terms of taking in larger chunks, or moving a little faster.

You could take your pen, for example, and mark dots on your page at various locations down the sides of the pages of your reading material before you start reading. When you start reading, you look toward those dots. Some people put their hands on the page, and just keep looking from thumb to thumb as they move their hands down the page.

Take a moment and make a strategy for shifting your own eye scanning pattern. In this case, you're giving your eyes instructions of what pattern to follow, as opposed to what words to look for. You are just trying to get your eyes set in a comfortable but more rapid scanning pattern. A little later on you will get a chance to check how this influences your reading speed and comprehension.

Reducing Sub-Vocalization and Internal Pronunciation

RD: Another way to accelerate your reading strategy is to reduce sub-vocalization and internal pronunciation. Now, this doesn't mean that you should never hear words in your head. The amount of participation of your auditory representational system depends upon your goal. If your goal is to find words that rhyme in a sentence, you're going to have to hear them. But if you're just trying to get a general meaning from it, you might not have to actually pronounce every word. You may need to hear or vocalize only selected words. For instance you can look for verbs, adjectives, adverbs and nouns, and can skip over articles, conjunctions, prepositions, etc. You can skip the little words and say or hear only the key words. Try it. Look over sentences and just hear the key words, don't hear all the "of's," "the's", or "it's." Just pass them over.

Another strategy you can try to in order to reduce sub-vocalization is to hold a pen or pencil between your teeth to help reduce reading aloud. For instance, take a pen, hold it in your mouth, look back over the last paragraph and read it keeping the pen in your mouth.

TE: You've got to keep the pen between your teeth. It's not enough to just put it between your lips, you have to get it in your teeth.

RD: Put the pen between your teeth, and read. Can you still understand what you're reading? People who do a lot of sub-vocalizing often find that this speeds up their reading because they are not mouthing all of the words. If you hold a pen between your teeth, you can't move your mouth. Remember that sub-vocalization, in which you actually move your mouth while you're reading, is different than internally hearing your voice saying the words. Sub-vocalization tends to be much slower. Putting the pen in your mouth will only short circuit the sub-vocalization. You might still hear the words in your mind.

Developing a Visual Comprehension Strategy

RD: We have already established the idea that the comprehension of written material is based on the mental map you derive from the text rather than from the actual surface structure of the words. Another important principle that can help you to accelerate your reading is that all written subjects are organized around a central theme. That central theme is the core for understanding the written material. The central theme is supported by the rest of the reading text. For speed in reading written material, visualizing is the most effective method for creating a mental map of the central theme and supporting information because it allows you to quickly grasp and add to the "big picture." In addition to the fact that they do not say the words they are reading, fast readers will make a

picture of what they are reading and then continue to fill in the
details of that picture as they continue reading. So that, rather
than trying to go over and read all the words, or hear all the words,
they'll make an image and whatever they read is related to that
image.

To develop this strategy, practice making your own visual map
of something you've been reading; perhaps even the material in
this book. On a piece of paper draw a picture or a diagram that
represents what you've been reading.

TE: Whatever the subject that you're reading about, draw some
picture that represents that subject to you. It doesn't have to be
anything that anybody else can understand. Just draw some
visual representation of the content of what you're reading.

RD: Again, this picture does not have to be understandable to
others. It only has to represent the information to you. Draw out
some of the key words of what you have read. What would be a
picture relating to key words? If you were reading about two
people, you could draw two stick figures. If you were reading about
the brain, you could draw a picture of the brain.

As an example, let's say I wanted to draw a visual map of my
understanding of this chapter on accelerated reading so far. I
might draw a book and put the words "Accelerated Reading
Strategies" as the core, and put the words "Pacing and Leading" as
the central theme. The rest of the text supports that core theme.
So I might draw a picture of eyes with arrows pointing to the sides
to represent the notion of "Expanding Peripheral Vision" and a zig-
zagging line to indicate "Selecting an Appropriate Eye Scanning
Pattern." I might draw a little stick figure holding a book up above
eye level to illustrate the notion of the influence "Book Position"
and draw a little "X" over the figure's mouth to indicate "Reducing
Sub-Vocalization."

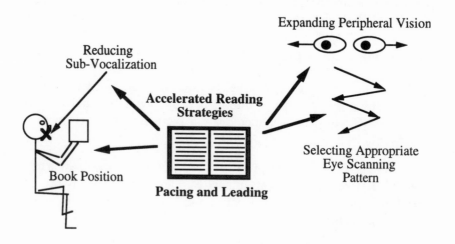

'Visual Map' of Chapter on Accelerated Reading

That is one way I might draw some of the key words that stand out to me from the paragraphs making up this chapter. You might draw your understanding completely differently from the way I did. In fact, give it a try right now. Get a piece of paper and draw a visual map for yourself of what you've read so far in this section on Accelerated Reading Strategies. We'll use this map as we continue with the rest of the chapter.

Going Through a Preorganization Strategy

RD: Another factor influencing reading speed is having some kind of 'preorganization' strategy. This involves reviewing and organizing what you already know regarding the subject you are reading about and setting a goal for what you're going to read next. Making your visual map is a part of this 'preorganization' process. The other part of it involves asking yourself a few simple questions before you begin reading. For instance, as you think about the subject area relating to your reading material, ask yourself the following questions:

1. *What is my goal in reading this material? What do I want to do with what I learn?*

2. *What is something that is interesting and important to me that I can learn more about from reading this material?*

3. *What do I already know about this subject?*

4. *What do I want to learn about the subject? What do I want to look for in the text? (i.e., Who? What? When? Where? Why? How?)*

As you ask yourself these questions, you will want to begin to build an image or movie in your mind's eye that represents and encapsulates what you already know about the subject. You can even begin to draw a visual map like you did in the previous section.

Asking these types of questions helps you to be better prepared and focused while you are reading. This way you can skip over parts that you already know, if you want to, and focus on what you want to learn from what you are reading. Rather than being passive, you will have some idea of what you want to look for in the text as you are reading. Given your goals, it may be more important to you to know 'who' is doing something or 'what' is being done. To accomplish a different goal, you may want to focus on 'how' it's being done, or 'where' it's being done.

This type of preorganization strategy will help you filter for the most relevant information. To get a sense of how this works you can try the following experiment. Pick something that you are reading and, as you are looking at it, just say in your mind over and over to yourself, "Who, who, who, who?" Don't try to actually 'read' anything. Just look at the page and ask, "Who, who, who, who?" in your mind, and look at the page. What most people find is that the names of people tend to immediately jump out at them. It is a way of using your unconscious mind to help you filter. Questions function like magnets. And if you're asking a question like, "How, how, how, who?" that type of information will tend to come into the foreground of your perception.   It also helps to short circuit sub-vocalization, because you are already filling up your auditory channel with something other than the pronunciation of the words.

Finding Your Optimal Physiological State for Reading

RD: We've gone over several important strategies for helping to accelerate your reading speed including, seeing word clusters, setting a new eye scanning pattern, reducing sub-vocalization, creating pictures and preorganizing your work. What integrates all of these various strategies together into a single workable process, however, is the state that you are in while you are reading.   When you are in the appropriate state, all of these different components function spontaneously and naturally without conscious effort or attention on your part.

Thus, given the goal that you have for reading something, you will want to pick a state that matches with that goal and the reading strategy or strategies you will be employing. For instance, if your goal is to enjoy what you are going to read, then you will want to get into an enjoyable state. If your goal is to get as much information as possible cognitively, then remember times when you were able to get cognitive information from reading before and put yourself back into the state you were in at those times. Essentially, you would find a reference experience for the state you want and put your body into the physiology that goes with that state.

The following are some common states utilized by speed readers. Try them out and notice which ones feel most comfortable and effective for you. You might want to shift them or vary them to fit your own style and goals. Think of experiences in which you were:

1. so excited and eager to learn about something that it seemed like you couldn't get enough - a time when it seemed like all of your mental processes were working at top speed.

2. able to be completely relaxed and open to any external information (i.e., watching a movie or a television program).

3. in such a state of heightened awareness that it seemed that the world around you was moving in 'slow motion' (such as a time you avoided an automobile accident).

Put yourself fully back into those experiences and pay attention to the feelings you had and, in particular, your posture, breathing rate and other physical attributes.

TE: What physiology goes along with that state? Would you be sitting? You may be standing and reading. You may be laying on the ground and reading. You may be walking and reading. As you try out these various states, think about your goals for reading. Determine what state best matches that goal, and what physiology goes along with that state.

RD: Incorporating all of the strategies and principles we have covered thus far, try reading utilizing each of the different states described above. Before you begin reading your material, put yourself back into that body posture as completely as you can. Read a page of material as quickly as you can. Have a partner note the time you began and ended, and determine your reading speed. Check your comprehension by having your partner ask you five questions about the material you have just read. Determine which states are optimal for different kinds of reading results (i.e., comfort, speed, comprehension, etc.).

Your goal is to try to stretch, to lead your reading a little bit more. If you want to just really go for it, that's fine too. You can try to go up to a couple thousand words per minutes if you want. Or you can try to just scan your eyes over as much text as you can and trust that you're going to get it.

TE: Before you start to read, remember the distance where you're going to get the optimal peripheral vision. Remember the eye scanning pattern that you chose. Remember the picture that represents what you've read so far. Remember your goals for what you want to read. Then get into the state you want to practice and begin.

RD: After each trial, count up the number of words that you've read and determine your reading speed. (At our Dynamic Learning seminars many people are able to get over 1000 per minute using these various strategies.) Then look back at the picture representing the core theme and see if there's anything new you'd add into that picture. For example, the following figure shows some additions that I might make to my visual map of this chapter.

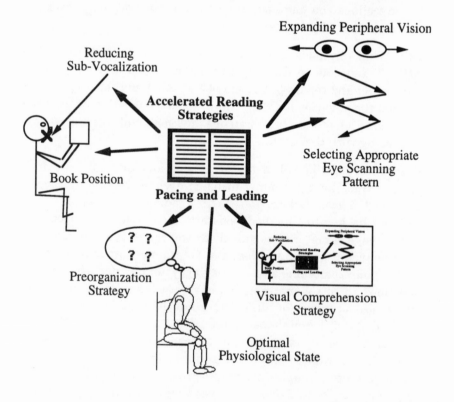

Additions to 'Visual Map' of Chapter on Accelerated Reading

Recalibrating Your New Natural Reading Speed

RD: As we pointed out earlier, the ultimate goal of these exercises is to help you to incrementally improve your natural reading ability—that is, the speed and effectiveness with which you read when you are not trying to do anything 'special' while reading. Check the effects the strategies and principles you have been developing have had on your natural reading speed by going through the following steps with your partner.

1. Find the state that will naturally and easily support what you want to learn and the way you want to learn it. Before you begin reading, put yourself in the physiology that represents that state.

2. Read a few paragraphs of material at a speed that feels natural and comfortable for you. Have your partner keep track of the time so you can determine your reading speed. (You may also choose to read comfortably for 30 seconds.)

3. Test your comprehension by having your partner ask you five questions about the material you just read.

Determine your new natural reading speed and your degree of comprehension. Using the methods we have gone over here, we find that many people are able to double their natural reading speed without any significant loss of comprehension. In fact, many people find that their comprehension as well as their speed actually improves.

Chapter 9

Creative Writing

Overview of Chapter 9

- Connectives
- Preparing to Write
- Determining Your Audience
- Creating Prompts
- Interactive Writing

Creative Writing

RD: "Reading" is about gathering information through written language. "Creative writing" on the other hand, is about expressing yourself through written media. Writing is one of the most basic and important means of communication; yet for many people it represents an area of difficulty and frustration. Many people are able to talk to others easily and effectively, but have a difficult time writing things down on paper. They wonder, "If I can talk about it so easily, why is it so laborious to write about it?"

Writing is a very different kind of process than speaking in many ways. Probably the main difference between writing and speaking is that speaking is such a highly interactive activity. Verbal interactions involve a lot of feedback; not only in terms of spoken responses from others, but also in terms of non-verbal reactions and 'meta messages, such as facial expressions, voice tone shifts, gestures, and so on. When you are writing, however, you are basically interacting with a piece of paper or a computer monitor.

The primary purpose of writing, like speech, is to communicate our experiences to others. Given that both written and spoken language are 'surface structures' whose job is to reflect experiential deep structure, the purpose of communication of any kind is to somehow transfer the deep structure representations that are in one person's mind into the mind of another person. In other words, the purpose of writing is to trigger experiences inside of other people, not just yourself. The key question in written composition thus becomes, "How do you go about arranging these little marks on a piece of paper such that they will trigger a picture, feeling, or set of sounds, that you have experienced, inside the mind of your reader?" The more effectively that you can accomplish this task, the better writer you will be.

Creative Writing is a matter of representing experiences through language and then connecting those experiences together in some kind of a sequential fashion. Just like spelling and reading, writing is a T.O.T.E. Your goal for writing is going to determine the selection of choices that you want to use as a means to accomplish that end. If you compare different writers such as James Joyce, William Shakespeare and Stephen King you can see that there are many different styles which can be used to trigger experiences in other people.

The Dynamic Learning Creative Writing Strategy is a simple but powerful method that will help you to add more choices in order to accomplish your writing goals. This strategy is based upon several fundamental assumptions.

1. People already have the content (experiences) that they need to write effectively. These experiences form the 'deep structure' of creative writing.

2. The process of writing is a matter of transforming or translating that experiential 'deep structure' into verbal 'surface structures' (words and sentences) representing those experiences. It is a matter of representing experiences through language and then connecting those experiences together in some kind of a sequential fashion.

3. Certain words can serve as *"prompts"* to help draw out and connect our representations of our experiences in an orderly way.

4. Engaging the other senses, such as touch and sight, facilitates the creative writing process.

5. Writing is as easy as talking. If you are communicating to someone your ideas flow more easily.

Connectives

RD: The Dynamic Learning Creative Writing Strategy for creative writing and composition (see also Dilts, 1983, 1994) leads a person to elaborate and enrich a beginning sentence into a paragraph by using key words or 'prompts' to draw out related ideas through the process of association. For instance "connectives" are words or phrases that link one idea to another; such as:

because	*therefore*	*after*
while	*whenever*	*so that*
in the same way that	*if*	*although*

We relate ideas together through these 'connective' words.

The crux of the Dynamic Learning Composition Strategy is that key words such as "connective" may be used as prompts to draw out and connect experiences together. That is, a word like "because" may be used to help form connections between different ideas and experiences. Let me demonstrate this briefly with Diane.

Diane, do you like to learn?

Diane: Yes, certainly.

RD: Great. Now, what I'd like to have you do is say the sentence: "I like to learn."

Diane: I like to learn.

RD: OK, next just finish the sentence that I am going to start for you. "I like to learn, *because* ..."

Diane: It's fun to improve.

RD: It's fun to improve, *because*...

Diane: It feels good to be more capable and confident.

RD: OK, it feels good to be more capable and confident, *because*...

Diane: It's exciting to do new things.

RD: It's exciting to do new things, *because*...

Diane: I enjoy having new experiences.

RD: Now I am going to to repeat back what Diane said, but drop out the connective word 'because'. "I like to learn. It's fun to improve. It feels good to be more capable and confident. It's exciting to do new things. I enjoy having new experiences." We have the basis of a paragraph on why Diane likes learning.

Notice how the connective word prompted Diane to take the next step. It's kind of compelling. It gets her to connect her previous thought to new experiences—which is exciting and fun, and means she is learning. The function of a word like "because" is to get you to 'connect' one idea or experience to another. It is kind of like asking the question "Why?" Except instead of posing it as a question, it's doing it through a prompt which is a little easier to answer.

Different types of connective words lead you in different directions. For example, Diane, start with the same sentence. Say, "I like to learn" again.

Diane: I like to learn.

RD: I like to learn *whenever*...

Diane: It's easy.

RD: It's easy *whenever*...

Diane: I'm not distracted by other things.

RD: I'm not distracted by other things, *whenever*...

Diane: I feel good.

RD: I feel good *whenever*...

Diane: I am able to be creative.

RD: OK notice that we started with the same beginning sentence but I used a different prompting word—'whenever'. This took Diane into a completely different direction of thinking than 'because', even though she started with the same idea. If we drop out the prompt word we get, "I like to learn. It's easy. I'm not distracted by other things. I feel good. I am able to be creative." Which is different from, "I like to learn. It's fun to improve. It feels good to be more capable and confident. It's exciting to do new things. I enjoy having new experiences." The different connective words lead to different chains of ideas.

Notice how we can leave out the prompt word itself and begin to get a sequence of sentences that form a paragraph which can be either added to or edited. Of course, you may decide that you want to keep the prompting word in some of the sentences, because it would help them to make sense. But the nice thing about these connective words, is that they are usually not necessary to keep in the sentence. Their purpose is to stimulate your thinking process and direct your thoughts in certain ways.

Let's try another connective. Let's start with "I like to learn" again Diane.

Diane: I like to learn.

RD: I like to learn *after...*

Diane: I get clear about my goals for learning.

RD: I get clear about my goals for learning *after...*

Diane: I get in the right mind set.

RD: I get in the right mind set *after...*

Diane: I know what I want to learn.

RD: I know what I want to learn *after...*

Diane: I am excited about a particular subject.

RD: OK, notice that we started again with the same beginning sentence, but by using a different key word, Diane created a different chain of ideas. Her new paragraph would read, "I like to learn. I get clear about my goals for learning. I get in the right mind set. I know what I want to learn. I am excited about a particular subject."

The connective "because" relates to reasons and justifications. "Whenever" is about contexts. "After" tends to put things together with respect to time. In these three paragraphs, Diane has begun to express the reasons that she likes to learn, the contexts in which she likes to learn and the sequence of things which leads her to enjoy learning.

If you look at different types of writing you will begin to see that they are based on different forms of these connective words. For instance, you might find that journalists tend to write more in the sequential fashion, commenting on observations of events connected by links such as "before" and "after". Editorial writing, on the other hand might be much more about reasons and justifications (ideas linked by connectives like "because"). Scientific writing may emphasize connectives like "whenever" that relate to the contexts surrounding events.

The point is that these certain key words draw out thoughts in a particular manner and get you to think about a particular subject in a certain way. Having access to these connective words is like carrying around a person in your mind who is sort of prompting you to keep going, to ask questions, and to say more. When you can do this, writing can become as easy as talking.

Preparing to Write

RD: We mentioned earlier that, rather than recording something on a piece of paper, the purpose of writing is to communicate your experiences to someone else. As with effective reading, this involves having a central theme. That central theme is the core for understanding the written material. The central theme is supported by the rest of the written text. In Diane's examples, the central theme would be "I like learning." The rest of the text supported that core theme in different ways.

Preparing to write effectively involves establishing a core theme or central idea. Before you start writing you want to identify the core feeling, or picture or idea that will be your central theme. Since this book is about Dynamic Learning you might want to pick "learning" as a central theme for your practice during this section.

The next issue is to determine whether your composition will primarily be about:

1. something you are remembering from the past; or

2. something you are making up.

In other words, if you are going to write about learning, are you going to be primarily looking to the future and writing about what you are going to be doing with the strategies you have learned in this book? Or are you going to look to the past and write about past learning experiences, such as what you have discovered about your own learning strategies? Since we're nearing the end of this book, you may want to start thinking about how your future learning experiences can be enhanced by the material in this book. What is learning going to be like for you in the future?

The next step would be to make a picture in your mind's eye of what you're going to write about. This image might not be very clear at first, and that's alright. You just want to start with some kind of picture of what it is that you're going to be writing about.

TE: Because even if the picture isn't very clear at first, the connective words will help you to fill it out. You'll find that the picture gets more focused and clearer as you write about it.

RD: So, make a picture in your mind's eye of what you want to write about. Look at the experience you want to write about from different points of view and through the eyes of the different people or characters and visualize what they might be seeing. As you do, add in the other representational systems as well:

1. Listen internally for any sounds or noises associated with what you want to write about.

2. Get in touch with any feelings you have regarding what you want to write about. What actions and emotions do you feel? Step inside of different characters and notice how your feelings change.

3. Listen to what words come to mind as you think about the experience. Ask yourself what different characters would say about the experience.

In a sense writing is like dramatizing. I've studied the strategies of a number of professional playwriters and novelists. All of them describe how important it is to put themselves inside of the key characters in their story. In other words, they take on the mind set and the feelings and everything else of the people inside the story. For example, award winning novelist Toni Morrison claims, "I try to enter the mind field of everyone there. Whether they're characters I approve of or not has nothing to do with it." Similarly, Edward Albee (author of *Who's Afraid of Virginia Woolf* and recipient of two Pulitzer Prizes) states:

> "When I sit down to write a play, I know the nature of the characters and their destination. The reality of what I'm doing is far more persuasive to me than what passes for other people as reality. The characters are more three-dimensional than my friends and loved ones. The reality of the environment that I'm writing in is more real than my own house...I must be both the character and at the same

*time be able to observe the character completely objectively
and from the outside of him. If you're only inside of him you
cannot exert artistic control. If you're only outside, you have
all the control, but there's nothing worth saying."*

You've probably all read material where you can tell that the
author was not involved and was only observing from the outside.
You can also tell when the author really knows what the characters think and feel. In these situations, you read the book and
think it is wonderful, but are disappointed with the movie version.
This is partially because it is more difficult for a movie to put you
inside of the characters, so that you feel the characters feelings or
think the character's thoughts. In a movie you are always
watching from the outside.

In our Dynamic Learning seminars we like to do this preparation phase interactively. This can be done by getting into groups
and having each person 'dramatize' their story. Let's say, for
example, that Diane was going to dramatize her story about how
she will be using what she learned from her Dynamic Learning
experience in the future. The first part of her picture that she
might want to clarify is where she will be. Diane, where are you
most likely to be using this information?

Diane: In a classroom.

RD: Next, figure out the key characters in this story about how
you will apply your learnings in the future. There's going to be
you, and there's going to be some other people. Will there be
certain types of other people? Will they all be the same kind of
person, or will there be different ones?

Diane: They'll be very different people.

RD: OK, let's imagine that you are there in the future. I'd like you
to think, "Here I am in this place in the future, applying what I've
learned with this group of people." It's kind of like you're stepping
onto a stage into this experience and ZOOM, you're going to be
there for a moment. Just fantasize what that's going to be like.
Imagine it has all these features you mentioned earlier, fun,
excitement, enjoyment and all those new experiences.

Now, while Diane is putting herself into this experience, her other group members are going to ask, "What are you seeing?" "What are you doing?" "What are you feeling?" "Are the other people saying things to each other?" "Are you saying things to them?" "What words come to your mind that might describe this experience?" "What actions and emotions do you experience?"

Diane, I'd also like you to think of a few key characters and go stand 'in their shoes' and look back at yourself.

TE: Pick some of those other folks in your future environment and experience what it would be like to see, hear, and feel the situation from their position.

RD: Start with one of these individuals. Put yourself in that person's perspective. Your group members will want to ask, "What are you seeing?" "What are you feeling?" "What are you hearing or saying?" "What kind of voice does this character have?" "What kind of actions and movements?" Then, pick another key character and put yourself in that individual's perspective. As this person, what do you see? What do you hear? What do you say to yourself? What do you feel? What do you do?

Now come out and be you again. I'll bet you didn't think writing could be this much fun.

Going through this process helps bring different aspects of your story to life. If you're going to write about something in the future, you want it to be alive inside of you. If you want to write about something that's rich and full and will be engaging to other people, then you want to have your reference experiences be rich, full and engaging as well. This way, when you are going to communicate about that experience, you have a robust foundation of feelings and pictures, and other 'deep structures' to draw upon.

Incidentally, if you really get into the experience, you may find that you reach a point where the story begins to sort of 'write itself'. Some writers talk about how, once their story gets started in this way, all they need to do is periodically check back on it to find out what the characters are doing. Once all the characters have enough life, they just check in occasionally and see what the characters have done since the last time they looked in on them. The author then runs the movie back and writes down what he or she sees in his or her mind's eye. As Edward Albee describes it:

"I have to use a pregnancy analogy. I discover from time to time that I am 'with' play. Somewhere along the line, without my being aware of it, I've gotten creatively 'knocked up', and there's a play growing in the womb of my head. By the time I became aware of a play I've obviously been thinking about it for quite a while because the characters and situation are forming and eventually crowd into my conscious mind...I follow it along, examine it, pop it back into my unconscious, bring it out again and see how it's developing. And I'll discover that it's a little bit further along."

The exercise can be done in groups of four. One group member, the 'author', will create a kind of 'stage' upon which to enact his or her learning situation of the future. That person is then to step into the perspective of himself or herself in the future and experience the situation. The 'author' is then to put himself or herself into any other key characters that might be involved and experience the situation from their point of view. Each of the other three people in the group will be responsible for a particular representational system. One of them be in charge of the visual aspects of the situation. The second will be in charge of the auditory aspects, and the third will be responsible for the kines-thetic elements. The task of the other group members is to be sure that the 'author' is thinking about what he or she would be seeing, hearing, and feeling from the various perspectives relevant to the situation.

Determining Your Audience

RD: It is important to remember that when you're writing, you're writing to someone. This is an important factor to consider in order to write effectively. It not only helps you to filter and select the appropriate language to use, but can also help you to produce ideas more readily. When you are communicating to someone, your ideas often tend to flow more easily and spontaneously. Some people have an easy time writing in their diaries, because they write to themselves, but have trouble trying to write for a 'general' audience. I remember talking to a woman who was taking a college writing course who complained, "I can write voluminous letters to my friends, but I can't write something for class. I don't understand it." But her problem really wasn't such a big mystery. When she was writing to her friends, she was writing to people that she knew. She knew what their reactions were going to be and she knew what to select from an experience that would appeal to that person. She assumed that they liked her and would be accepting of her ideas. But when she wrote for a teacher, she was writing to somebody that she didn't know who was going to judge her work rather than consider it as a personal communication.

The reason that people will be able to write fluently in a certain area and experience a tremendous writing block in another area is often because of what they're hallucinating about the audience who is going to read their work—and the audience's reactions to their writing. It is more difficult to write for someone that you imagine will be critical of your work; especially if you are imagining the criticism to be on the values or identity level instead of the level of capability. If somebody reads something you've written and goes, "This is trash. You're no good!" You experience it differently than if they say, "Well, you could clean up your spelling and grammar a little."

The point is that if you're going to write a book for children, it's a lot different than if you're writing to the Union of Astro Physicists, or a group of motorcycle aficionados. You may be more familiar with one of those groups than the others. The whole purpose of writing, like in any other form of communication, is communicating *to someone*.

Therefore, before you start writing, it is useful to visualize who you want to write for or who might be interested in reading about your topic. Think about what kinds of reactions you would want them to have about your composition. As you begin to put your experience into words, picture how this person might respond to what you are writing. What pictures or images could you paint with your words that would elicit the kinds of reactions you want.

1. Think of what sounds or noises you could write about that might elicit the kinds of reactions you want.

2. What feelings could you describe or put your reader in touch with that would get them to feel the way you want them to feel as they are reading your composition.

3. Think of what kinds of words you would use if you were telling your reader about your experience. What words might you choose to get the reactions you want from your reader?

For instance, it will be different to write about what you've learned from your Dynamic Learning experience to the administrative staff of a school than to a friend. You will select different aspects of what you've learned and present it to the two audiences in different ways.

TE: Remember that your audience is different from the characters in your mental play. Your audience will not be in the play that you constructed in the last exercise, but rather will be watching it through your words. To get your audience's perspective, you have to climb down off the stage, go down the stairs, and walk out into the auditorium. That's where the audience is.

RD: When your audience is reading your story, they're trying to see this whole dramatization—except they can only see it through the words on the paper. The readers can't actually watch the play, they can only look at the paper and try to imagine what's happening in that play.

So, the next step in our Dynamic Writing exercise would be to select who you are going to write to about your Dynamic Learning experiences. To whom would you like to communicate about your experiences? Who is your audience going to be? Then, get back into your group of four, give them a quick description of your intended audience and show them what this person would be like. Then you are going to assign somebody in your group to role play the person who will be your reading audience. Pick a group member that would most be like the person you are writing to and have that person be your audience.

TE: Select the person in your group that you think could best play that role; maybe they look just like, or sound like, or can some way emulate the person that will be your audience.

RD: Help this group member to understand your audience. Make sure he or she can be the skeptical doctor, the interested peer, the supportive boss, the critical part of you, or whoever it is that you are writing to.

TE: As Robert said, the key issue here is that the piece of paper is actually between your audience and the play. In other words, the play on your mental stage is for you. Your audience never gets to watch the play, they only get to read the play or read about the play. Your audience is not going to get to watch the play being performed. They're going to be reading the description of the performance. Keep that in mind as you get into your groups, pick your audience and assign somebody to role play that audience.

Creating Prompts

RD: Now that you have finished your preparation, by reviewing what you're writing about and who you're writing for, it's time to begin the fun part—which is actually getting your ideas organized and written down. I realize that many of you may not consider this to be 'fun' based on your past experiences with writing; but remember, this is Dynamic Learning. The emphasis of composition strategy is on increasing both fluency and creativity in writing. The core of the strategy involves using certain key words which help stimulate and link thinking processes. The 'author' uses the words to help generate sentences and ideas while writing. The key words may be organized in specific sequences in order to draw out particular pathways of associations or may be referred to randomly in order to increase spontaneity.

The following table shows a listing of possible connectives, perspectives and representational system words that can be combined to make prompts for effective writing.

Column A	Column B	Column C	Column D
		Representational System	
Connective	*Perspective*	*and Time Frame*	
because	I	see(s) - saw - will see	that
therefore	We	hear(s) - heard - will hear	like
after	You	feel(s) - felt - will feel	how
while	She	look(s) - looked - will look	as if
whenever	He	sound(s) - sounded - will sound	
so that	They	touch(es) - touched - will touch — *GOALS*	
if	It	show(s) - showed - will show	
although		say(s) - said - will say	
in the same way that		move(s) - moved - will move — *METAPHORS*	

Column A contains a list of Connectives. As we have already mentioned, the purpose of the **Connectives** words is to help us connect our thoughts and experiences together in different ways. Different connectives will tend to lead our thinking in different directions. Words like "while," "if" and "whenever", for instance will lead us to think in terms of contexts and constraints relating to a topic. Words like "before" and "after" will probably lead us to think of the past and future in terms of linear cause and effect relations. A phrase like "so that" would lead us to think in terms of goals and purposes; whereas a phrase like "in the same way that" will prompt us to think in terms of metaphors and analogies.

The purpose of the **Perspective** words in Column B is to help you explore moving into different points of view as you are writing. Right now, reflect back on the experience from your past when you were able to communicate your ideas very effectively. As you think of the experience, remember a number of different parts of the experience starting each memory with the word "**I**." Then, remember some other parts of the past experience, but this time begin each memory with the word "**We**." How does this change the way you are experiencing that past situation? Does it shift your perspective about what was happening? Now review the past experience starting each memory with the word "**You**." Continue this process of remembering your past experience until you have gone through all of the words in Column B. Notice how the different words make you think about the experience from different points of view. These words get you to move to new perspectives and standpoints in your mind.

We can also direct our associations to perceptions involving different sensory representational systems and different time frames by adding some additional prompts after the connective and perspective. For example, adding the words "because I see that" will lead us to focus on our own visual perspective. Adding the words "because he said that" will direct us to another perspective and representational modality.

Column C contains various **Representational System** words. As you look at the words in the column you will notice that they have to do with your senses - seeing, hearing and feeling. One of the core beliefs behind Dynamic Learning is that everything that we remember, imagine or experience in the present is represented in our minds through our senses. When we are writing to communicate our ideas to others our goal is to create these sensory experiences in their minds

through our words. We must *"paint a mental picture"* for them, put them *"in touch"* with a particular feeling or *"give voice"* to a particular idea or character. At other times we must connect certain images together, communicate the feeling behind a set of words or create a mental movie of a particular incident. The success of our writing depends upon how clearly and solidly we can get our readers to access their senses as they are mentally representing our ideas. If our words are too vague our reader may say that our writing is not *"clear"* or does not *"make sense."*

Smell and taste are, of course, important senses as well and should be incorporated into your ideas as you write. We have found, however, that the majority of ideas are represented and communicated through the three senses of *sight, sound and touch.*

The particular sense that you use to represent your experience to a reader can also greatly effect the impact it has on your reader. Describing how something looked will leave a different impression than describing how something felt or sounded. To experience this, go back to the situation we were exploring earlier in which you were able to communicate your ideas effectively. As you remember that scene from the past, read the word **"see."** What do you see in your mind as you remember that experience? Now shift to the word 'hear' and review the same experience. What did you hear in that past experience? Continue reviewing the past situation using the perceptual mode indicated by each word in the column. Notice how each word helps to bring out a different aspect of what occurred in that memory by leading you to perceive the same experience through your different senses. How does that change or enrich your experience of your topic? Did it add some new perceptions about the experience that you had not been aware of before?

Notice that Column C also contains each representational system word phrased in terms of both past and future tense, as well as present tense. Each of the three tenses, ***past-present-future,*** prompts us to use our senses in a different way and will change the focus and impact of our writing.

TE: Go through all of them and determine which one best expresses what you want to convey in your story.

RD: The purpose of the words in Column D is to help you to make a complete sentence without having to use any of the words from the other columns to make your sentence grammatical. In fact, the goal of the **Composition Strategy** prompts is to help you to create your own sentences without having to use any of the words from the columns in your sentence. This will assist you in using the maximum amount of your creativity. For instance, the words, **"that"** or **"like"** will lead you to make a complete sentence when following a prompt.

As an example, to complete the sentence *"I like to write about my experiences* **because I see...**" you might fill in the words **"because I see** *an exciting adventure in my mind's eye."* If I just put down the words *"an exciting adventure in my mind's eye,"* without also adding the words **"I see,"** I have only a sentence fragment that is not grammatical. On the other hand, to complete the sentence *"I like to write about my experiences* **because I see that...**" you might fill in something like **"because I see that** *you will be very interested in my exciting adventure."* Here, the words *"You will be very interested in my exciting adventure,"* make a complete sentence without you having to include any of the words contained in the prompting sentence.

Sometimes the word *"like," "how"* or *"as if"* will fit better with certain representational system words than others. For instance, **"because I sound like..."** fits better than, **"because I sound that..."** As you are writing, feel free to find the word that fits the best for you.

Of course, it is possible to come up with some sentences that are not complete even when you add the word "that" or "like." If, when you read the words you have filled in, you have not made a complete sentence, then you should either reword your answer so that it does make a complete sentence or include the words from Columns B and C with the words that you have filled in.

In the following exercise you will be combining the words from Column A, B, C and D in order to write a composition. Keep in mind that the purpose of these exercises are merely to help you get acquainted with the prompts and how to use them. The real power of the Dynamic Composition Strategy will be most evident when you use it without the formal exercise structure. The exercises are simply to familiarize you with the process of how to use the prompting words.

Interactive Writing

RD: The exercise may be done in either a written form or interactively in groups. To do it interactively, you would return to the group of four you have been working with previously. In your group of four, each 'author' has identified a person to play his or her 'audience'. The remaining two group members are going to assume two other functions necessary for interactive writing; a 'prompter' and a 'recorder'. The 'prompter' is going to prompt the author using connective words, as I demonstrated earlier with Diane. The 'recorder' is going to write down the author's answers to the prompts.

Let's say that Todd, myself, Joelle and Marsha were all members of a group. Joelle will be the 'audience', Marsha is the 'recorder', I'm the 'prompter' and Todd is the 'author'. Todd has created his mental 'play' that he is going to communicate about to Joelle. I am going to prompt Todd to make various descriptions of his play using the various key words in columns A, B, C and D, and Marsha is going to write down Todd's answers. We sometimes like to call this the 'Chinese Menu' method of writing, because you can choose one from column A, one from column B and one from Column C, and so on; or you can just have the appetizer from column A.

TE: You can have them all, but you only get a small amount of each thing. (Laughter) You're always hungry when it's over. Then you'll want to write again because you feel so unsatisfied that it's not finished yet.

RD: To begin the 'meal', Todd needs to come up with a beginning sentence.

TE: I want to write about learning a foreign language.

RD: So Marsha writes down, "I want to write about learning a foreign language." Marsha can either write in Todd's book, or he can give her a piece of paper with his name on it that indicates its his composition. Joelle is going to be Todd's audience. Todd, who is the audience that you want Joelle to role play and what is your goal for writing to that person?

TE: My audience is a government official. And my goal is to convince that person to fund second language education.

RD: OK. Now my job is to pick a cluster of prompting words and add them to the end of Todd's beginning sentence. I just take one from each of the columns. For instance, I might prompt Todd by saying, "I want to write about learning a foreign language *because I see that...*"

TE: It's important for world communication.

RD: As the 'recorder', Marsha would write down, "It's important for world communication."

Now since Todd's core theme is 'learning a foreign language', I would continue to hold his beginning sentence constant and shift the cluster of connective words in order to pull out another element of that theme for his paragraph. I choose another word from each of the columns and prompt Todd by saying, "I want to write about learning a foreign language *because you will hear how...*"

TE: Important it is to learn about other people's cultures.

RD: OK. Now in this case, the 'recorder' has to apply a little editorial license, because it is not grammatical to write, "Important it is to learn about other people's cultures." For the sentence to be grammatical, Marsha will also have to include some of the prompting words. She will need to write, "You will hear how important it is to learn about other people's cultures." She could also just change the first few words around a little and write, "It is important to learn about other people's cultures."

Again, we started with a central theme, 'learning a foreign language', and even though we have used two different types of prompts, the resulting sentences both support the central theme of the paragraph. By using different prompts, but always starting each sentence with the central theme, we can draw out a variety of supporting ideas.

For instance, I could prompt Todd in another direction by saying, "I want to write about learning a foreign language *whenever we will move as if...*"

TE: Whenever we will move as if we really care about each other.

RD: Marsha would now write, "We will move as if we really care about each other".

We would continue this process with Todd either a) an arbitrary number of times (such as four or five repetitions) or b) until it becomes difficult to make any other associations. Then, we can collect together his group of associations and make them into a paragraph by simply leaving out the prompting words and capitalizing the first word of each phrase. At that point, Todd may want to change, rearrange or edit his answers a little bit.

The group would then help Todd make a second paragraph about learning a foreign language. For the second paragraph, Todd can either a) start with a new beginning sentence and we repeat the process using the same prompts or b) use the same beginning sentence as his first paragraph and we use new prompts. When Todd has completed his second paragraph, we repeat the process one more time. So Todd ends up with three paragraphs relating to his core theme. He can then edit or draw from those 3 different paragraphs to make the final version of the story or article or memo etc., that he is going to submit to this government official who he chose as his audience.

What's interesting about the prompts is that they create a direction of thinking that forces you to move through your brain in a different way. Sometimes you have to be quite creative in order to complete the sentence. What is remarkable, however, is that even though you generate all of the sentences independently, when you are done they often hang together as the basis for a reasonable paragraph. For instance, if we take all of Todd's sentences together we get:

"I want to write about learning foreign languages. It's important for world communication. You will hear how important it is to learn about other people's cultures. We will move as if we really care about each other."

It actually makes the beginnings of a pretty interesting paragraph. There are several different perspectives supporting a central theme. Of course you can always go back and edit it later. The purpose of the prompts is to get you started.

TE: The prompts can be used to force people into a perspective that they wouldn't normally use. I especially enjoyed the last set of prompts—"we will move as if." I enjoyed them because they pushed me to think in a really different way in order to complete the sentence. It was a stretch for me, but as long as the theme I had in my mind was constant, I could work around it without getting lost. It was just a matter of finding what I had in the story that fit with the prompts that he just gave me.

RD: As Todd is thinking of his answers he is drawing upon his mental picture of his play in order to fill in this verbal 'vacuum' we've created by the prompt.

TE: As the writer, I found it very useful to look back and forth between my audience, Joelle, and the picture of my story. I was kind of filtering what Robert said through my picture in order to come up with something I thought might make sense to my audience. I didn't search for words first, I looked at the picture and thought, "What makes sense?"

Also, if you're the prompter, it can be helpful to repeat the prompting sentence. This gives the writer's brain a chance to begin sorting through their experience the first time, so that the second time through, the answer can come spontaneously.

RD: Incidentally, if you are working with children, you may want to start with simple prompts first— using only connective words from Column A for example. One basic strategy is to continue to repeat the beginning sentence and shift through all of the connectives in Column A. In that case you might get a sequence that goes something like, I want to write about learning a foreign language *because* it's important for world communication. I want to write about learning a foreign language *therefore* it is important for me to have more effective strategies for learning. I want to write about learning a foreign language *whenever* I feel connected or close to other people.

Again, if you leave out the various connectives you'll have an interesting paragraph that develops a central theme through different pathways of association. "I want to write about learning a foreign language. It is important for world communication. It is important for me to have more effective strategies for learning. I feel connected or close to other people."

Keep in mind that this is intended to be a first draft, as opposed to a final product. The Dynamic Learning Creative Writing Strategy is not designed to teach the proper use of grammar and punctuation but rather to help students organize their thinking so that they can be creative and productive. It assumes that the student has some familiarity with the basic rules of grammar and punctuation. One of the primary objectives of the Dynamic Learning Creative Writing Strategy is to encourage self learning and independent thinking. Its fundamental purpose is to help people write with more ease, creativity and speed. It also facilitates motivation to write because it is success oriented and focuses on immediate results.

TE: I heard somewhere that Jack Kerouac wrote the first draft of his books on a roll of paper rather than single sheets. He bought a roll of paper, stuck one end of it in the typewriter and just started typing. He ended up with a roll of paper on the one side of which was his story. I think he took it to fifteen or twenty publishers, and nobody would publish it. You can imagine what it would be like if some guy came in with a roll of paper and rolled it out on your desk. The spelling was poor, the grammar was atrocious, it wasn't even put into paragraphs, but the story was wonderful. During an interview someone once asked him, "How come you don't check your grammar, spelling, etc., etc." He said, "I just write the story. They pay people to know how to spell and to know how to do grammar, I don't have to do that." That was his attitude, which I don't think was all that healthy. But it shows that creativity need not be held back by correct spelling or grammar or anything else. You can always go back and do that later on.

RD: By the way, you can also use variations of this strategy to help teach subjects like history. After a history lesson, you can have students tell a story about what they read by piecing the information together through selected prompts.

One of my beliefs is that these different clusters of prompts could actually be used to account for and teach the styles of different well known writers. For instance, if you take people like Hemingway, F. Scott Fitzgerald, or James Joyce, you would find that what makes the difference in their styles could be traced to the habitual, though unconscious, use of certain groups of connectives in their thinking strategy. If you look carefully at their writings you can almost tell which connectives, perspectives and representational systems they are unconsciously using as prompts as they're putting their sentences together. I have always thought it would be interesting to have something like a 'Hemingway generator'. To create it, you would go over the sentences in his novels and figure out which clusters of connective words would fit in between each sentence. Once you determined the pattern you could actually prompt people to write paragraphs using the connectives perspectives, representational systems and the time frames that Hemingway used to produce his own writings.

Think about it for a moment. What makes a writing style consistent is that there are certain perspectives, representational systems, and a certain orientation in time that a writer consistently takes to expand upon a particular central theme. Hemingway, for instance, didn't spend that much time in the future. He mostly wrote about the present or the past. He talked about his own feelings quite often, but he didn't describe other people's feelings very much.

Take some time now and try out this strategy for yourself. The following pages will help guide you to create a composition if you are not able to do it interactively or want to try a self directed approach.

Column A	Column B	Column C	Column D
		Representational System	
Connective	*Perspective*	*and Time Frame*	
because	I	see(s) - saw - will see	that
therefore	We	hear(s) - heard - will hear	like
after	You	feel(s) - felt - will feel	how
while	She	look(s) - looked - will look	as if
whenever	He	sound(s) - sounded - will sound	
so that	They	touch(es) - touched - will touch	
if	It	show(s) - showed - will show	
although		say(s) - said - will say	
in the same		move(s) - moved - will move	
way that			

1. Write a beginning sentence for your paragraph in the space below. You can start simply with something like: *"I want to write about...(your topic),"* or *"(Your topic)...is fun,"* or *"You will be interested in...(your topic)."*

_____ .

2. Read the sentence you have written above. Then read (silently) one word from each of the columns listed at the top of the page and mentally fill in the words that come to you most easily to complete the sentence you have started. Write them on the line below. (Do not write down any of the words from the columns.)

_____ .

3. Now read the sentence you have written above and once again silently add four words chosen randomly from columns A, B, C, and D above. Fill in the new sentence you have begun and write it below leaving out the words from the columns.

_____ .

4. Repeat the above process again using different words from each of the columns.

_____.

5. Read the sentences you have written on the line above one after the other.

a. If what you have written does not adequately represent the experience you started with or does not seem like it will get the kind of reaction you want from your intended reader, go back to step #1 and repeat the process again with the same beginning sentence. Experiment with different combinations of words from each of the columns.

b. If you are satisfied with the flow of ideas then you may refine or add to them in order to make them into a paragraph.

c. Write the finished sentences in the spaces provided below to make a complete paragraph.

_____.

_____.

_____.

_____.

_____.

d. Start a new paragraph by writing a new beginning sentence at the top of the next page and follow the strategy from step #1.

<u>Column A</u>	<u>Column B</u>	<u>Column C</u> *Representational System* *and Time Frame*	<u>Column D</u>
Connective	*Perspective*		
because	I	see(s) - saw - will see	that
therefore	We	hear(s) - heard - will hear	like
after	You	feel(s) - felt - will feel	how
while	She	look(s) - looked - will look	as if
whenever	He	sound(s) - sounded - will sound	
so that	They	touch(es) - touched - will touch	
if	It	show(s) - showed - will show	
although		say(s) - said - will say	
in the same way that		move(s) - moved - will move	

1. Write a beginning sentence for your paragraph in the space below. You can start simply with something like: *"I want to write about...(your topic),"* or *"(Your topic)...is fun,"* or *"You will be interested in...(your topic)."*

_____.

2. Read the sentence you have written above. Then read (silently) one word from each of the columns listed at the top of the page and mentally fill in the words that come to you most easily to complete the sentence you have started. Write them on the line below. (Do not write down any of the words from the columns.)

_____.

3. Now read the sentence you have written above and once again silently add four words chosen randomly from columns A, B, C, and D above. Fill in the new sentence you have begun and write it below leaving out the words from the columns.

_____.

4. Repeat the above process again using different words from each of the columns.

_____.

5. Read the sentences you have written on the line above one after the other.

   a. If what you have written does not adequately represent the experience you started with or does not seem like it will get the kind of reaction you want from your intended reader, go back to step #1 and repeat the process again with the same beginning sentence. Experiment with different combinations of words from each of the columns.

   b. If you are satisfied with the flow of ideas then you may refine or add to them in order to make them into a paragraph.

   c. Write the finished sentences in the spaces provided below to make a complete paragraph.

_____.

_____.

_____.

_____.

_____.

   d. Start a new paragraph by writing a new beginning sentence at the top the next page and follow the strategy from step #1.

Column A	Column B	Column C	Column D
		Representational System	
Connective	*Perspective*	*and Time Frame*	
because	I	see(s) - saw - will see	that
therefore	We	hear(s) - heard - will hear	like
after	You	feel(s) - felt - will feel	how
while	She	look(s) - looked - will look	as if
whenever	He	sound(s) - sounded - will sound	
so that	They	touch(es) - touched - will touch	
if	It	show(s) - showed - will show	
although		say(s) - said - will say	
in the same way that		move(s) - moved - will move	

1. Write a beginning sentence for your paragraph in the space below. You can start simply with something like: *"I want to write about...(your topic),"* or *"(Your topic)...is fun,"* or *"You will be interested in...(your topic)."*

   _____.

2. Read the sentence you have written above. Then read (silently) one word from each of the columns listed at the top of the page and mentally fill in the words that come to you most easily to complete the sentence you have started. Write them on the line below. (Do not write down any of the words from the columns.)

   _____.

3. Now read the sentence you have written above and once again silently add four words chosen randomly from columns A, B, C, and D above. Fill in the new sentence you have begun and write it below leaving out the words from the columns.

   _____.

4. Repeat the above process again using different words from each of the columns.

_____.

5. Read the sentences you have written on the line above one after the other.

a. If what you have written does not adequately represent the experience you started with or does not seem like it will get the kind of reaction you want from your intended reader, go back to step #1 and repeat the process again with the same beginning sentence. Experiment with different combinations of words from each of the columns.

b. If you are satisfied with the flow of ideas then you may now refine or add to them to make them into a paragraph.

c. Write the finished sentences in the spaces provided below to make a complete paragraph.

_____.

_____.

_____.

_____.

_____.

6. On the following page, write all three paragraphs that you have composed on the previous pages.

_____.

_____.

_____.

_____.

_____.

_____.

_____.

_____.

_____.

_____.

_____.

_____.

_____.

_____.

As you look over the paragraphs above, adjust, edit or modify them in the way that would be most effective and appealing for the audience you are writing for.

Chapter 10

Dynamic Assessment

Overview of Chapter 10

- The Dynamic Assessment Process
- Dealing with Resistances and Interferences to Learning
- Conclusion

Dynamic Assessment

RD: There are two types of assessment that can be made with respect to learning - those related to the *products* of the learning, and those related to the *processes* of learning. Assessment related to the 'products' of learning is generally done at the end of an activity and serves to filter learners according to standards and competency thresholds. Assessment related to learning 'processes' is done on an ongoing basis throughout the learning activity and serves to provide feedback for teachers and learners with respect to how they might more effectively reach their learning goals.

The purpose of feedback is to provide the information necessary to adapt operations in order to reach the desired goal. When teaching operations are overly standardized and rigid they match the needs and strategies of only a few learners, yielding a 'bell shaped' distribution curve of success in reaching the goal. When procedures are held constant it is hoped that they become optimized to reach the greatest number of average learners and only leave out the extremes — the 'gifted' and 'handicapped' learners — who will experience difficulties.

According to the T.O.T.E. model, when learning goals are held constant, teaching operations must be varied in response to feedback in order to maximize the probability of success in reaching the goal. Operations must be varied to account for different types of learners, learning contexts, etc.

Of course, one of the reasons schools and organizations standardize programs is because it is thought to be easier and less costly to hold operations constant rather than to change them. With the advent of cooperative learning, computers, multi media and other adaptable self-learning tools, however, this assumption has become less and less valid. When learners have feedback they can engage in their own individual processes to improve performance.

This emphasizes the need for effective assessment processes which can provide ongoing relevant feedback. It also emphasizes the need for teachers to change their attitudes about the role and the importance of evidence and evidence procedures in relation to achieving learning goals. Many people still assume that the primary role of assessment is to act as a filter in relation to the 'products' of learning.

A good example of this type of presupposition is illustrated in the book *The One Minute Manager*. The authors give an example about a manager who goes to speak to his child's teacher because the child is having some problems at school. In his discussions with the teacher he points out that as a manager it is important for the company to make sure that all of members of the organization are successful in their tasks. And that he has discovered that if he gives his collaborators clear goals and evidences they perform better. He then offers the suggestion to the teacher that perhaps he should give the children the questions for the final exam at the beginning of the course, so that they would know what was going to be important in the class, what to study for, and how to assess their progress.

The teacher was appalled and flabbergasted, exclaiming, "I can't do that. Then everybody would get an 'A' (the best grade)!"

The implication of the teacher's response is that the problem with the manager's suggestion is that everyone would, in fact, do well. Then it would not be an effective filter. This probably reflects our assumptions about how particular thinking and learning styles and strengths tend to support different roles. People who have strengths or weaknesses in particular areas belong in certain roles and not others. Academic performance is what determines whether someone is going to be a doctor or a mechanic. 'Intelligence' has historically been an important measuring stick - one that has been closely associated with roles and power. More often than not, tests are set up to sort or filter out people. Rather than being tested on your ability to think creatively or productively, you are getting tested on how well you understand and accept the values and presuppositions of the system.

Another implication of the teacher's response is that giving the students the final evidence at the beginning of the course would be equivalent to 'cheating'. It provides the students 'too much' of an opportunity to be successful. It makes success 'too easy'.

These presuppositions are deeply embedded in our culture. We believe that to implement truly effective learning, however, these assumptions must be reconsidered.

The Dynamic Assessment Process

As we gain greater knowledge about the learning process and create better tools for learning, the less effective learning needs to be dependent on the natural 'intelligence' of the particular learner. An effective educational experience must provide people with the maximum 'opportunities' to learn and make it 'easy' for them to learn. This requires a shift of emphasis with respect to assessment and feedback.

In the late 1980's and early 1990's Todd and I were involved in a project within the California School system called "Dynamic Assessment" in which we applied the kinds of tools described in this book to help children who had been diagnosed with learning disabilities. The Dynamic Assessment program was originally designed to help children of Hispanic origin who were non-native speakers of English and were found to have some kind of learning handicap. The purpose of the Dynamic Assessment program was to provide an alternative to the typical forms of the assessment and treatment of learning problems.

The school district in which it was implemented had a large Hispanic population, primarily from migrant working families. The learning problems among the Hispanic population had become so severe that the school district was in danger of losing its accreditation. Like many school systems they were not set up to teach people how to think. In most schools you rarely, see anybody get a good grade for how they thought about a problem. The grade isn't for how you thought about it, it is for what your answer was. If your answer matches the standard, then you must be smart. Rather than being tested on the ability to think productively or creatively, students are tested on how well their learning strategies naturally fit the standard methods of teaching.

One of the reasons they began the Dynamic Assessment program was because they discovered that many of the typical learning and intelligence tests were so full of cultural presuppositions that rather than measuring intelligence they were really measuring differences in cultural values. There are many presupposed values in our approach to education. Unfortunately, most of them are not about how to think, but rather about what to think and how to behave.

The idea of the Dynamic Assessment program was to assess the intelligence of the child, not on what they knew in response to test questions, as is typically done, but rather on a different level. They were assessed on their ability to learn how to learn - that is, on how much progress they could make in the process of learning. The focus was on the 'dynamic' process aspects of learning rather than simply on the 'products' of learning.

TE: In school people are generally assessed with respect to the behavioral 'products' of learning. But, as Albert Einstein said, the solutions to our problems cannot come from the same level as the problems. The solutions must come from a different level. If the behavioral problem is that the student cannot spell "geography", having the student practice the word over and over again is not necessarily going to make the child be a better speller. How many times do we hear comments like, "You're not studying hard enough. You haven't done it enough times. Repeat it again." I know people who are 50 years old and are still trying to figure how to spell 'geography'. And they repeat it every day. It's not the amount of time you spend that determines your success in learning; it's not even how hard you work. It's whether or not you have the strategies you need in order to successfully accomplish the tasks presented to you.

If you think about the spelling strategy, it involves many visualizations. When you teach a child to visualize when spelling a word, you are not just teaching spelling, you're teaching a child how to visually manipulate images. This is the basis of what we call intelligence in the United States and in most western countries. Your ability to manipulate images determines whether or not you achieve a high score on an I.Q. test; because the questions are all oriented toward a certain representational system. Most learning in school is oriented toward the visual representational system. So, when you teach a skill to a child, like the spelling strategy, in essence you have just opened up a part of their brain that they might never have used much before. You're teaching them how to use visual imagery. That goes far beyond spelling. I've seen people learn to spell, and all of a sudden their history grades go up. It doesn't have anything to do with the fact that they are spelling their history words better. I've seen people learn the

math strategy (in Appendix D) and suddenly have their geography grades go right through the ceiling. Because capabilities generalize much more easily than behaviors.

RD: In a Dynamic Assessment, instead of giving the student a test, categorizing their disability and handing them their "life sentence", the special education teacher or psychologist was to interact with the student, coaching him or her as much as possible and trying to see how much progress could be made in a single session. We taught the teachers and psychologists how to elicit the learning strategies of the students who were having problems and then simply try to widen or enrich that strategy. The idea was to get the psychologists and teachers to think creatively along with the students in order to discover and enhance the thought process that the student was using in the problem area.

TE: If you are a science teacher and biology is fun and easy for you, it is most likely because (1) you have some positive feeling state that you associate with biology which makes it seem fun and easy; and (2) you have a strategy for organizing that information that also makes it easy for you to use it. If you want your students to enjoy biology in the same way that you do, you have to equip them with both pieces. You have to give them a part of what makes it so exciting for you — to create that state in them. Secondly, you have to give them the way that you think about biology. What makes it easy for you? How do you organize it?

If you are a math teacher and you're teaching geometry and geometry is easy for you, how do you do it in your own mind? Because it is what you do in your head in order to make it easy, the way you sort it out and chunk it for yourself, that's the first thing your geometry students need to learn—not what's the area of a square or a triangle. What makes it easy is that strategy; that's the first thing you teach—then you teach the content. Because once you have them in the state and you've given them the strategy, the rest of the course is the content.

RD: On the other side, if you're a student and you go to your chemistry teacher and your chemistry teacher says "Well, the only way to learn chemistry is to study hard and it will be difficult for you but you just hang in there and keep working and you'll eventually get it;" boy, you don't want that guy's strategy. The person whose strategy you want is the guy that stays up all night till four o'clock in the morning before the test partying, and then comes in and aces it and he hasn't studied at all. He's the one whose strategy I want, because he does it naturally. With the minimum amount of information and effort, the guy can get an "A". That's the strategy you want; not necessarily the life style, but the strategy.

TE: One goal of Dynamic Assessment was to take teachers, resource specialists, speech pathologists, psychologists, all the people involved with these students, and teach them all the same language. We taught everybody NLP, to one degree or another. That way a teacher would know enough about eye movements to observe a child and notice what happens when the student has difficulties. Then, when the teacher went to the school psychologist, he or she could talk to that person in the same language.

RD: Before this, the teachers, psychologists and special education personnel didn't speak the same language. A child would have a problem in the classroom and the teacher would send him to the psychologist, mainly to get him out of the classroom. Rather than interact with the teacher about what had been going on with the student, the psychologist would just run the student through a bunch of tests and come up with some kind of diagnosis like "central auditory processing deficit" and turn him over to the resource specialist. This person would take one look at the diagnosis, shrug her shoulders and start trying whatever she could to help the student learn. If she were successful in pacing his learning style so that he could improve, she would send him back to the same classroom and teacher and the cycle would begin again.

The problem with a label like 'central auditory processing deficit' is that it doesn't address the complex dynamics that are involved with the real human being and the system that that human being is in. If you look at a problem myopically, under a microscope, you can find all kinds of things that you can label, but that may not be useful in helping the student improve. Whenever you measure one part of the system, you can find all kinds of deficits in it, but unless you look at the whole system you may not be able to find the solution to those problems. As an analogy, if you have a problem in one part of your car, it might occur because of interference from another part, but if you never look at the whole thing you won't know it. Imagine if your car wouldn't start because the gas ran out of the tank, but because your mechanic was an air cleaner specialist, the only thing that he ever looked at was the air cleaner. "I just can't figure it out—let's put a new air cleaner in."

TE: This car is just not ready to run. It's a resistant automobile.

RD: Unfortunately there is nothing in the label 'central auditory processing deficit' that tells you what to do to change it. With Dynamic Assessment the way that we assess whether somebody is having trouble spelling automatically tells us what to do to improve the spelling. With many other methods of testing there is no way to go from the diagnosis to any kind of intervention. The diagnosis is just the diagnosis. "We have this diagnosis, what should we do?"

TE: Give them rytalin.

RD: The whole point is, the way that I tell that the child has a problem and the way that I treat the problem need to be related. The assessment and intervention have to go together. So that if I assess that the child is having a problem spelling because his or her eyes are going down and to her left, I can tell the child, "Put your eyes up and to the left and you'll spell better" — and she will. In a Dynamic Assessment, if I tell the student "Change what you just did," it will have an impact on the results that you are measuring.

Many standard assessments involve the student answering a bunch of questions. Based on the answers a diagnosis is made. But you can't then say to the student, "Here, just change your answer to these questions and you'll get better. It doesn't work that way."

TE: Changing the answers to those questions just changes what's on the paper. It doesn't change the child at all. With Dynamic Assessment, when you change the thing that the child was doing that indicated the problem, it's sure to change the results immediately.

RD: It goes both ways. Dynamic Assessment is based on distinctions that will create change not just distinctions whose purpose is to label and categorize.

TE: A Dynamic Assessment starts by asking, "What is the capability that this child needs in order to be able to accomplish this learning goal successfully?" For instance, if the goal is to teach a student to spell the word "geography," the question is, "What capability does the student need in order to be able to spell that word?"

Sometimes I'll draw the figure "Δ" on the board and ask people, "What is that?" 99% will immediately say, "It's a triangle, that's what that is." But I like to point out that it's not really "a triangle." It is an intersection of three lines at three given angles—which we call "a triangle." The question you need to ask for yourself is, "What needs to be there to call it a triangle?" Similarly, in the process of learning, we need to ask ourselves, "What needs to be there to call a process 'spelling'?" What is the capability that spelling is based on? Notice that this is very different than asking, "What are the behaviors that would indicate to us that a child was spelling a word correctly?" Dynamic assessment processes focus on the capabilities needed for learning regardless of the content of what you want to put through those capabilities.

So when you think about assessing the student, the question you need to ask yourself, is regardless of the subject you're teaching, "What's the skill the child needs to be able to learn it?" Not "What's the content?" Not "What does the lesson plan say?" To spell, for instance, the student needs to be able to have enough visual skill to form an image of that word in his or mind.

The next question is, "How do I test to find out whether this child can develop this capability?" In a Dynamic Assessment, what I do is to interact with this child and find out if there is any place in this child's life where he or she can already visualize to the degree required to be able to spell. If that kid can describe to me in detail how he robbed the local liquor store, and as he tells me his eyes are up and to the left and doing all the things that show me that he has the ability to visualize, then I've got my answer. My Dynamic Assessment tells me that this kid can be taught to spell. I don't need an IQ test, or any other tests, to tell me whether this child has what he needs. If the child doesn't currently have any visualizing skills, then that tells me where I need to start with him. Whether or not he can already spell "geography" is irrelevant with respect to whether or not he is capable of learning to spell. If you judge a child's capability based on their current behavior, you will never get to what it is that you really need to look at and ask about.

RD: The purpose of Dynamic Assessment is to address different levels of learning processes. Process level assessment allows learners to either a) utilize their own preferred learning strategies or b) be aware of their strategies in such a way that they can be enriched and changed.

Process level feedback involves having a constant goal and evidence procedures that allow for ongoing assessment so that the operations of both the teacher and the learner can be most quickly and effectively adapted to reach the goal under a greater variety of conditions.

TE: Dynamic Assessment is based on the NLP notion of 'pacing and leading'. As an example, let's say that a child is having difficulty in the classroom but loves working on motors. To pace the child, the first thing I might ask is, "What kind of motor is it?" Let's say the kid replies, "It's a Ford." To begin to lead a bit I might ask, "How do you know it's a Ford, does it say anything anywhere on it?" Maybe he says, "Yeah, it is written on the valve covers; F-O-R-D." I might say, "Great. Let's assume that they said, 'XYLP', would they look differently?" In other words, I'm using the motor as a resource rather than a distraction. You can eventually get to the point where you can put whatever letters you want the kid to remember on the motor.

Another example might be a child who claims, "I can't spell," but can describe his or her bicycle in utter detail. You can pace and lead this child as well. For instance, some bicycles have the license plates on the back of the seats. You can ask, "What does it say on your license plate?" Maybe the child responds, "It has my name, 'Bobby'." I can say, "Good, supposed it said 'Cat'. Have you ever seen a license plate that had 'C-A-T' on it? How many licenses have you seen?"

In other words, you pace by starting with something that is already easy for the child to remember. It doesn't need to have anything to do with school at all. The reason for this is that I want to first attach what we're doing to something that is familiar. If the child's bicycle is familiar, then I want to attach the task of visualizing to his or her bicycle because it's familiar and even fun to ride a bicycle.

RD: A good example of this kind of approach is the case of a child at the Pajaro Valley school district who was three or four grade levels behind in math. The young Hispanic psychologist who was working with him made a brilliant intervention that I think characterizes what Dynamic Assessment is all about.

In beginning the assessment process, the psychologist noticed that the boy was using the typical strategy of counting on his fingers to try to solve math problems. This strategy seemed to be slowing him down immensely and limiting his degree of performance.

A typical response in the classroom to such a situation is to reprimand the child, tell him not to count on his hands (in the old days the hands were slapped with a ruler), but offer no concrete or effective alternative.

Instead, the psychologist lead the boy to discover the limits of this strategy on his own and then to enrich the strategy by jumping outside of the typical presupposed limits of it.

"What is three plus two?" he asked.

- "One, two...three, four , Five!"

"Great!" the psychologist said. "What's thirteen plus four?"

"One, two, threeee....I don't know!"

Instead of telling him at that point that his strategy was wrong or ineffective, the psychologist tried to help the child think of a way to expand his strategy to be able to add thirteen plus four.

The psychologist offered a suggestion. "I have an idea! Whatever the two numbers are, **you** always be the biggest number and count the smaller number out on your fingers. If it is thirteen plus four, then you are the thirteen. Now hold up four fingers and count."

-"Fourteen, fifteen, sixteen...seventeen!"

"Now, What is thirteen plus ten? Remember you be the bigger number." The child was able to add the two numbers.

"OK. What is a hundred and twenty five plus seven?" Initially the child hesitated. The numbers seemed so 'big'.

The psychologist reminded him, "You are the hundred twenty five. Now hold up seven fingers and count."

- "A hundred and thirty two!" came the delighted response.

Suddenly this child had made a quantum leap in the amount of numbers he could add by adding one simple step to his strategy. They went on from there to realize that even when you are adding columns of multi-digit numbers, if you learn to carry, you never have to add more than two numbers at a time. So this child who had never been able to add up numbers whose sum was higher than ten was suddenly doing multi-digit addition. His sense of excitement and self-esteem was tremendous.

Perhaps more important than his improved ability with math was the child's response to his mother when she asked him if he was happy that he had learned to count.

He said, "I learned something a lot more important than that. I learned that I could learn how to learn! I can learn in different ways."

The amazing thing was that this child's grades in all his other subjects began to improve too. And he became interested in other strategies for doing not only math but his other subjects.

This is a whole different approach to the process of teaching. It helps the student build confidence in his own learning abilities and to appreciate his own learning strategies. And on another level it builds the belief that there is more than one way to learn. This is not just the teacher's way or a way that someone prescribed in a book, there are many ways of doing it.

Of course, an initial objection was made by the regular classroom teachers that this method required a lot of personal attention and that they were too overwhelmed with their daily workload to provide their students with this kind of feedback. Their assumption, however was that they needed to provide the feedback. We introduced the idea of team learning in the classroom and showed them that, given the right "how to" technology, students could teach each other more effectively in many cases than teachers could. They began implementing cooperative learning programs, where students shared their learning strategies with each other. In fact, the most effective spelling teacher in their entire school district was an eleven year old girl. She could teach anyone to spell!

Dealing with Resistances and Interferences to Learning

RD: Sometimes resistances or interferences to learning arise that are not simply a matter of pacing and leading a person's existing learning strategy.

TE: There was a lady that I worked with once who was great with math. She loved computers and as far as numbers went she was great, no problem at all. But when it came to spelling, forget it. She was convinced she couldn't spell. She felt badly every time she tried to spell or even if you mentioned spelling to her. The interesting thing was the strategy she used for doing her math and computer programming was exactly the same strategy that she should have been using to spell. They were exactly the same thing. You know what got in her way? The word "spelling." It wasn't the activity of spelling. It was the word spelling and what it meant to her.

A good speller and a poor speller will often operate from a completely different starting state. When a teacher says, "OK, it's time for our new spelling words for the week." You can just watch around the room and observe which kids go "Yuck" and which ones go "Alright, spelling" and pull out their spelling books. From the very beginning, there's a starting state and a belief about whether it's even possible to do it. If you start by going, "OH, we're going to do spelling. This is something I can't do. I already know I'm going to fail at this before I even start." That starting state is never going to let you through that door, even if you're given the strategy. Because the starting state determines where you go.

RD: The basic Dynamic Learning approach to dealing with resistances is to find out the positive intention or purpose behind the resistance and then identify other more appropriate choices for satisfying that positive intention. In Dynamic Learning we assume that everybody responds with the best choices available to them at the time. If you look deeply enough you will find that the intention behind any response is positive in some way. Problems arise when people don't have a choice that's most appropriate for a particular situation.

For example, when people are trying to spell visually they often become aware of a voice in their head that keeps trying to sound out the words. Typically people try to deal with this internal voice by telling it to "shut up." The result is that it just gets louder. Instead of just trying to get rid of the voice, we would ask it, "What are you trying to do for me?" I had the same problem myself, and what I discovered was that this voice was trying to help me to 'do it right'; and of course "right" meant the way that I was taught. So I asked my inner voice, "What will 'doing it right' do positively for me?" The answer came back, "To spell correctly." The next question to this voice was, "Is what you're doing actually getting the result that you want? If you sound it out do I actually spell it correctly?" I know it sounds funny, but I actually explained and demonstrated to my own inner voice that I could spell more accurately when I didn't sound out the words. And since the voice wanted to help me to 'do it the right way', I asked it to remind me to visualize the word.

TE: You can utilize the fact that there is a voice. It isn't that you have to get rid of the voice. If you want to be making pictures in your head and you have a voice that stops you from making those pictures, why not have it be talking to you about what's supposed to be in the pictures?

A friend of mine who was a drummer was studying to be a pharmacist. He was studying to be a pharmacist because he had three kids and a wife, but he wanted to be a drummer because that's what was fun to him. Becoming a pharmacist involved a lot of reading, a lot of memorization of formulas and all kinds of medical information. He came to me because every time he sat down to read this technical material, he'd get three pages into it and have absolutely no idea what was going on. The problem was that, like a lot of musicians, he'd sit down to read and he'd open the book up and he'd get through the first sentence and he'd be singing a song. Before he knew it, it was twenty minutes later and he was still on the same sentence. He'd get into the "rhythm of it" and that rhythm would match with another rhythm which would match with a drum beat and before long he had a song going, and what was in the book had gone 'out the window'. So he told me wanted me to take the songs out of his head.

Instead, I asked "Do these songs have words?" He said "Sure, I sing the words." So I told him to pick his favorite songs, remove the words from the songs, and play that music while reading. Instead of hearing the words for the song he was to sing the words on the page. I had him choose different songs for each subject matter, so that when he needed to remember the material for the test, he just needed to remember what song it went with. He could punch that one up on his mental 'CD' and start playing it. If he needed to get to a place that was halfway through the chapter, he could 'fast forward' to the right place then slow it down again, get the answer and write it down. The neat thing was, it worked for him.

RD: This is the essence of pacing and leading. You take what is creating a problem, you turn it around the other way.

TE: You utilize what's going on, as opposed to trying to fight it.

RD: You start with where the person is going anyway and then you gently lead to the next place. Start where a person wants to start; where they're going to start naturally. Then lead. In NLP the term "reframing" refers to the process of taking something that seems like a block and turning it into a resource. Instead of fighting your own processes, you pace and lead them.

In our spelling demonstration, for example, Patty experienced a resistance to spelling based upon her personal history. She had been told as a little girl that she was tone deaf and that it made her a bad speller. Instead of trying to ignore Patty's past, we did an intervention with Patty known as "changing personal history" in NLP. We 'paced' where Patty was going naturally by inviting her to go back in her mind to that little girl that didn't know that she could believe anything different. In order to 'lead', the adult Patty acted as 'big sister' to the younger Patty and told her that she could now believe something different about her ability to spell.

The following set of steps represent a typical NLP approach to addressing resistances to learning related to past events.

1. Identify the specific feeling of resistance.

2. Identify the earliest experience of the resistance.

3. Disassociate from the experience—that is, see the experience as if you were watching a movie of yourself.

4. Find the positive intent of the resistance in the context of the past experience.

5. Identify the resources or choices that you needed then and did not have but have available to you now.

6. Replay the movie seeing yourself with the resources that you needed and then put yourself back into the experience.

TE: Not all resistances to learning come in response to past experiences. Some are related to current events in a person's life. For example, a young girl was brought to me who had been having a problem with her math studies in school. She was accompanied by her mother, who was very insistent that her daughter had a severe problem with math and was about to fail. She told me that the girl had been seen by a counselor and a math specialist in the school and they were not able to correct the situation. The mother brought the written records of all the test results, conclusions and interventions that had been tried to that point.

Rather than focusing on the paper, I spent the first part of my interview observing the way she solved math problems. I gave her a number of simple addition, subtraction, multiplication and division problems that were at her grade level. She was able to successfully solve the problems I provided for her. I noticed, however, that when I gave her the division problems, she first looked down and to her right and paused for some time before she went on to complete the problems. To check my observation, I presented her with a few more examples of each type of problem. Again, when she got to the division problems, she looked down and right, paused and then went on to complete the problems successfully. It became obvious to me that this young girl was able to correctly complete all the math problems and exhibited no real difficulty during the process. In fact I observed that she had a very well developed visual strategy for solving the problems. However there was evidence from her math test scores that she was having some kind of difficulty.

It seemed obvious to me that whatever was going on with this girl wasn't about math strategies or visualization skills. So I decided to ask her if she understood why her mother had brought her to see me. She very sheepishly responded that she *thought* it had something to do with a problem she was having with math. At this point I asked her if she actually was experiencing any difficulty with division problems. She told me that she could do the problems just fine but she "felt bad about division." Notice that she did not say that she had any difficulty with math. What she said was that she "felt bad about division." She did not say that she didn't know how to do a specific division problem, didn't know the process or strategy for division, nor that she had difficulty learning. Instead, she made a statement about herself in relationship to "division." I began to wonder, "How is it possible that a 10 year old girl could be feeling bad about "division?" How many meanings are there to the term "division?"

At this point, I went out of my office to the next room to talk to the girl's mother. I asked if she and her husband had been recently separated or divorced. She said that they had been separated for about 10 months. As it turns out, this was the approximate length of time that the girl had been experiencing her so-called "difficulty with math." Her mother proceeded to tell me about the circumstances surrounding the separation and subsequent placement of the children.

For the next several hours I talked with the young girl about her family and her friends and her relationships. Interestingly enough, I found out whenever she thought about division it brought back memories of how the children in the family were separated from each other and how the family was divided. "Division" to her meant breaking things down into smaller units which was a metaphor for the divorce of her parents and the subsequent separation of the children. Her two brothers lived with her father and she lived with her mom. Just thinking about things being divided made her feel uncomfortable. She described to me how it was impossible to imagine things being divided up any more that they already were.

I helped her to find the positive intention of her bad feeling about division and find some other resources for dealing with it. By the end of our talk she felt much better. She said that talking to me about her family situation had helped her to recognize and sort out her feelings about her family from her feelings about math. As a result of this session, her grades soon returned to normal.

The point is, attempting to help this young girl with her difficulty by approaching it as a problem with learning or math (as the counselor and math specialist had done) would not have addressed the true nature of the problem. The issue was on the level of beliefs about what "division" meant. The problem was solved by addressing the relationship issues around her family system and sorting out her beliefs about the meaning of "division".

Man: What type of strategies would you use to help kids who don't have enough auditory acuity to pay attention and follow instructions?

RD: I think you have to first check for any issues that create resistances to paying attention. First, find out whether it is a 'how to' or a 'want to' issue.

TE: The point being that 'paying attention' may have little or nothing to do with auditory input. As an analogy, let's say a student has the capability to make pictures, and you're trying to teach him the spelling strategy, and every time you tell that student to put his or her eyes up and to the left the person starts resisting and becoming agitated. It is probably not an issue of being able to visualize a word. More likely it's because the child doesn't want to look at what ever's up there. Perhaps the child has pictures of some kind of trauma, and the spelling words are getting mixed up with these disturbing images. It's not because they don't want to visualize words per se, it's because they have made the generalization that 'looking at pictures' means 'feeling bad'. It may have nothing to do with spelling. So you may need to ask, "What else is going on in that child's life?"

RD: I was talking to a teacher about a girl in her class who had trouble listening in class because in her mind all she constantly heard a type of of 'hissing' sound. The teacher was wondering if I could use NLP to turn down that sound and get that "SSHHH" out of the girl's head so that she would be able to listen better. After asking the teacher a few questions, however, I discovered that this child lived in an abusive family. Her mother was a prostitute who was hit all the time by the various men she had around her. All of a sudden that "SSHHH" sound took on other potentially significant implications. The child's not paying attention might be a survival issue. The things you do to get that kid to pay attention in class are going to potentially have an impact on other aspects of the child's life.

In Dynamic Assessment it is important to look at the broader space encompassing the total child. Because, when you look at the problems that kids have in school—it's not that they come to school out of a void. Their system is larger than the classroom.

Man: Would you want to have them let go of that at school, and perhaps turn it back on when they go home?

RD: Yes you can do that, but notice in order to do that you have to understand that child. You have to have a trusting relationship with that child. Ecologically speaking, we're talking about making it safe for the child—not just turning her ears off or on.

Man: I'm talking about making her understand the process to some extent by which that happens so that she can turn it on when it's useful and turn it off when it's not.

TE: It would be really simple to teach them how to turn it on and off. The question is whether or not it would be safe or ecological

RD: Imagine, all of the knowledge it would take to know *when* to turn it on or off

TE: I think in this case it is important to distinguish between what is expected from a teacher versus when a psychologist is needed. I don't necessarily expect a teacher to handle certain kinds of problems. A teacher may not have the skills or the time to be put in the position of doing psychotherapy. I think that teachers and psychologists need to understand what their position is in the larger system and need to form an alliance.

RD: There are other books (such as *Changing Belief Systems with NLP*) that cover NLP therapeutic techniques. Our goal with this book, and with Dynamic Assessment, is to focus on those issues and elements related to the process of learning. However, we encourage you to use your new learning skills to widen your understanding of NLP as much as possible.

Conclusion

RD: Assessment methods should concentrate on the process of learning as much as the products of learning. The emphasis on the process of learning requires several different levels of assessment. In addition to assessing specific behaviors, it is also important to assess cognitive processes such as learning strategies, beliefs, values and motivation. These aspects of the learning 'process' require that assessment be more ongoing and geared to providing feedback than oriented toward 'filtering' and 'failure'. Every 'opportunity' must be provided for 'everyone' to succeed and 'get an A'. When this is done, even individuals who have been considered 'handicapped' can excel.

The Dynamic Assessment program at the Pajaro Valley School District was very successful. I mentioned earlier that the Dynamic Assessment program was originally implemented as a means to help children of Hispanic origin who were non-native speakers of English and were found to have some kind of learning handicap. As a result of the success of this approach with these problem learners, Dynamic Learning principles soon spread throughout the school district as the fundamental paradigm for learning. The teachers adopted the slogan "Creating a school to which children choose to belong." The overall performance of the school district went from being one of the lowest in California to being the second highest in the state. Christine Amato, the woman who spearheaded the project in that school system, was later appointed to review educational legislation for the entire state.

Chapter 11

Conclusion

Conclusion

RD: We hope that, through this book, you have been able to get a sense of the vision, the mission and the fun that we had in doing Dynamic Learning. Since Dynamic Learning is about learning through experience and this is only a book we encourage you to try out these strategies behaviorally, experientially and interactively with others.

Todd used to like to say that NLP was not 'written as a solo', but rather as a 'duet'. NLP came out of the dynamic interaction between Richard Bandler and John Grinder. I think that Dynamic Learning also plays best as a duet.

At the conclusion of our seminars, Todd often liked to read a quotation from the book *A River Runs Through It* by Norman Maclean. Two brothers are talking about the type of strategies that are necessary to be a successful fisherman. One of the brothers is telling the other about the importance of thinking in being able to fish. The other brother asks what he means by "thinking." The first brother responds:

> *"All there is to thinking," he said, "is seeing something noticeable which makes you see something you weren't noticing which makes you see something that isn't even visible..."*

This is perhaps the deepest metaphor for Dynamic Learning.

This book itself symbolizes a number of conclusions for me—most significantly the passing of Todd Epstein. It seems only fitting to end this book with a few final words about Todd.

It is perhaps only once in a lifetime (if one is lucky) that a person is blessed with a true friend. In my life that friend was Todd Epstein. For the past fifteen years he has been a major part of me; personally, professionally and spiritually. John Grinder once said that friendship could be measured by the number of different parts of yourself that you could freely express when you were around a person. By that measurement, Todd was far and away my greatest friend.

Through simply being himself, Todd was able to draw from me my best and then add to it; whether it was teaching, creating, writing, or just 'shooting some hoops' on the basketball court. His down-to-earth style helped me to grow as a teacher; his curiosity and practicality helped me to grow as a developer and writer; and his humanity and strength helped me to grow as a man.

Todd's intelligence, intensity, inquisitiveness and creativity burst through in everything he did: his music, his questions, his humor, and his contributions to the many things he and I created together. Wherever he is, I know that Todd will be playing music, teaching and asking a lot of questions.

In our seminars, when discussing his view of life and his perception of his own life's mission, Todd often referred to the earth as "a little blue ball floating in space," and always carried with him a photograph of the planet taken from deep in space as a reminder and an inspiration. I derive some comfort from knowing that he will now always be able to see the earth and the people he loved from this perspective.

Todd sometimes lightheartedly expressed his sense of 'God' and spirituality in terms of "the goo that holds everything together." It brings me a deep sense of peace to know that he and I and those he loved will be connected as parts of that cosmic "goo" for eternity.

To my partner, my friend, my brother, good bye.

Afterword

I hope you have enjoyed this exploration into *Dynamic Learning*. As we indicated during the course of the book, many tools and resources exist to further develop and apply the models, strategies and skills described within these pages.

The Dynamic Learning Center / NLP University is an organization committed to bringing the highest quality trainings in basic and advanced NLP skills and to promoting the development of new models and applications of NLP in the areas of health, business and organization, creativity and learning. Each Summer The Dynamic Learning Center and NLP University hold residential programs at the University of California at Santa Cruz.

Dynamic Learning Publications publishes articles and monographs which represent the leading edge of the growing and changing field of Systemic NLP.

If you would like to receive further information regarding these publications and programs or any future developments related to *Dynamic Learning*, please contact:

The Dynamic Learning Center
NLP University
P.O. Box 1112
Ben Lomond, California 95005
Phone: (408) 336-3457
Fax: (408) 336-5854

Appendix A:
Levels of Learning

Gregory Bateson (1973) proposed a categorization of different 'logical levels' of learning based on Bertrand Russell's mathematical theory of logical types - which stated that a class of things cannot be a member of itself. The central thesis of this theory is that there is a discontinuity between a class and its members. The class cannot be a member of itself nor can one of the members be the class, since the term used for the class is of a different level of abstraction—a different 'logical type'—from terms used for members.

For example, the class of even numbers cannot itself be an even number; the class of cats cannot be a cat. Likewise a single example of a cat cannot be the class of cats. Bateson applied this logical theory to biology and behavior. A tissue that is made up of a group of cells, for instance, is a different logical level than the individual cells - a brain is not the same as a brain cell. The two can effect each other through indirect feedback - i.e., the functioning and connections of the overall brain can influence the behavior of a single brain cell and the activity of a single brain cell contributes to the overall functioning of the brain. Indeed, a cell may be said to effect itself through the rest of the brain structure.

In human behavior, Bateson identified a series of levels of learning—each responsible for making corrective changes and refinements in the other class of learning upon which it operated.

"Zero learning is characterized by specificity of response [i.e., having a specific behavior in a specific environment - RD] which - right or wrong - is not subject to correction.

"Learning I is change in specificity of response by correction of errors of choice within a set of alternatives.

"Learning II is a change in the process of Learning I, e.g., a corrective change in the set of alternatives from which choice is made, or it is a change in how the sequence is punctuated.

"Learning III is change in the process of Learning II, e.g., a corrective change in the system of sets of alternatives from which choice is made."

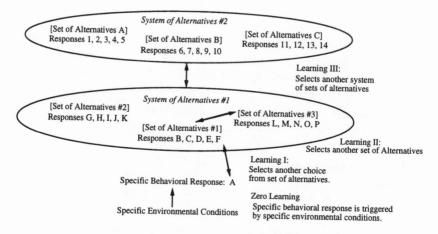

Bateson's 'Logical Levels' of Learning

In this framework, a simple, mechanical reflex would be a case of zero learning. Habituation, behavioral conditioning and psycho-motor learning would be operations relating to particular behavioral alternatives - learning I. Perceptual learning, latent learning skill acquisition and modeling would relate to operations which address sets of alternatives - learning II. Insight learning and 'imprinting' would relate more to the establishment of change of whole systems of alternative behaviors - learning III.

In NLP Bateson's logical levels of learning are expressed in terms of the following categories:

A. Who I **Am** - *Identity*
    Mission   Who?

B. My **B**elief system - *Values and Meanings*
    Permission & Motivation   Why?

C. My **C**apabilities - *Strategies and States*
    Maps & Plans   How?

D. What I **D**o or have **D**one - *Specific Behaviors*
    Actions & Reactions   What?

E. My **E**nvironment - *External Stimuli*
    Constraints & Opportunities   Where? When?

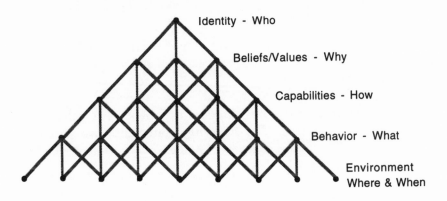

Identity - Who

Beliefs/Values - Why

Capabilities - How

Behavior - What

Environment
Where & When

Levels of Influences on Learning

The environment level involves the specific external stimuli and conditions in which our behavior takes place. Behaviors without any inner map, plan or strategy to guide them, however, are like knee jerk reactions, habits or rituals. At the level of capability we are able to select, alter and adapt a class of behaviors to a wider set of external situations. At the level of beliefs and values we may encourage, inhibit or generalize a particular strategy, plan or way of thinking. Identity, of course, consolidates whole systems of beliefs and values into a sense of self. While each level becomes more abstracted from the specifics of behavior and sensory experience, it actually has more and more widespread effect on our behavior and experience.

In summary:

* *Environmental factors* determine the external opportunities or constraints a person has to react to. Relates to the **where** and **when** of learning.

* *Behavior* is made up of the specific actions or reactions taken within the environment. Relates to the **what** of learning.

* *Capabilities* guide and give direction to behavioral actions through a mental map, plan or strategy. Relates to the **how** of learning.

* *Beliefs* and *values* provide the reinforcement (motivation and permission) that supports or denies capabilities. Relates to the **why** of learning.

* *Identity* factors determine overall purpose (mission) and shape beliefs and values through our sense of self. Relates to **who** is learning.

The different levels of learning and experience are reflected in our language patterns. The following statements are potential examples of these different levels of response to a student who has done poorly on a spelling test.

A. Identity - *"You are a stupid person."*

B. Belief - *"If you cannot spell well you cannot do well in school."*

C. Capability - *"You are not very good at spelling."*

D. Specific Behavior - *"You did poorly on this particular test."*

E. Environment - *"The noise in the room makes it difficult to take tests."*

Appendix B: Summary of Learning Strategies

Identifying an Effective Learning State

Body Posture and Learning

Remember a time in which you were able to learn easily and effectively. Put yourself fully into that experience and notice what happens to your physiology. Circle which of the pictures below most clearly represents the posture you assume when you are in that effective learning state.

Remember a time in which you were trying to learn but became stuck or distracted. Put yourself back into that experience and notice what happens differently with your physiology. Put a square around the pictures that most represent your posture when you are stuck or distracted (choose both a front and a side view).

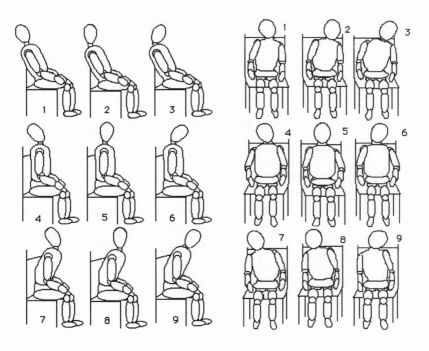

Gestures and Learning

Again, put yourself back into the experience in which you were able to learn easily and effectively and notice your physiology. Circle the picture among the following group that represents the gestures you use most often in an effective learning state, or draw the gestures on the picture provided on the right.

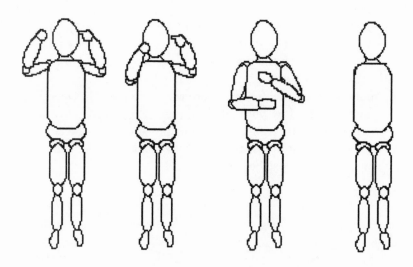

Gestures for Effective Learning State

Return to the experience in which you were stuck or distracted. Put a square around the picture among the following group that represents the gestures you use most often in a stuck or distracted state, or draw the gestures on the picture provided on the right.

[Note: If you are a more auditory or kinesthetic learner, you may want to have a partner observe you, or look in a mirror when you are in the effective or distracted learning states.]

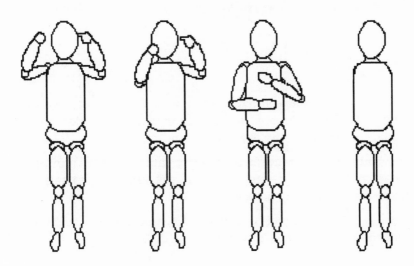

Gestures for Stuck or Distracted State

Eye Position and Learning

On the diagrams below indicate a) which eye position(s) are most associated with your effective learning state and b) which eye position(s) are most associated with a stuck or distracted state. If there is more than one, indicate the sequence or order that the eye movements typically follow. You may use either numbers or arrows.

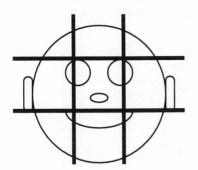

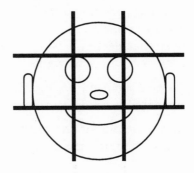

Effective Learning State   **Stuck or Distracted State**

Remembering Names

Beliefs

A. A person's name has something to do with the person. A name is not just a formality, but has something to do with a statement of relationship or quality of relationship.

B. You "validate" someone through using their name. It's important to remember someone's name if you are going to talk to them about something personal.

C. Learning a name is not a function of focusing on the sound or what the name is, but of focusing on the person.

Steps

1. Start with the feeling that you want to get to know that person.

2. Make eye contact and try to really hear the name. Visualize the person's face, and attach the face to their name. For example, make a picture of the person's face in your mind, hear the person's name and then make a visual image of the person's name on a name card and stick it on the forehead of the person.

3. Focus on a characteristic of the person. Find a feature that fits that person and the make up of that person; not necessarily his or her dress, but rather something that represents the way that person is — i.e., the style of dress or hair, or the way he or she acts, walks, talks, etc.

4. 'Try on' some of the characteristics of that person. Take in the ones that you find attractive.

5. Get a feeling for the person and use the name as a point of association for the distinguishing features related to that person.

Some other helpful strategies are:

a. Associate the person with other people who have a similar name and with whom you are already in a key relationship. This attaches the name to something that is already important to you — things that belong in long term memory rather than short term memory.

b. Make up names for people if it is difficult to remember their actual name. If you can't get somebody's name, because it doesn't evoke something, then make up a name or nickname for them—such as 'Tiger', or 'Cookie'.

c. Add to the name; such as calling Lisa, "Lisa-Bonita."

Memory Strategy Exercises

The purpose of this set of exercises is to help you determine which of your senses or combination of representational systems is most highly developed for memory. This will be done by leading you through the same learning task three times but limiting your input and output channel to a different representational system each time.

PREPARATION

Make a copy of the Memory Strategy Worksheet. At the top of the sheet are printed the digits from 0-9 and the letters from A-Z. Starting with the segment labeled "VISUAL," fill in the blank spaces provided under the heading "ORIGINAL SEQUENCE," with a series of randomly chosen letters and digits. You should end up with a total of ten random characters. Be sure to write legibly so someone else can read it.

Repeat this same process for the sections titled "AUDITORY" and "KINESTHETIC" choosing a *different* sequence of random characters for each "ORIGINAL SEQUENCE." Leave the spaces under the heading "GUESS" blank for now. Divide the worksheet into four parts by tearing or cutting along the dotted lines in between each segment.

MEMORY STRATEGY WORKSHEET

	0	1	2	3	4	5	6	7	8	9
	A	B	C	D	E	F	G	H	I	J
	K	L	M	N	O	P	Q	R	S	T
	U	V	W	X	Y	Z	*	#	?	!

ORIGINAL SEQUENCE: **VISUAL**

— — — — — — — — — —

GUESS:

— — — — — — — — — —

ORIGINAL SEQUENCE: **AUDITORY**

— — — — — — — — — —

GUESS:

— — — — — — — — — —

ORIGINAL SEQUENCE: **KINESTHETIC**

— — — — — — — — — —

GUESS:

— — — — — — — — — —

MEMORY STRATEGY PROGRESS REPORT

Round 1

Rep. System Tested	No. of Characters	Time(s) Presented	Number Correct	Number Out of Order
Visual				
Auditory				
Kinesthetic				

Round 2

Rep. System Tested	No. of Characters	Time(s) Presented	Number Correct	Number Out of Order
Visual				
Auditory				
Kinesthetic				

Round 3

Rep. System Tested	No. of Characters	Time(s) Presented	Number Correct	Number Out of Order
Visual				
Auditory				
Kinesthetic				

PROCEDURE

Get together with two other people (making a group of three) and test each other's memory strategies with the following procedure:

A. Part 1 - VISUAL

1. INPUTTING - Start with the section of paper marked "VISUAL." The 'teacher' will show the 'learner' a sequence of 10 characters for up to 30 seconds, no longer. During this time, the 'observer' is to carefully watch the learner for any significant patterns of micro-behavioral cues. If the 'learner' thinks that he or she has memorized the sequence in less time you may stop before 30 seconds. Record the time in the box marked "Time(s) Presented" on the MEMORY STRATEGY PROGRESS REPORT provided on the previous page.

2. RETRIEVING - Have the 'learner' point (without speaking) to the sequence of characters in the order he or she remembers them on the segment of paper containing the list of all the numbers and letters. Write down the sequence in the spaces under the heading "GUESS" as the 'learner' points it out. Then compare it to the ORIGINAL SEQUENCE.

3. SCORING - Record the number of characters the 'learner' remembered correctly (regardless of whether or not they were in the right order) in the box marked "Number Correct" on your MEMORY STRATEGY PROGRESS REPORT. Then record the number of characters that were in the wrong sequence in the box marked "Number Out Of Order."

[NOTE: If the 'learner' has simply left out a character it does not mean that all of the ones following it are in the wrong sequence. So if your sequence is: DLC65W7U8N and the 'learner' forgets the "W" and points to DLC657U8N their score is 9 guessed correctly and 1 in the wrong place (the "7" is out of order). If the 'learner' points to a character that was not in the original sequence that is counted as a character that is "Out of Order."]

4. ELICITATION - Find out what kind of memory strategy the 'learner' used to try to remember the characters by discussing what she or he did mentally during the time you were showing the characters. The observer begins by recounting what he or she saw happening while the 'learner' was attempting to commit the characters to memory. It is important that the observer simply report what he or she has seen or heard, not attempt to interpret those observations. Then both the observer and the 'teacher' may start asking the 'learner' what was happening internally in relation to the observed behavioral cues. What was the 'leaner' aware of? Did the 'learner' attempt to make a picture of the characters in his or her mind's eye? Did s/he say them to his/herself? Observe the eye movements and other non-verbal behaviors that can help you tell which representational system(s) the 'learner' was using. Note how well this strategy worked by referring to the score. Discuss how the strategy could be refined or improved.

Then switch roles so that a different person is 'learner', 'teacher' and 'observer'. Repeat the process until all three members of the group have been in each role. (The process should take about ten minutes per person.)

B. PART 2 - AUDITORY

The 'teacher' is to sit behind the 'learner' and the 'observer' will sit facing the 'learner'. The 'teacher' is to read aloud the sequence of characters on the section of paper marked "AUDITORY." The 'teacher' should read the characters at a consistent rhythm (without any attempt to chunk them for the 'learner'—so that the 'learner' may chunk them in his or her own way). The 'learner' may request to hear the sequence again (either faster, slower or at the same rate) but may hear it no more than three times. The 'teacher' is to record how many times the 'learner' needed to hear the sequence in the box marked "Time(s) Presented." Without looking at the characters, the 'learner' will then verbally repeat the sequence that was previously read aloud by the 'teacher'. The 'teacher' will write down the 'learner's' recollection in the spaces beneath "GUESS" and score it as you did in the previous exercise.

Then the 'observer' will make his or her observations and the group will explore the 'learners' mental strategy for memorizing this sequence. For instance, you can ask, "Does it differ from the strategy used for the visual task? How well did it work for this type of memory?"

Once again, rotate the roles until all three group members have had a chance to try the auditory memory task.

C. Part 3 - KINESTHETIC

The 'teacher' instructs the 'learner' to close his or her eyes and is to guide the 'learner's' hand through the act of writing the sequence of characters. The character to be used will be the set that you created for the section marked "KINESTHETIC" on the Memory Strategy Worksheet. The 'learner' may choose to use a pen or his or her index finger. The 'learner' could also choose to have the 'teacher' write out the sequence of characters on his or her back or the palm of the hand. As with the auditory test, up to three repetitions may be requested. Then, with eyes closed, the 'learner' is to write out the sequence of characters on a piece of paper.

Scoring is done the same way as in the previous exercises.

When you are finished, the observer is make comments on what he or she has observed. The 'observer' and the 'teacher' will then help to elicit the memory strategy that the 'learner' used for this task and compare the process and results to the previous exercises.

Repeat this process over several days in order to measure how much your memory ability expands. You may extend your memory ability by either 1) adding more characters to your memory task, or 2) shortening the time it takes you to commit characters to memory. Use Round 2 and Round 3 of the MEMORY STRATEGY PROGRESS REPORT to keep track of your improvement.

Developing Visual Skill

Get into pairs of two people (**A** & **B**):

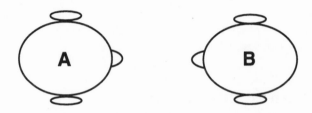

STEP 1. **A** and **B** stand facing one another. **A** gives instructions to **B** to visualize **A**'s body position and look up to the left (for right handers) or the right (for left handers) to remember it.

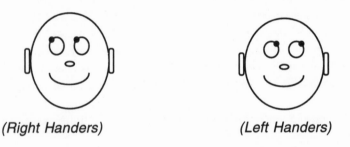

(Right Handers)   *(Left Handers)*

STEP 2. **B** closes his or her eyes. **A** moves some part of his or her body (i.e. hand, leg, finger, head tilt, etc.) while **B**'s eyes are closed.

STEP 3. **A** then tells **B** to open his or her eyes. **B** looks up to the left (or right) and compares what he or she sees to the remembered image and guesses which part of the body **A** moved.

STEP 4. If **B** misguesses then **A** instructs **B** to close his or her eyes again. **A** does not tell **B** what part was moved but goes back to the original body position and then instructs **B** to open his or her eyes once more and guess (go back to STEP 2).

Developing Auditory Skill

Form a group of four people (**A,B,C & D**)

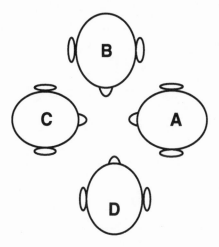

STEP 1. **A** sits or stands and **B,C & D** stand around **A** in a semi circle. **B, C & D** each in turn make a sound (i.e. snap fingers, tap a chair with a pencil, clap hands; as long as each person makes the same kind of sound) and as they do each repeats his or her name following their sound. **B, C & D** repeat the sound and name until **A** indicates she can identify each person by their corresponding sound.

STEP 2. **A** closes his or her eyes and **B, C** or **D** makes the sound. **A** is to guess which of them has made the sound.

STEP 3. If **A** misguesses then **B, C & D** repeat the original sound and his or her name until **A** indicates he or she can identify the match between name and corresponding sound. The group then repeats STEP 2.

STEP 4. To add an interesting twist, persons **B, C & D** can attempt to imitate each others sounds and person **A** must guess who is imitating who. For example, **A** may guess "**B** is imitating **C**" or "**B** is imitating **D**."

Developing Kinesthetic Skill

Form a group of four people (**A,B,C & D**)

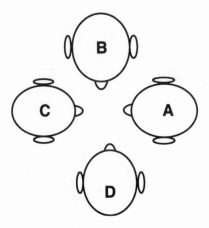

STEP 1. **A** sits or stands and persons **B, C & D** stand around in a semi-circle.

STEP 2. Person **A** is to orient his or her eyes down and to the right (or to the left if **A** is left handed) and take a deep breath in order to promote the maximum access to his or her feelings.

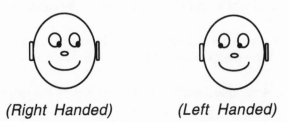

(Right Handed)   *(Left Handed)*

A is then instructed to close his or her eyes and **B, C & D** each take turns touching person **A**. They should each touch person **A** in the same place. Initially, **B, C & D** will each say his or her own name while touching person **A**. This is so that **A** can associate each person's touch with that person's name.

For example: **B, C & D** touch **A** on the back of the hand with their fingers or hands. **B, C & D** could also use an inanimate object such as a pencil or a piece of plastic. The important thing to remember is that each person needs to use the same object and touch **A** on the same area (i.e. **B, C & D** could touch **A** on the right first knuckle with their index fingers as they say their name). This process is repeated until **A** indicates that he or she can identify the touch associated with the name.

STEP 3. While **A** keeps his or her eyes closed either **B, C** or **D** will touch **A** without saying his or her name. **A** must then guess the name of who just touched him or her. Specifically, **A** looks down and right (or left) and compares the feelings of the touch he or she just received with the memory of the three touches he or she experienced previously. **A** picks the one that matches most closely and says aloud the name he or she has associated with that touch.

STEP 4. If **A** is unsuccessful in correctly guessing who just touched him or her, **A** should "recalibrate" by repeating STEPS 2 and 3. When **A** has guessed the correct person three times in a row proceed to the next section for the next level of the exercise.

STEP 5. **A** is again instructed to close his eyes and orient his eyes down and to the right or left. While **A** has his eyes shut **B, C &** **D** each touch **A**, in sequence, without verbally identifying themselves. **A** has to then match the names with the touches and guess the appropriate sequence. The sequences should be random, for example, <**B, D, C**> or <**C, D, B**>, etc.

STEP 6. If **A** is unsuccessful in identifying the correct sequence he or she may call for a "recalibration" by repeating STEP 2 (associating touches with names). When **A** has correctly identified three sequences in a row proceed to the next step.

STEP 7. In order to really stretch **A**'s ability to use his sense of touch, **B, C & D** can try to imitate each other's touch. With his eyes closed, **A** should attempt to guess who is imitating who. For example, **B** tries to make his quality of touch match that of **D** and **C** attempts to touch like **B**.

Exploring Perceptual Filters

Visual

1. Find a phenomenon that you can see in your external environment that is either stable or repetitive. Look at it for about 10 seconds.

2. Stop looking at the phenomenon and make a drawing of what you saw.

3. Find a partner and compare your drawings.

4. Take turns asking each other about the internal representation you used to make your drawing. i.e., Is your drawing exactly the same as your internal representation? If not, how are they different?

5. Especially check for any key features of the drawing that seem to be different from the external phenomenon.

6. Referring to the table of "submodalities" provided below, Go down the list of VISUAL submodalities with your partner. For each submodality distinction, look at the phenomenon focusing on that particular filter.

7. Compare your perceptions of where the phenomenon fits along the range of qualities defined by each submodality distinction using a scale of 1 to 10 (e.g., dim =1, bright =10).

8. Explore with your partner what reference point you assumed or presupposed in order to determine the scaling of the submodality distinction. (e.g., "Brighter than what?" "Bright compared with what?" The room? Other objects nearby in the environment? The light outside?)

9. Once again, stop looking at the phenomenon and make a drawing of what you saw.

10. Compare your new drawing with your partner and note what has changed.

11. Explore any changes in the internal representations you used to make your drawings by examining which submodality distinctions had the most impact and influence on your perception (internal cognitive map).

VISUAL SUBMODALITIES
BRIGHTNESS: dim—bright
SIZE: large—small
COLOR : black & white—*color*
MOVEMENT: *fast*—slow—still
DISTANCE: near—far
FOCUS: clear—*fuzzy*
LOCATION

Auditory

1. Find a phenomenon that you can hear in your external environment that is either stable or repetitive. Listen to it for about 10 seconds.

2. Stop listening to the phenomenon and find a way to auditorily reproduce what you heard using your own voice.

3. Find a partner and compare your reproductions.

4. Take turns asking each other about the internal representation you used to generate your reproductions. i.e., Is your voicing exactly the same as your internal representation? If not, how are they different?

5. Especially check for any key features of the reproduction that seem to be different from the external phenomenon.

6. Referring to the table of "submodalities" provided earlier, go down the list of AUDITORY submodalities with your partner. For each submodality distinction, listen again to the phenomenon paying attention to that particular filter.

7. Compare your perceptions of where the phenomenon fits along the range of qualities defined by each submodality distinction using a scale of 1 to 10 (e.g., quiet =1, loud =10).

8. Explore with your partner what reference point you assumed or presupposed in order to determine the scaling of the submodality distinction. (e.g., "Louder than what?" "Loud compared with what?" The other sounds in the room? Another memory you have of that sound?)

9. Once again, stop listening to the phenomenon and make a reproduction of what you heard using your own voice.

10. Compare your new voicing with your partner and note what has changed.

11. Explore any changes in the internal representations you used to make your reproduction by examining which submodality distinctions had the most impact and influence on your perception (internal cognitive map).

AUDITORY SUBMODALITIES
VOLUME: loud—quiet
TONE: **bass**—*treble*
PITCH: high—low
TEMPO: *fast*—slow
DISTANCE: close—far
RHYTHM
LOCATION

Kinesthetic

1. Find an object that you can touch in your external environment that is either stable or repetitive. Physically feel it for about 10 seconds.

2. Stop touching the object. Reproduce the physical sensations associated with what you touched, using parts of your hands or arms such that another person could experience the sensations by touching the reproduction(s) you have created using your hands or arms. (You may reproduce different features separately and guide your partner's hands.)

3. Find a partner and compare your physical reproductions.

4. Take turns asking each other about the internal representation you used to create your reproduction with your hands or arms. i.e., Is your reproduction exactly the same as your internal representation? If not, how are they different?

5. Especially check for any key features of the reproduction that are the most different from the external object.

6. Referring to the table of "submodalities" provided earlier, Go down the list of KINESTHETIC submodalities with your partner. For each submodality distinction, touch the object focusing on that particular filter.

7. Compare your perceptions of where the object fits along the range of qualities defined by each submodality distinction using a scale of 1 to 10 (e.g., smooth =1, rough =10).

8. Explore with your partner what reference point you assumed or presupposed in order to determine the scaling of the submodality distinction. (e.g., "Smoother than what?" "Smooth compared with what?" The skin on your hand? Other objects nearby in the environment?)

9. Once again, stop touching the object and make another reproduction with your hands or arms.

10. Compare your new reproduction with your partner and note what has changed.

11. Explore any changes in the internal representations you used to make your reproductions by examining which submodality distinctions had the most impact and influence on your perception (internal cognitive map).

KINESTHETIC SUBMODALITIES
INTENSITY: **strong**—weak
AREA: large—small
TEXTURE: rough—smooth
DURATION: constant—intermittent
TEMPERATURE: *hot*—cold
WEIGHT: **heavy**—light
LOCATION

'Telephone' Strategy Game

The following exercise is a multiple representational system version of the child's game 'telephone' which demonstrates some important features of cooperative learning and cognitive strategies.

Form group of four (**A**, **B**, **C**, & **D**).

1. Person **A** demonstrates a particular action or posture to Person **B**.

2. Person **B** draws a picture of Person **A**'s posture or behavior. Persons **B** & **C** do not get to see Person **A**'s original posture.

3. Person **B** shows his or her picture to Person **C**. Person **C** verbally describes the picture to Person **D**. Person C may only use words; he or she is not allowed to show the picture to Person D or demonstrate anything with his or her body.

4. Person **D** enacts person **C**'s description with his or her body.

5. Person **A** then reshows his or her initial posture and compares it with the posture of Person **D**.

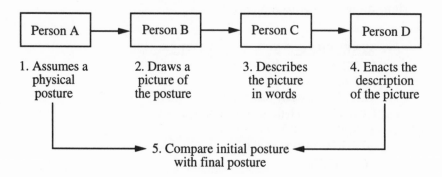

Diagram of 'Telephone' Strategy Game

There are a number of variations of this exercise. One typical structure is that the input and the output be the same representational system - i.e., visual in/visual out or auditory in/auditory out or physical in/physical out, movement in/movement out. In between the input and the output, you pass the information through one or two other representational systems. For instance, you could make a variation of this game in which Person B would draw a picture of Person A's posture and Person C would also have to draw a picture from looking at Person B's picture. So that you would have one picture being transformed into a second picture. Instead of describing it, Person C would give her drawing to Person D, and Person D would have to figure out how to enact that picture.

You could also have Person A start with a verbal description, Person B has to represent those words in pictures, Person C has to act out what he or she saw in the picture and Person D has to put that action into words. In this case you would have words coming in and words going out.

You could also change the relationships between the steps by changing their order. For example, you could have Person B describe Person A's posture to Person C, who would then have to draw a picture from Person B's description and show it to Person D.

To make the game more challenging you can allow Person A to move. The input would then be much more multi-faceted. It is also challenging to start with something purely tonal, like a quacking sound, and translate it through visual, kinesthetic or verbal representations.

This exercise is a basic metaphor for a strategy and can help you build intuitions about what makes a good strategy. If the group of people represented a brain, the sequence of transformations might be a learning strategy. Each person in the group is like a step in somebody's strategy for learning something.

To make a more effective sequence you can allow feedback loops in various places. For instance you may let Person A look at Person B's picture and ask, "What about this part of my posture? You might want to do it this way." This typically leads to a more accurate representation of the original input.

You may use this type of exercise to try to externalize and 'model' a particular mental strategy so you can study it. For instance, what type of 'telephone' game would you make if you were attempting to replicate the mental processes behind spelling?

Another interesting way to use this 'telephone' process is to attempt to construct a 'learning disabled' group.

Exploring The Structure of A Learning Strategy

To explore the structure of one of your own learning strategies, take a few moments and answer the following questions as completely as you can.

1. What is the subject that you are attempting to learn?

2. What are the learning goals or objectives that you are attempting to accomplish with respect to this subject?

3. What do you use as evidence to know that you are accomplishing those learning goals?

4. What do you do to get to the goals - what are some specific steps and activities that you use to achieve your learning goals with respect to this subject?

5. When you experience unexpected problems or difficulties in achieving your learning goals with this subject, what is your response to them? What specific activities or steps do you take to correct them?

Look back over your answers to the T.O.T.E. questions and see which R.O.L.E. Model elements you can identify.

1. Context:

What perceptual aspects of the context or subject were most involved in stimulating you to learn effectively?

Something you saw?
Something you heard?
Something you felt?
Something someone said?
Something you said to yourself?

2. Goals:

How did you cognitively represent your goals in this context?

Visualized them in imagination?
Remembered them visually?
Drew them?
Verbalized them to someone else?
Verbalized them to yourself?
Recalled something verbally?
Felt them?

3. Evidence:

What cognitive or sensory processes did you use to assess your progress toward your goals?

Something you saw?
Something you imagined?
Something you heard?
How you felt?
Something someone said?
Something you said to yourself?

4. Operations:

Which cognitive or perceptual processes did you use in relation to achieving your goals?

Fantasizing?   Self talk (inner dialogue)?

Intuitive Feelings?   Visual memory?   Emotions?

Drawing?   Discussing?   Touching?

Watching?   Listening?   Moving/Doing?

Recalled words or instructions?

5. Response to Problems:

Which cognitive or perceptual processes did you activate in response to problems?

Imagining options?   Self talk (inner dialogue)?

Intuitive Feelings?   Visually remembering options?

Recalled words or instructions?   Emotions?

Drawing?   Discussing?   Touching?

Watching?   Listening?   Changing Actions?

Cooperative Learning Exercise

Effective strategies may be transferred between two people. For example two teachers, or two musicians, or two spellers may have different strategies for accomplishing the same kind of task in the same context. Eliciting and sharing goals, evidence procedures and operations can help to widen and enrich the range and scope of your creative abilities.

Find a partner and choose a common task or a situation that requires learning. Each of you fill in the T.O.T.E. information on the chart below and compare your answers for the similarities and differences. Imagine what it would be like to add your partner's operations, evidence procedures, goals or responses to problems to your own strategy. How might it change or enrich the way you approach the situation?

Context: _____

	Person #1	Person #2
What are your goals?		
How do you know you are achieving your goals?		
What do you do in order to reach your goals? *What do you do if you are not satisfactorily reaching your goals?*		

Spelling Strategy

I. Beliefs

A. Spelling is a visual recognition skill that can be easily learned. This skill is a function of a mental strategy not an innate talent determined by the development of a "spelling gene."

B. Phonics, while it may be a useful backup system, is a less accurate and slower method to use for spelling than visualizing. (If you spelled "phonics" phonically you might end up with "f-o-n-i-x.")

II. Preparation

A. Think of something that is so familiar to you that you are confident you will never forget it (e.g., Your middle name, your telephone number, the front of your home, etc.). Pay close attention to the feelings of familiarity and confidence that you get from that memory that let you know you will never forget it. (K^r_1)

B. Think of something you have already successfully learned or accomplished that was an enjoyable challenge for you (e.g., your favorite sport, solving a puzzle or learning a new game, etc.). Remember the feelings of curiosity and challenge that motivated you to continue learning or accomplishing that goal. (K^r_2)

III. Steps

1. Look at the word you want to learn to spell. Make sure you are far enough away from the word that you can easily see all of the letters at once. (V^e_1)

2. Look up and to the left and visualize the letters as you just saw them. See if you can picture them in your favorite color. Keep looking at the written or printed word and putting your eyes up and left until you can see the letters clearly in your mind's eye. (V^r_1)

3. If you have difficulty visualizing the letters you may:

a. First picture something familiar to you - like a favorite movie scene, painting, toy, person, etc. Once you have that image clearly in your mind's eye, overlap the letters of the word you want to spell on top of that image that is already easy to see. $(V^r_2 \longrightarrow V^r_1)$

b. Break the word you want to spell into chunks that are each three letters long. Visualize the first three letters until they are clear enough that you can easily see them. Then add the next three and focus on them until you can see the first six letters. Continue adding the chunks of three letters to the letters you can already see until you have finished the whole word. $(V^r_2 \longrightarrow V^r_1)$

4. Compare the feelings you get as you look at the word in your mind's eye to the feelings of familiarity and confidence you remember from something that you will never forget. If the feelings do not match the feeling of curiosity and challenge you felt with the earlier successful learning experience then go back to **step #1** and repeat the process. $(K^i/K^r_1 \longrightarrow K^r_2)$

5. Put the spelling word you are learning out of sight. Copy down or read off the letters you see in your mind and compare the result with the correct spelling. If they do not match, remember again the feeling of curiosity and challenge from your past success, return to **step #1** and repeat the process. $(V^r_1 \longrightarrow V^e_2/V^e_1 \longrightarrow K^r_2)$

6. Look at the word in your mind's eye and once again compare the feelings you get as you look at it to the feelings of familiarity and confidence you get from something you will never forget. If the feelings do not match, strengthen and clarify the image in your mind. $(V^r_1 \longrightarrow K^i/K^r_1)$

7. Remove the spelling of the word you are learning from sight. Spell the word backwards by copying down or reading the letters you see in your mind in reverse order - that is, starting with the letter farthest to the right and moving to the left. If you are writing them down, place them on the paper from right to left also so that when you are finished the word looks correct. $(V^r_1 \longrightarrow V^e_2)$

8. Check the letters you have produced against the correct spelling. If they do not match, go to **step #7** and repeat the process. (V^e_2/V^e_1)

IV. Notation

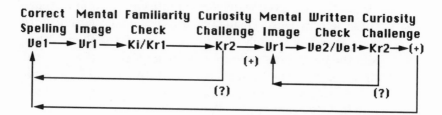

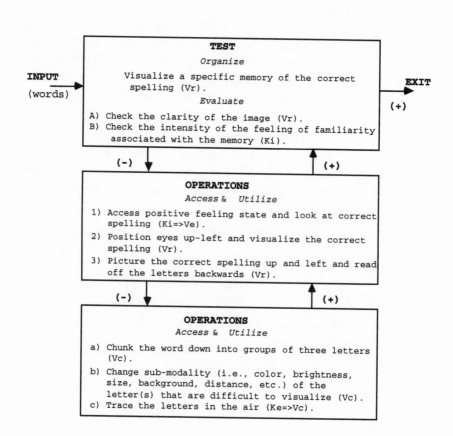

Basic Spelling Strategy
(Short Version)

1. Place the correct spelling of the word to be learned either:

    a. directly in front of you at about eye level; or

    b. above eye level and to your upper left (or right if you are left handed).

2. Close your eyes and think of something that feels *confident, familiar and relaxing*. When the feeling is strong, open your eyes and look at the correct spelling.

    a. If you placed the correct spelling in front of you, move your eyes up and to the left (or right) and picture the correct spelling in your mind's eye.

    b. If you placed the correct spelling to your upper left, remove the correct spelling, but keep your eyes up and to the left and continue to see the correct spelling in your mind's eye.

    (If you have difficulty use the __Helpful Hints__ on the following page.)

3. Look up at your mental image and verbalize (or write) the letters you see. Check what you have verbalized or written with the correct spelling. If any letters are missing or incorrect, return to *step #1* and use the Helpful Hints to help clarify your mental image.

4. Look up at your mental image and spell the word backwards *(i.e., verbalize or write the letters down from right to left)*. Compare what you have verbalized written with the correct spelling. If you have difficulty or any letters are missing or incorrect, go back to *step #2* and use the Helpful Hints to assist in clarifying your mental image.

HELPFUL HINTS

A. Picture the word in your *favorite color.*

B. *Make any unclear letters stand out* by making them look different than the others in some way - e.g. *bigger, brighter, closer, a different color, etc.*

C. Break the word into *groups of three letters* and build your picture three letters at a time.

D. Put the letters on a *familiar background.* Picture something like a familiar object or movie scene and then put the letters you want to remember on top of it.

E. If it is a long word, make the letters small enough so that you can *see the whole word easily.*

F. *Trace the letters in the air* with your finger and picture in your mind the letters you are writing.

Basic Language Learning Strategies

A. 'Second Position' Modeling

1. Find a person who is a native speaker of a language that you do not already know. This person is to utter a phrase, question or greeting, engaging whatever cultural nonverbal communication goes along naturally with that phrase.

2. A second person in the group is to 'step into the native speaker's shoes' and imitate the non-verbal and verbal communication.

3. A third person will be watching to make sure that the imitation is a good match.

4. After the second person has done this type of 'second position modeling' a few times, then he or she gets to guess what it is that he or she has been saying.

5. The native speaker will then tell person number two whether or not he or she was accurate. Accuracy is not to be judged solely by guessing the content of the statement, but also on the 'meta message' of the statement.

B. Simple Vocabulary

1. Find a native or expert speaker of the language you want to learn to use as a model. The same strategy will work for a foreign language as well as English.

2. Have the model make a list of six specific objects (e.g. door, chair, book, wall, etc.) and six actions or activities (e.g. run, jump, touch, hold, etc.) that are in the immediate environment or are easy to act out.

   Note: Include articles, etc., if they are a necessary part of the name.

3. Have the model show and pronounce the word and then either draw or point to it (if it is an object) or act it out (if it is an action). Repeat three times.

4. Have the model say and/or show the name of one object and one action (or vice versa depending on the syntax of the language).

   a. If the word is spoken, the student must pretend that he or she is the model and mimic the pronunciation and expression (including gestures) of the model. (NOTE: This is different than trying to pronounce the word "correctly.")

   b. If the word is shown, the student must copy the characters that make up the word. Initially you may allow the student to look at the characters as she or he is copying it. Later you can require that it be done from memory.

   c. Once the students are familiar with the words you may (1) show the words and require the students to pronounce them; or (2) say the words and require the students to write them.

5. The student must act out the indicated action to or with the indicated object. If the student makes a mistake, the model presents the words again and demonstrates the appropriate behavior.

6. Once the student has mastered all of the combinations created by pairing single objects with single actions, the model may string together combinations of object-action pairs (adding in articles and conjunctions as needed).

7. To continue building basic vocabulary, repeat the process adding other sets of objects and actions.

C. Adjectives *(e.g. green, round, tall, etc.)*

1. Show 3 different objects, that the student has already learned, that share the named quality. For instance, if the adjective you are teaching is "green," you would show a "green" pencil, a "green" chair and a "green" ball.

2. Show 2 objects that are exactly the same except in the quality named. (e.g., a "green" pencil and a red pencil.)

3. Use the basic structure applied for 'objects and actions' to present the words to the student.

4. Test comprehension by having the student identify (a) a different object that shares the named quality (e.g., a "green" shirt), and (b) a similar object that differs in the named quality (e.g., a blue pencil).

D. Adverbs and Prepositions *(e.g. fast, up, left, over, etc.)*

1. Do 3 examples of different actions, that the student has already learned, keeping the named quality the same. For example, if the adverb is "fast," you could walk fast, crawl fast and dance fast.

2. Demonstrate 2 examples of the same action varying only the named quality. (e.g., walk fast and walk slowly).

3. Present the new words to the student using the procedure applied for 'objects and actions'.

4. Test comprehension by having the student demonstrate (a) a different action that shares the named quality, and (b) the differences in quality by varying that quality in an action as he or she names it.

E. Obstacle Course

1. Build a simple obstacle course out of chairs, books, boxes, etc.

2. Provide the group members with basic directional signals in the other language; i.e., 'fast', 'slow', 'stop', 'go', 'frontwards', 'back-wards', 'left', 'right', etc. Demonstrate the actions associated with each directional word.

3. Each learner is to choose a partner. One member of the pair is to close his or her eyes or be blindfolded. The other is to be a kind of guide or 'guardian angel' who can only speak in the other language that you've been learning.

4. The 'guardian angel' is to guide the 'explorer' through the obstacle course using only the directional words from the other language.

F. Nominalizations, Abstractions *(e.g. communication, love, relationship, etc.)* and **Unspecified Verbs** *(e.g. help, find, hurt, go, etc.)*

These types of words indicate a) classes or compounds of the more simple objects and actions, b) processes involving groups of objects or actions or c) relationships between objects or actions.

1. Give at least 3 examples that fall into the category, compound, process or relationship named.

2. Give 2 examples that are similar except that they differ in the type of category, process, compound or relationship.

3. Repeat the modeling process described earlier to present the words.

4. Test comprehension by having the student provide examples that fit and examples that do not fit the category, compound, process or relationship named.

G. Idioms

1. Pick one or two idioms, or idiomatic phrases, that you may have only heard in the language to be learned.

2. Create a context in which that idiom will get meaning; i.e., illustrate the meaning through a created situation, or through the meta messages. Initially, the goal is to convey the overall sense of the idiom. This is probably best done using the 'second position' modeling method described in the first language exercise.

3. Translate the idiom or use descriptions or explanations to give learners a more precise sense of the idiom.

H. Simple Syntax

1. Introduce syntax initially in 3 part sequences (i.e. subject-predicate- object, or whatever basic order is appropriate for the particular language). Demonstrate the changes in meaning that occur as you change the order.

   (e.g. "The boy runs to the chair." "The chair runs to the boy.")

2. Distinguish between grammatical and semantic errors.

   a. It is grammatically correct to say or write *"The chair ran fast to the door,"* but grammatically incorrect to say or write *"The boy the ran chair to."*

   b. It is semantically incorrect to say or write *"The rock drank the chair,"* although it is grammatically correct.

3. Demonstrate why these are considered errors by comparing correct and incorrect sequences and have the student try to act them out.

4. Test by having the student say or write and then act out correct and incorrect sequences.

I. Role Playing

Create several role plays, contextualizing verbal interactions to common situations that the learner might encounter while speaking the other language. For instance, pretend to be a waiter or waitress in a restaurant. The learner sits in a 'booth' at the restaurant while you show and describe various foods. The learner would then try to order a meal from you.

Another possibility would be to give the learner directions to some location in the language to be learned. The learner would try to find that location based on your directions.

Accelerated Reading Strategy

I. Calibrate Your Natural Reading Speed

1. Read a few paragraphs of written material at the speed that seems most natural and comfortable for you. Have your partner look at a watch or clock and note your starting time.

2. When you are finished, signal your partner to check the time. Record the number of seconds it took you to read the material. Count up the number of words you have read. (If you need to, you can estimate it by counting the number of words in one line, counting the number of lines and multiplying the lines by the number of words per line.)

3. Determine your reading speed by dividing the number of words you read by the number of seconds it took you to read them and then multiplying by 60: *Reading Speed* = (# of words/# of seconds) X 60.

    Another strategy is to read for 30 seconds, figure out how many words you read during that time and then double it. That will give you a sense of how many words per minute you are reading. (The average adult reading speed is about 275 words per minute.)

4. Check your comprehension by having your partner ask you five questions about the material that you have read. Note the accuracy of your answers.

II. Beliefs About Reading.

A. It is possible to recognize words and derive meaning from them without having to pronounce them verbally to yourself.

B. Seeing is instantaneous.

C. The human nervous system is capable of registering much more than is available in conscious awareness.

III. Expand Your Peripheral Vision to See Word Clusters.

Fix your eyes on a certain spot and see how many words you can see on either side of that spot, without moving your eyes. For instance, consider the words below. Fix your eyes on the 'X' in the middle and notice if you can see the words on either side of it as they become progressively farther apart.

	blue	**X**	ball	
	red	**X**	car	
green		**X**		sea
brown		**X**		horse

Something similar can also be done with flash cards. Words may be written on small cards which can then be held farther and farther apart. For instance, you can have your partner focus on your nose, and then hold up a card in each of your hands, holding them on either side of your face. You can help your partner develop more peripheral vision by holding the cards progressively farther apart.

Other variations include using cards with numbers or colors written on them. Rather than read the words, your partner is to tell you the result of combining the two words (i.e., the sum of the numbers or the result of mixing the two colors).

IV. Choose an Appropriate Eye Scanning Pattern.

1. Holding a book, locate the position in which you can see the most number of words easily —that is, where you can see word clusters as opposed to individual words. Make sure you are able to keep your arms comfortable (you may want to prop your book against a chair or something).

2. Have your partner watch your eyes while you read and help you identify your habitual eye scanning pattern. The most common pattern is to move the eyes, or the eyes and head, across the page from left to right, scanning each line on the page. A faster reader, may move his or her eyes in a less linear way, allowing them to drift around a paragraph or scanning it diagonally instead of looking at it line by line. You might not even have any clear set pattern of eye movement while you read.

3. Apply the principle of 'pacing and leading' to shift your eye scanning pattern a little. Take your current scanning pattern and shift it a little bit, so that you are reading just a little bit faster in such a way that it feels natural. For instance, instead of looking at each word or each line, you might want to try looking at several words or several lines at once. Instead of scanning across each line, you may try looking straight down the page. You may want to try scanning straight down the page looking back and forth between two parallel points slightly in from left and right edges of the paragraph. You can even move your eyes in a diagonal pattern from right to left across the page, in order to prevent any attempt at sounding out.

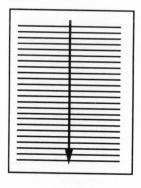 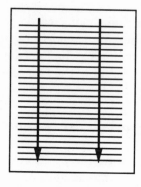 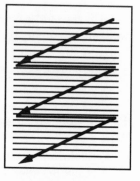

Scanning straight   Scanning between   Zig-zagging from
down the center   two parallel points   right to left
of the page

Some Possible Eye Scanning Patterns

V. Reduce Sub-Vocalization and Internal Pronunciation

Try to hear or vocalize only selected words. For instance, read only selected words. Look for verbs, adjectives, adverbs and nouns. There is no need to read every word. You can skip over articles, conjunctions, prepositions, etc. You can also hold a pen or pencil between your teeth to help stop reading aloud.

VI. Develop a Visual Comprehension Strategy

A. Comprehension of written material is based on the mental map you derive from the text rather than from the actual words.

B. All written subjects are organized around a central theme. That central theme is the core for understanding that written material. The central theme is supported by the rest of the reading text.

C. For speed in reading written material, visualizing is the most effective method for creating a mental map of the central theme and supporting information because it allows you to quickly grasp and add to the "big picture."

To develop this strategy, practice making your own visual map of what you've read. On a piece of paper draw a picture or a diagram that represents the core theme and the key supporting information. This picture does not need to be understood by others. It only has to represent the information to you. Go over the key words of what you have read and draw a picture illustrating key words. For instance, if you were reading about two people, you could draw two stick figures. If you were reading about the brain, you could draw a picture of a brain.

VII. Preorganization Strategy

A. As you think about the subject area relating to your reading material ask yourself the following questions:

1. *What is my goal in reading this material? What do I want to do with what I learn?*

2. *What is something that is interesting and important to me that I can learn more about from reading this material?*

3. *What do I already know about this subject?*

4. *What do I want to learn about the subject? What do I want to look for in the text? (i.e., Who? What? When? Where? Why? How?)*

B. As you ask yourself these questions begin to build an image or a movie in your mind's eye that represents and encapsulates what you already know about the subject.

VIII. Finding Your Physiological State for Reading

A. Think of experiences in which you were:

1. so excited and eager to learn about something that it seemed like you couldn't get enough - a time when it seemed like all of your mental processes were working at top speed.

2. able to be completely relaxed and open to any external information (i.e., watching a movie or a television program).

3. in such a state of heightened awareness that it seemed that the world around you was moving in 'slow motion' (such as a time you avoided an automobile accident).

Put yourself fully back in the experiences and pay attention to the feelings you had and, in particular, your posture, breathing rate and other physical attributes. Before you begin reading your material, put yourself back into that body posture as completely as you can.

B. Using the strategies and principles described previously, try reading utilizing each of the different states described above. Read a page of material as quickly as you can. Have a partner note the time you began and ended, and determine your reading speed. Check your comprehension by having your partner ask you five questions about the material you have just read. Determine which states are optimal for different kinds of reading results (i.e., comfort, speed, comprehension, etc.).

IX. Recalibrate Your New Natural Reading Speed

Check the effects of the strategies and principles you have been developing have had on your natural reading speed by going through the following steps with your partner.

1. Find the state that will naturally and easily support what you want to learn and the way you want to learn it. Before you begin reading, put yourself in the physiology that represents that state.

2. Read another page of material at a speed that feels natural and comfortable for you. Have your partner keep track of the time so you can determine your reading speed. (You may also choose to read comfortable for 30 seconds.)

3. Test your comprehension by having your partner ask you five questions about the material you just read.

Speed Scanning Strategy

Identify a topic that you need to gather information about (e.g. "leadership," "cancer," "reading," "learning disabilities," etc.). Review what you already know about this topic and build an image or movie in your mind's eye that represents and encapsulates what you already know about the subject. (V^r)

Gather a series of books or articles relevant to the topic you are researching.

Steps

1. Look at the title of the book or article to be read. (V^e)

2. To find the central theme, construct an image based on what experiences are triggered by the words in the title. (V^c_1)

3. Compare the constructed image to the picture you already formed regarding your subject matter. (V^c_1/V^r)

4. Decision Point (K^i -> A_d)

   a. If you have no constructed picture or it has only a vague similarity to your remembered image of your subject, feel that you want to clarify the relationship and say, *"I'm curious,"* and continue with **step #5**.

   b. If there is already a complete match then say, *"I already know that,"* and look through your other reading material.

5. Look again at the words in the next sub-heading in the reading material. (V^e)

6. Compare the image you construct out of the associations with these printed words with the image you initially constructed when you looked at the title. (V^c_2/V^c_1)

7. Decision Point (K^i)

   a. If these images match, then feel that you are reading relevant material and go on to **step #8**.

b. If the images do not match then get the feeling that what you are reading is not relevant and look for another word in the heading or skip to the next heading and go back to **step #5**.

8. Move the index finger of your right hand down the center of the page you are reading. Parallel to this, and at the same rate of speed, move your left hand down the left margin. This movement will help to maintain a rapid reading pace. (K^e)

9. Look at words and groups of words in the text. (V^e)

10. Fill in and add to the constructed image, that you began when you looked at the sub-heading, with any new images associated with the words you are seeing in the body of the text. (V^c_2)

11. Compare the filled out image with the picture you initially formed of the relevant subject matter. (V^c_2/V^r)

12. Decision Point (K^i)

a. If there is a match or coordination of the two images then feel good that you are learning and mark the new image with a positive feeling so it will be easy to remember later. Continue the scanning process at **step #8** until you reach the next sub-heading. When you reach the next sub-heading go to **step #5**.

b. If there is a mismatch or uncertainty about the images, then feel that the new pictures don't fit, clear your mental screen and either go to **step #5** and skip the rest of the material under the current sub-heading or rescan the text by repeating **step #8**.

If you rescanned the material once already and it still does not fit with the constructed image representing the central theme then go to **step #5** and skip the rest of the text under the current sub-heading.

Notation

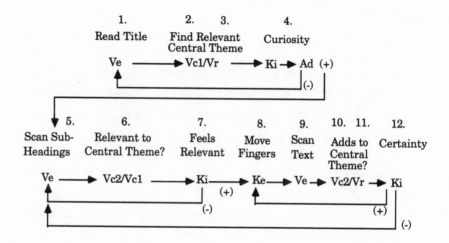

Creative Writing Strategy

I. Beliefs

A. Everyone already has the content (experiences) that they need to write effectively. These experiences form the 'deep structure' of creative writing.

B. The process of writing is a matter of transforming or translating that experiential 'deep structure' into verbal 'surface structures' (words and sentences) representing those experiences. It is a matter of representing experiences through language and then connecting those experiences together in some kind of a sequential fashion.

C. Certain words can serve as *"prompts"* to help draw out and connect our representations of our experiences in an orderly way.

D. Engaging the other senses, such as touch and sight, facilitates the creative writing process.

E. Writing is as easy as talking. If you are communicating to someone your ideas flow more easily.

II. Preparation

A. Write down the name of what you will be writing about.

B. Think of whether the composition will primarily be about:

   1. something you are remembering from the past; or

   2. something you are making up.

C. *Make a **picture in your mind's eye** of what you want to write about.* Look at the experience you want to write about from *different points of view* and through the eyes of the different people or characters and visualize what they might be seeing.

   1. Listen internally for any **sounds or noises** associated with what you want to write about.

2. Get in touch with any *feelings* you have regarding what you want to write about. What *actions and emotions* do you feel. Step inside of different characters and notice how your feelings change.

3. Listen to what *words* come to mind as you think about the experience. Ask yourself what different characters would say about the experience.

D. *Visualize who you you want to write for* or who might be interested in reading about this topic. Think about what kinds of reactions you would want them to have about your composition. As you begin to put this experience into words, *picture how this person might respond to what you are writing.* What *pictures or images* could you paint with your words that would get the types of reactions you want.

1. Think of what *sounds or noises* you could write about that might get the types of reactions you want.

2. What *feelings* could you describe or put your reader in touch with that would get them to feel the way you want them to feel as they are reading your composition?

3. Think of what kinds of *words* you would use if you were telling your reader about your experience. What words might you choose to get the reactions you want from your reader?

Column A	Column B	Column C	Column D
Connective	*Perspective*	*Representational System and Time Frame*	
because	I	see(s) - saw - will see	that
therefore	We	hear(s) - heard - will hear	like
after	You	feel(s) - felt - will feel	how
while	She	look(s) - looked - will look	as if
whenever	He	sound(s) - sounded - will sound	
so that	They	touch(es) - touched - will touch	
if	It	show(s) - showed - will show	
although		say(s) - said - will say	
in the same way that		move(s) - moved - will move	

1. Write a beginning sentence for your paragraph in the space below. You can start simply with something like: *"I want to write about...(your topic),"* or *"(Your topic)...is fun,"* or *"You will be interested in...(your topic)."*

   _____.

2. Read the sentence you have written above. Then read (silently) one word from each of the columns listed at the top of the page and mentally fill in the words that come to you most easily to complete the sentence you have started. Write them on the line below. (Do not write down any of the words from the columns.)

   _____.

3. Now read the sentence you have written above and once again, silently add four words chosen randomly from columns A, B, C, and D above. Fill in the new sentence you have begun and write it below leaving out the words from the columns.

   _____.

4. Repeat the above process again using different words from each of the columns.

_____.

5. Read the sentences you have written on the line above one after the other.

    a. If what you have written does not adequately represent the experience you started with or does not seem like it will get the kind of reaction you want from your intended reader, go back to step #1 and repeat the process again with the same beginning sentence. Experiment with different combinations of words from each of the columns.

    b. If you are satisfied with the flow of ideas then you may refine or add to them in order to create a paragraph.

    c. Write the finished sentences in the spaces provided below to make a complete paragraph.

_____.

_____.

_____.

_____.

_____.

    d. Start a new paragraph by writing a new beginning sentence at the top of the next page and follow the strategy from step #1.

Column A	Column B	Column C	Column D
		Representational System	
Connective	*Perspective*	*and Time Frame*	
because	I	see(s) - saw - will see	that
therefore	We	hear(s) - heard - will hear	like
after	You	feel(s) - felt - will feel	how
while	She	look(s) - looked - will look	as if
whenever	He	sound(s) - sounded - will sound	
so that	They	touch(es) - touched - will touch	
if	It	show(s) - showed - will show	
although		say(s) - said - will say	
in the same way that		move(s) - moved - will move	

1. Write a beginning sentence for your paragraph in the space below. You can start simply with something like: *"I want to write about...(your topic),"* or *"(Your topic)...is fun,"* or *"You will be interested in...(your topic)."*

_____.

2. Read the sentence you have written above. Then read (silently) one word from each of the columns listed at the top of the page and mentally fill in the words that come to you most easily to complete the sentence you have started. Write them on the line below. (Do not write down any of the words from the columns.)

_____.

3. Now read the sentence you have written above and once again silently add four words chosen randomly from columns A, B, C, and D above. Fill in the new sentence you have begun and write it below leaving out the words from the columns.

_____.

4. Repeat the above process again using different words from each of the columns.

_____.

5. Read the sentences you have written on the line above one after the other.

   a. If what you have written does not adequately represent the experience you started with or does not seem like it will get the kind of reaction you want from your intended reader, go back to step #1 and repeat the process again with the same beginning sentence. Experiment with different combinations of words from each of the columns.

   b. If you are satisfied with the flow of ideas then you may refine or add to them in order to create a paragraph.

   c. Write the finished sentences in the spaces provided below to make a complete paragraph.

_____.

_____.

_____.

_____.

_____.

   d. Start a new paragraph by writing a new beginning sentence at the top of the next page and follow the strategy from step #1.

Column A	Column B	Column C	Column D
		Representational System	
Connective	*Perspective*	*and Time Frame*	
because	I	see(s) - saw - will see	that
therefore	We	hear(s) - heard - will hear	like
after	You	feel(s) - felt - will feel	how
while	She	look(s) - looked - will look	as if
whenever	He	sound(s) - sounded - will sound	
so that	They	touch(es) - touched - will touch	
if	It	show(s) - showed - will show	
although		say(s) - said - will say	
in the same way that		move(s) - moved - will move	

1. Write a beginning sentence for your paragraph in the space below. You can start simply with something like: *"I want to write about...(your topic),"* or *"(Your topic)...is fun,"* or *"You will be interested in...(your topic)."*

_____.

2. Read the sentence you have written above. Then read (silently) one word from each of the columns listed at the top of the page and mentally fill in the words that come to you most easily to complete the sentence you have started. Write them on the line below. (Do not write down any of the words from the columns.)

_____.

3. Now read the sentence you have written above and once again silently add four words chosen randomly from columns A, B, C, and D above. Fill in the new sentence you have begun and write it below leaving out the words from the columns.

_____.

4. Repeat the above process again using different words from each of the columns.

_____.

5. Read the sentences you have written on the line above one after the other.

   a. If what you have written does not adequately represent the experience you started with or does not seem like it will get the kind of reaction you want from your intended reader, go back to step #1 and repeat the process again with the same beginning sentence. Experiment with different combinations of words from each of the columns.

   b. If you are satisfied with the flow of ideas then you may now refine or add to them in order to create a paragraph.

   c. Write the finished sentences in the spaces provided below to make a complete paragraph.

_____.

_____.

_____.

_____.

_____.

6. On the following page, write all three paragraphs that you have composed on the previous pages.

_____.

_____.

_____.

_____.

_____.

_____.

_____.

_____.

_____.

_____.

_____.

_____.

_____.

_____.

As you look over the paragraphs above, adjust, edit or modify them in the way that would be most effective and appealing for the audience you are writing for.

Appendix C:
Research Studies on the NLP Spelling Strategy

In many ways the NLP orientation toward 'mental program-ming' makes it easier to adapt effective learning strategies to computerized instruction. In fact, I (Dilts) have made the basic spelling strategy into a computer program. The program follows the basic format described in Chapter 6. It shows the st :dent the correct spelling of a word in a color selected by the student. The student is instructed to look up and to their left hand side and visualize the word in his or her mind's eye. After typing in the word left-to-right, the student is instructed to type in the spelling starting on the right hand side and moving to the left. The program is quite simple but has demonstrated significant results.

In fact, this program was researched at the University of Moncton in New Brunswick, Canada (see abstract) in order to test the basic tenets of the strategy - and the NLP model. The research began with the selection of 44 average spellers as determined by their scores on a PRETEST composed of made-up nonsense words. All of these students had scored roughly the same on the test.

The research procedure consisted of using four variations of the computerized spelling strategy (this served to avoid differences in the influence of the experimenters in giving instructions). The first version showed the various spelling words and gave the instruction to visualize the word while looking up and to the left (**VUL**). The second version had the instruction to visualize the words and look down and right (**VDR**) - a position the NLP model associates with feelings instead of imagery. The third version instructed students simply to visualize the words with no reference to any eye position (**VIS**). The final version simply instructed the students to study the word in order to learn it (**STU**), thus using whatever strategy they were already using. The students were divided randomly into four groups of eleven. Each different group used one of the different computer programs to learn made-up nonsense words (so there would not be any chance that they would already know the word). They were then tested on the words they had learned (POST-TEST).

The results showed a **20-25% increase** in the correct spellings of the students who had looked up and to the left and visualized (**VUL**), a **10% increase** in the ones who had been instructed to visualize only (**VIS**), the students who were instructed to study the words (**STU**) - thus using their previous learning strategy - stayed roughly **the same**, as one would expect, but the scores of the students who were instructed to look down and to the right (**VDR**) while visualizing (i.e., to an inappropriate accessing cue) **worsened by about 15%.** *(See diagram.)*

THE EFFECT OF EYE PLACEMENT
ON ORTHOGRAPHIC MEMORIZATION
François Loiselle
Faculté des sciences sociales Université de Moncton

Abstract. After reviewing research on mental imagery and eye movements, F. Loiselle (1985) presents the Neuro-Linguistic Programming model (Grinder, Bandler, Dilts) and one of its applications to education, a spelling strategy developed by Behavioral Engineering (Dilts) that uses eye placement to facilitate visualization. Using variations of this strategy and a control group, Loiselle studies the relationship between eye placement, instructions to draw up visual images and capacity for orthographic memorization of nonsense words.

Forty-four subjects were divided into four groups, identified by primary instruction given: visualize looking up and left (VUL), visualize looking down and right (VDR), visualize (VIS), study (STU). The VUL group was instructed to look up to the left and form a visual image of the sequence of letters in the words used as stimuli. The VDR group received the same instruction, except that they were instructed to look down and right. The VIS group was instructed to form a visual image of the sequence of the letters in the words without an eye position suggested. Finally, the STU group was instructed to study the words.

Results indicate significant interactions and an analysis for simple effects (Kirk) show that the VUL group was the only one to increase significantly the number of words spelled correctly for immediate (post-test) and short-term (final test) retention. The VUL group also made more eye movements toward positions 1,7, and 8 (up left, up right, up center) relative to other groups. Finally, the VUL group did not use more training time than other groups who underwent training.

In conclusion, results appear to indicate that a high eye position, particularly a high left, facilitates orthographic memorization.

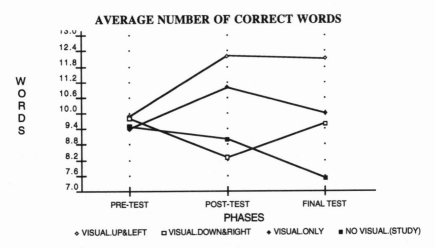

AVERAGE NUMBER OF CORRECT WORDS

Prepared by L.Y. Bourque (1987) with F. Loiselle's authorization.

A further indication of the impact of the NLP principles came when students were tested for retention (FINAL TEST). This test was given to see how much students had retained from their POST-TEST words. The students were simply retested on the words and were not required to do any particular process to remember. The results of this test showed close to **100% retention** of the words memorized by the group who were instructed to both visualize and look up and left (**VUL**). This group also showed more spontaneous eye movements to the upward eye position they had been trained in. The group who had been given the instructions to visualize only (**VIS**) had a **drop off in their scores of about 7%.** The control group (**STU**) who had not been instructed in any strategy in particular, showed a **decline** in their scores of about **15%** (the standard drop according to the normal statistical learning curve). The group that had been instructed to visualize but look to the inappropriate position (**VDR**), however, actually showed an **improvement** in their scores of about **10-15%!** According to the NLP model, this would make sense because they were no longer required to put their eyes in a position that was incompatible with the cognitive process they were being instructed to perform. The final difference in retention between the control group and the group using the visual spelling strategy was over **61%.** This could easily make the difference between a failing and a passing test score.

There are a number of important implications of this research. In addition to demonstrating the importance of visualizing as the most appropriate cognitive strategy for spelling (all of the groups told to visualize ended up with better retention than the control group), it showed the importance of the relationship between accessing cues and underlying mental processes. Subtle physiological behaviors can support or inhibit specific mental steps. In fact, one of the important implications of this research is that the worse place a student should keep their eyes while taking a test is probably on the paper in front of them (i.e., down as opposed to up) as they are usually instructed. In fact, students attempting to visualize are often reprimanded or ridiculed with statements such as, *"Do you think the answer is written on the ceiling? Keep your eyes on the paper in front of you."* The research described above indicates that this can actually inhibit access to information the person actually knows. Obviously, NLP principles have important implications in how the process of education occurs in our society.

Another research study conducted at the University of Utah (see abstract) compared a more complete version of the NLP spelling strategy with a control group (who were given no strategy at all) and a group using a phonetically based auditory rule learning strategy. Again average spellers with similar test scores were utilized as subjects. As with the other study, students using the visual spelling strategy improved their scores by **20-25%** (some reaching perfect scores) with almost **100% retention.** That much improvement would easily raise a "C" student to an "A" student. The group using the auditory rule learning strategy (which is actually different from simple 'sounding out') improved by **15%** but showed a **drop off** in retention of over **5%**. The control group, as expected, showed **no improvement.** (See diagram.)

The groups were also tested with a new set of words to learn but were offered no instructions for how to learn them in order to see how much the strategy would automatically generalize without any further instruction. Once more, the visual spelling strategy showed more significant generalization to new lists of words than the auditory rule learning strategy. These results again demonstrate the superiority of the spelling method based on the NLP modeling principles.

COGNITIVE STRATEGIES AND A CLASSROOM PROCEDURE
FOR TEACHING SPELLING

Thomas E. Malloy
Dept. of Psychology
University of Utah

Abstract - Using the techniques of NLP, Robert Dilts developed a spelling strategy with visualization as a key element. Dr. Malloy adapted this strategy into a cognitive spelling package for the classroom. In an experiment evaluating the effectiveness of the cognitive spelling package one group was taught to spell via the spelling package, a second group via standard spelling rules, and a third group was not trained. Both training groups showed significant improvement in spelling pre-to-post-tests compared to the no training control. The spelling package group showed generally larger gains than did the standard training group. Only the spelling package group showed significant generalization to new lists of words. The usefulness of parallel visual and phonetic spelling strategies is discussed. The spelling package is used as an example to discuss several general theoretical principles in designing methods to teach cognitive strategies.

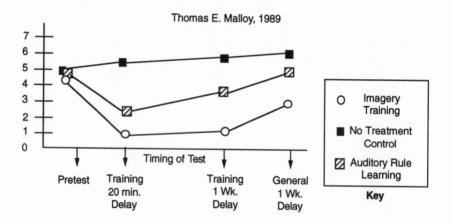

People often complain that there is no research to support the basic tenets of NLP. The studies described above validate not only the specific application of NLP for the improvement of spelling, but also the fundamental principles of accessing cues, representational systems and strategies.

Appendix D: Math Strategy

Math strategy uses the interplay between eye movements and memory to teach an effective strategy for memorizing basic addition, subtraction, division and multiplication tables. People who are good at memorizing and equations use their mind's eye to form a clear mental image of those equations. Math Strategy shows you how to learn equations by forming mental pictures of them.

1. Place the correct equation in front of you so you can see it easily.

2. Close your eyes and think of something that feels *familiar and relaxing*. When the feeling is strong, open your eyes and look at the correct equation.

3. *Move your eyes up and to the left* and picture the correct equation in your mind's eye. *(If you have difficulty use the* **Helpful Hints** *on the following page.)*

4. Look up at your mental image and write down the numbers and symbols you see. Check what you have written against the correct equation. If incorrect go to **step #1.**

5. Look up at your mental image and read off the numbers and symbols backwards *(write the equation down from right to left)*. Check the equation. If incorrect, go to **step #3.**

HELPFUL HINTS

A. Picture the equation in your *favorite color*.

B. *Break the equation in half.* Once you can clearly see the letters and symbols on one side of the "=" then add the numbers on the other side.

C. Make any unclear numbers or symbols stand out by making them look different than the others in some way - e.g. *bigger, brighter, closer, etc.*

D. Put the equation on a *familiar background.* Picture something like a familiar object or movie scene then put the equation you want to remember on top of it.

E. If it is a long equation, make the numbers and symbols small enough so that you can *see the whole equation* easily.

F. *Trace the equation in the air with your finger* and picture in your mind the numbers and symbols you are writing.

Appendix E:
The Writing Cubes Program

The *Writing Cubes Program* is a multi-sensory, hands-on program which stimulates creative and productive writing. Designed by Robert Dilts and Kolman Korentayer, the Writing Cubes Program is based upon the Dynamic Learning creative writing strategy described in this book. The core of the program involves key words placed on the faces of specially designed cubes. The purpose of the cubes is to help people focus their attention and then stimulate and link thinking processes through movement and sensory-motor activity. The student uses the words and cubes to help generate sentences and ideas while writing. The key words on the cubes may be organized in specific sequences in order to draw out particular pathways of associations or may be referred to randomly in order to increase spontaneity.

The Writing Cubes Program was developed by combining principles of Dynamic Learning with the *Feldenkrais Functional Integration Process*. The Feldenkrais Functional Integration method, developed by Moshe Feldenkrais, explores the impact of the body and movement on the mental processes of creativity and learning. Both the Feldenkrais Method and Dynamic Learning acknowledge the importance of multi-sensory learning and the continual development and uniqueness of the individual.

By connecting touch and movement with the other senses during learning, the Writing Cubes Program adds significantly to the educational experience. The Writing Cubes Program allows students to learn kinesthetically, visually and auditorally and helps them to enrich their variety of expression. The Writing Cubes Program is 'user friendly' and simple to use. It encourages self learning and independent thinking, and at the same time, fits well within the existing educational curriculum. It can also be used to help students with writing problems or learning disabilities.

This has been validated by several projects involving the Writing Cubes Program that have been conducted in Santa Cruz County, California—one with the California Writing Project and the other with UC Santa Cruz Disability Resource Center.

Professor Don Rothman of UC Santa Cruz, director of the *Central California Writing Project*, commented:

> *"These blocks provide a creative way for teachers to work with students on the generation of sentences and, therefore, on the creation of new ideas. My enthusiasm is prompted by the response from UCSC students who worked with [the Writing Cubes Program] in the Disabled Student Services office, including a writing student of mine who is dyslexic. They found [the Writing Cubes Program] to be very beneficial...[the Writing Cubes] offer a very positive alternative to standard material. They are a playful way to encourage language development."*

Another project was focused at the Disability Resource Center at the University of California at Santa Cruz. Several workshops were done through the Disability Resource Center for learning disabled college students. Individual students were also seen on a one-to-one tutoring basis and taken through the Writing Cubes Program. According to Sharyn Martin, LD Program Coordinator at the Disability Resource Center:

> *"All of [the students] were enthusiastic in their response and happy with the progress they have made in their writing skills. There was unanimous agreement that this approach dramatically increased their ability to express their ideas and organize their thoughts. The word generator blocks were consistently mentioned as key to "unblocking" their writing process. Students commented that the most valuable part of the experience was that they felt the freedom to express themselves, and develop a free-flowing thought process where they could "just write." I believe there is exciting potential here, at the university level, for students with learning disabilities."*

For further information on the Writing Cubes Program, contact:
Text Blox c/o Strategies of Genius
P.O. Box 67448
Scotts Valley, CA 95067-7498

Appendix F:
Typing Strategy

I (author Dilts) was once involved in the modeling of a piano player who could immediately sight read and beautifully perform any piece of music that was placed in front of him, as if he had played it many times before. By exploring his internal strategy, we discovered that, when he was learning to play the piano, he would visualize the piano keyboard in his mind. As he was learning to sight read he would look at individual notes in their written form and would picture which of the keys on his mental keyboard was to be depressed to make that note. He would look at a particular note, and imagine which key was to go down. After a while he could look at any particular written note and see the corresponding key automatically going down on his mental keyboard. Pretty soon he could look at two or three notes at once and see the corresponding keys being depressed. He was eventually able to see the notation for whole chords and imagine the cluster of keys being depressed that made up that chord.

By overlapping his mental image of the piano keyboard with the actual piano keys, he would then use his fingers to press on the keys that he saw were supposed to be depressed. He explained that, "Now when I sight-read music it's very easy - it is like playing a player piano. I look at the notes, see the keys going down and I just stick my fingers in the slots."

This is a strategy based on the development of associations between an externally represented code (musical notation) and a personal internal image (the imaginary keyboard). There is then an association made from activity on the mental keyboard (notes being depressed) to the kinesthetic act of pressing the corresponding key on the actual physical keyboard. The specific steps involve: 1) see specific note; 2) picture key on imaginary keyboard; 3) move finger to corresponding position on actual keyboard; 4) produce sound.

I used this strategy as the basis for a computer program to teach people to touch type. In this program, the computer screen shows a picture of your hands and of the computer keyboard. It begins by displaying individual letters, and highlights which key on the keyboard corresponds to that letter and which finger should be used to depress that key. So you see the letter, the location on the keyboard and the finger to be used. Keeping your eyes on the computer monitor, you are to try to press the highlighted key with the indicated finger. If you hit the wrong key, that key is highlighted in a different color than the target key, so you can see where your finger is with respect to where it should be, without having to look down at the keyboard.

In order to encourage the self-organizing processes required to effectively acquire any psychomotor skill, such as typing or playing a musical instrument, you need to provide *feedback*. The problem is that the most direct way to get feedback while typing or learning a musical instrument is to look at what you fingers are doing. Unfortunately this is disruptive and inefficient because 1) you have to look away from the written source for what you are trying to type or play, and 2) it does not facilitate the development of an internal representation of the keyboard or musical instrument.

This computer program encourages you to fumble around kinesthetically by continuing to press the keys with your fingers until you see that you hit the right key. It keeps showing you the relationship between the target key, the finger to use and the key you've actually hit. As a result you naturally build an image of the keyboard and develop the synesthesia between eye and hand without having to look down. As your skill increases, individual letters are extended to form words, sentences and finally whole paragraphs.

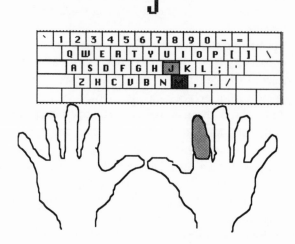

Sample Screen From 'Typing Strategy' Program

Obviously, a similar kind of program could be developed to help people to learn the strategy to sight-read for musical instruments. Notes could be displayed on the computer screen together with a replica of the instrument to be played and a pair of hands. Individual notes could be shown and the key, string or valve required to produce that note could be highlighted in some way along with the finger(s) to be used. The actual instrument could be connected or wired to the computer in some way so that it was able to ascertain which note you were actually playing in order to complete the feedback loop.

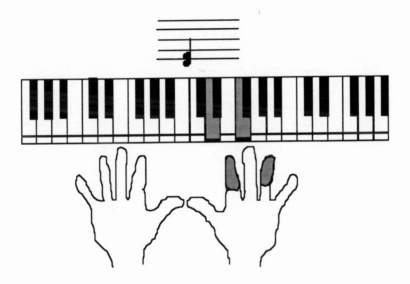

Example of Music 'Sight Reading' Program

Appendix G:
The NeuroLink

The *NeuroLink* is a tool, developed by author Robert Dilts, that can be used to achieve optimal states for learning and performance. The NeuroLink device is designed to detect subtle changes in a person's body caused by shifts in his or her internal state. It works by measuring a number of important physiological responses associated with the autonomic nervous system - the body's inner regulatory system. The NeuroLink detects heart rate, skin temperature and what is called the 'galvanic skin response', or GSR— the electrical activity, or conductivity, of the skin. These measures are used both in biofeedback and lie detection and are sensitive indicators of a person's internal states.

The NeuroLink comes with software that combines these key measurements of nervous system activity with artificial intelligence and NLP methods and principles in order to help people achieve and maintain desired states. NeuroLink software includes programs and games that can help you become more aware of your internal state and learn how to focus and direct it. Applications include programs for enhancing memory and developing better concentration.

The NeuroLink programs are both fun and informative, and have even been used to help children who are hyperactive or have other attention problems.

The NeuroLink device and software operates on both Macintosh and IBM PC compatible computers. For more Information contact:

NeuroLink International
343 Soquel Ave. #334
Santa Cruz, CA 95062
(408) 438-5679
Fax (408) 438-5649

Bibliography

Applications of Neuro-Linguistic Programming, Dilts, R., Meta Publications, Capitola, Ca., 1983.

Effective Presentation Skills, Dilts, R., Meta Publications, Capitola, Ca.,1994.

Frogs into Princes, Bandler, R. and Grinder, J.; Real People Press, Moab, Utah, 1979.

Introducing Neuro-Linguistic Programming, O'Connor, J., Seymour, J., Aquarian Press, Cornwall, England, 1990.

Megateaching and Learning, Van Nagel, C., Reese, E., Reese, M., Siudzinski, R., Southern Inst. Press, Indian Rocks Beach, FLA, 1985.

Meta-Cation Vols. I, II, III, Jacobson, S., Meta Publications, Capitola, Ca., 1983, 1986, 1987.

Mind and Nature, Bateson, Gregory; E. P. Dutton, New York, NY, 1979.

Neuro-Linguistic Programming: The Study of the Structure of Subjective Experience, Volume I; Dilts, R., Grinder, J., Bandler, R., DeLozier, J.; Meta Publications, Capitola, California, 1980.

"NLP In Training Groups", Dilts, R., Epstein, T., Dynamic Learning Publications, Ben Lomond, Ca., 1989.

On the Soul, Aristotle, *Britannica Great Books,* Encyclopedia Britannica Inc., Chicago Ill., 1979.

The One Minute Manager; Blanchard & Johnson; Berkeley Books, New York, 1983.

The PhotoReading Whole Mind System, Scheele, P., Learning Strategies Corporation, Wayzata, Minn., 1994.

"The Parable of the Porpoise: A New Paradigm for Learning and Management", Dilts, R., Dynamic Learning Publications, Ben Lomond, Ca., 1990.

Plans and the Structure of Behavior, Miller, G., Galanter, E., and Pribram, K., Henry Holt & Co., Inc., 1960.

Principles of Psychology, William James, *Britannica Great Books,* Encyclopedia Britannica Inc., Chicago Ill., 1979.

Righting The Educational Conveyor Belt, Grinder, M., Metamorphous Press, Portland, OR, 1990.

Skills for the Future, Dilts, R. with Bonissone, G., Meta Publications, Capitola, Ca., 1993.

Steps to an Ecology of Mind, Bateson, G.; Ballantine Books, New York, New York, 1972.

Strategies of Genius Vols. I, II,& III, Dilts, R., Meta Publications, Capitola, Ca.,1994-1995.

The Structure of Magic Vol. I & II, Grinder, J. and Bandler, R.; Science and Behavior Books, Palo Alto, California, 1975, 1976.

Tools for Dreamers, Dilts, R. B., Epstein, T., Dilts, R. W., Meta Publications, Capitola, Ca.,1991.

Using Your Brain, Bandler, Richard; Real People Press, Moab, Utah,1984.